INTONATION IN DISCOURSE

EDITED BY CATHERINE JOHNS-LEWIS

CROOM HELM
London & Sydney

COLLEGE-HILL PRESS, INC.
San Diego, CA 92105

© 1986 Catherine Johns-Lewis
Croom Helm Ltd, Provident House, Burrell Row,
Beckenham, Kent BR3 1AT
Croom Helm Australia Pty Ltd, Suite 4, 6th Floor,
64-76 Kippax Street, Surry Hills, NSW 2010, Australia

British Library Cataloguing in Publication Data

Intonation in discourse.
   1. Intonation (Phonetics)
   I. Johns-Lewis, Catherine
   414   P222

   ISBN 0-7099-1423-7

College-Hill Press, Inc.
4284 41st Street
San Diego, CA 92105

Library of Congress Cataloging in Publication Data
Main entry under title:

Intonation in discourse.

   Based on papers written for a seminar at the University
of Aston in Birmingham, under the auspices of the British
Association of Applied Linguistics, Apr. 5-7, 1982.
   Bibliography: p.
   1. Intonation (phonetics) 2. Prosodic analysis
(linguistics) 3. Discourse analysis. I. Johns-Lewis,
Catherine. II. British Association for Applied
Linguistics.
P222.1465   1985   414   84-19929
ISBN 0-88744-121-1

Printed and bound in Great Britain by
Biddles Ltd, Guildford and King's Lynn

CONTENTS

PREFACE

Intonation in Discourse is the outcome of a conference on intonation which took place in April 1982 at the University of Aston in Birmingham, under the auspices of the British Association of Applied Linguistics. Contributors came from a variety of backgrounds - mainly linguistics, phonetics and psycholinguistics - and the papers presented reflect different orientations and methodologies curently employed in the field of intonation research.

This volume is not a record of the conference proceedings, nor is it in any sense a synthesis, although the introduction tries to relate the contributions to each other and to the field in general. Some papers given at the conference are not included in this book (those by Ilse Lehiste, David Crystal, David Brazil, Elizabeth Couper-Kuhlen, Harold Fish, Gerry Knowles, Esther Gebara, Michael Pickering, Paul Tench and Ian Thompson) either because they have since been published elsewhere, or because they represented work still in progress. The papers included have been substantially revised, and to the collection have been added three by others who did not present papers at the conference (Wiktor Jassem, David Graddol and Ben Maassen). The effect of these additions is to make the volume more representative of the current diversity of approaches.

The book does not, obviously, represent all ongoing research on intonation. Cross-language comparison is largely absent (an exception being Williams' paper on the perception of stress inEnglish and Welsh); and a number of areas are under-represented (language acquisition, clinical linguistics and sociolinguistics) considering their importance. However, the collection does give a sense of the breadth and focus of activity in the field. Contributions range across psychoacoustics, conversation analysis, discourse analysis, syntax and semantics,sociolinguistics, psycholinguistics, clinical linguistics and social psychology.

The collection owes its origin to the 1982 Aston conference, and I should like to thank a number of bodies which generously helped to fund that conference: the British Academy, the British Council and the British Association of Applied Linguistics. Several organisations also indirectly supported the conference through advertising in the conference brochure and exhibiting: Academic Press, Basil Blackwell, Cambridge Electronic Design Ltd, Cambridge University Press, Collins (Publishers), Croom Helm (Publishers), Edinburgh University Press, Edward Arnold Ltd, Pergamon Press, F J Electronics ApS, K Elemetrics Corporation, Jessop Acoustics Ltd, Longman, Millgrant Wells Ltd and Texas Instruments Ltd. To all these bodies I should like to express appreciation of the support given.

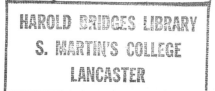

The preparation of the book would have been even more time-consuming than it was without the professional expertise of the secretarial staff of the Modern Languages Department at Aston. Most of the burden of the work has fallen on Joy Fenton, without whose skill and patience this book would never have emerged from the departmental word processor. To her I owe a special debt. I should also like to thank Aston Graphics for dealing with the artwork, figures, graphs and tables and Communitype for type-setting.

Assistance with proof-reading at various stages was given by Sharon Rimmer, Salwa Farag and Farouk El-Batanouny, and I am grateful for their help.

The comments of colleagues Suzanne Romaine and Anne Cutler on aspects of the collection were greatly appreciated; and encouragement from Wiktor Jassem and Francis Nolan went a long way towards ensuring that the book appeared.

Finally, I must thank my long-suffering family, who have put up with protracted absenteeism and distraction with great tolerance.

Catherine Johns-Lewis
Aston University
Birmingham, England

ACKNOWLEDGEMENTS

Thanks are due to Foris Publications, Dordrecht for permission to reprint Carlos Gussenhoven's paper; and to the Journal of Pragmatics, for permission to print an amended version of the paper by Peter French and John Local.

INTRODUCTION

Catherine Johns-Lewis

1. Basic terms; 'prosody' and 'intonation'

The first issue we must confront is the implication of the term *intonation* in the title of this book. Is there a dividing line between *intonation* and *prosody*? The answer, as with so many terms, is that it depends who is using the terms. Where 'concrete' measurement is involved, the three physical parameters most commonly given as being *prosodic* are **fundamental frequency** (perceived as pitch), **intensity** (perceived as loudness) and **duration** (perceived as length). (See Gimson 1980:60; Cutler and Ladd 1983:1). Lehiste (1970:1) remarks that *prosody* is 'used more or less synonymously with suprasegmental', and identifies the same three physical parameters of duration, fundamental frequency and intensity/amplitude as criteria for suprasegmentals (1970:4). However, even if *prosody* and *suprasegmentals* refer to the same physical phenomena, an alternative, more abstract view of prosody is possible. Prosody may be seen not as 'features of segments' but 'features of structure' (Liberman, 1978:169), so that

> the acoustic nature of prominence may be explained in part by assuming that the physical realities are organised cognitively into a rhythmic structure, which in turn affects our perception of physical realities.

(Ladd, 1980:50)

As Cutler and Ladd (1983:14) argue, activities in the field fall into two categories: concrete measurement and experimentation, which relies on the three basic physical parameters, and abstract theorisation, which focuses on systems and meanings. A complicating factor is the overlap of the terms *intonation* and *prosody*. This is commented on by Crystal. He notes that

> scholars in the field have been anxious to restrict the formal definition of intonation to pitch movement alone (although occasionally allowing in stress variation as well).

(Crystal, 1969:195)

Crystal views intonation not as a single system of pitch levels, pitch contours, etc, but as

> ... a complex of features from different prosodic systems ... the most central (of which) are *tone, pitch range*, and *loudness*, with *rhythmicality* and *tempo* closely related.

(Crystal, 1969:195)

Prosodic systems, for Crystal, include not only the above, but also *pause* and *tension*, *tension* falling also into the category of *paralinguistic* systems, which include *tension*, *voice qualifiers* and *voice qualifications*. (*Voice qualifiers* - e.g. whispery, breathy, husky - and *voice qualifications* - e.g. sob, laugh, giggle - are not always distinguished by those who use the term *voice quality*.)

There is, then, considerable overlap between *intonation* and *prosody*, *intonation* acting as a collective label for a subset of prosodic systems, all of which co-occur simultaneously with segmental information on continually varying parameters. The amount of overlap will be determined by the way in which a definition of *intonation* such as Crystal's will produce a greater amount of overlap with *prosody* than a narrow definition of intonation as involving *rises and falls in pitch level* (Gimson, 1980: 264).

The fact that concrete measurement in *prosody* **and** *intonation* can focus on the **same three** physical parameters, fundamental frequency (Fo), intensity and duration, may suggest an apparent interchangeability of terms. Yet certain facts suggest that the terms are both necessary, although the relationship between them is problematic.

First, as we have seen, *prosody* covers some phenomena which cannot be included in *intonation as a system*. Prosody includes not just *pause phenomena* (frequency, duration and distribution of pauses), but also the time domain of non-speech in interaction - in other words the relative amount of time occupied by articulatory activity as opposed to non-activity. Silence, its duration and distribution does not figure in statements of intonation but may be a useful prosodic parameter, which can distinguish between types of discourse. In addition, voice quality (Crystal's voice qualifiers) lies outside the intonation system, since it is not simply an overlaid function of fundamental frequency. Some voice quality features **are** related to vocal fold activity (creak, for instance, which results from vibration falling below about 40 cps (in males) in a largely aperiodic fashion) while others (vocal laxness, for instance, resulting from damping in the vocal tract) are independent of mode of vibration of the vocal folds.

Second, the perception of "the intonation system" is undoubtedly affected by phonetic and linguistic phenomena that fall outside the domain of 'rises and falls in pitch'. The most reliable acoustic cue for stress perception in English is, as has been known for some time (Fry, 1958), change in fundamental frequency. The language specific character of stress perception is demonstrated by Williams (this volume) who shows that amplitude correlates better with perceived stress in Welsh, and who additionally finds that pitch prominence in Welsh requires a linguistic and historical explanation. The intimate relationship between stress perception and pitch prominence in English, with duration also a contributory cue, has been known for some time. It is now clear that the **perception** of aspects of the *intonation system* may be affected by phonetic phenomena which, strictly speaking, belong to *prosody*.

Pitch phenomena (maximum pitch range and kinetic tone) which have been shown to be active cues in marking intonational prominence in English operate in parallel with *tempo phenomena* (pause, lengthening (drawl) and speech rate) and *loudness phonomena* (Wells, this volume). Segmental lengthening is known to occur as a marker of sentence finality, paragraph finality, and conversation turn finality (Lehiste, 1975). Two other cues, creak (laryngealisation) before a boundary, and pause length are associated with the perception of boundaries. There is, however, a trading relationship between them such that even if a pause is relatively short, provided there is laryngealisation and significant pre-boundary segmental lengthening, a boundary will still be perceived (Lehiste, 1979). It seems then that *lengthening* enters into *prominence*, which is part of the intonation system, but also functions at the syntactic and discourse levels to assist in marking boundaries between sentences, between paragraphs/topics and between conversational turns. *Creak* often but not necessarily enters in the perception of boundaries between sentences, between paragraphs/topics and between turns. In addition, pitch phenomena (maximum range and kinetic tone) which have a significant role in marking out prominence in the intonation system **also** enter into boundary marking at the sentence level, and at the discourse level.

Pitch marking of the initial boundary of the sentence takes the form of *sentence declination*, whereby the fundamental frequency (Fo) tends to decline with time across the utterance in the unmarked case. Sentence declination has been studied in a number of languages: English (Maeda, 1976), Dutch (Cohen and 'tHart, 1967), Italian (Magno-Caldognetto et al, 1978), Japanese (Fujisaki et al, 1979) and tone languages (Hombert, 1974). Declination has already entered abstract modelling of sentence production (Gårding, 1983: Ladd, 1983) and perception (Pierrehumbert, 1979), various bases for the relative scaling of Fo peaks having been proposed. Pitch height is thus a marker of utterance initiality. It is **also** a marker of paragraph/topic initiality. Lehiste (1975) showed that listeners recognised sentences as paragraph initial which exhibited a relatively high Fo peak. High pitch marking of topic initiality has been suggested by others (e.g. Brazil, 1975, 1979, who proposes this function for 'high key'). However, recent work (Schaffer, 1984) suggests that pitch heightening is not uniquely associated with new topic. Conversation participants regularly use pitch heightening in reply to a question, and Schaffer found using Fo to be a strong cue for topic **continuation**, but not topic beginning. It is not clear whether high, rising Fo peaks have an interactive function **other than** the marking of topic or tun initiality. Further investigation may throw some light on this.

Cues to turn finality include not only segmental lengthening and creak but also pitch characteristics. Cutler and Pearson's study (this volume) shows that the acoustic cue most reliably associated with turn-finality was downstepped contour in the final series of tone units in the turn. (This is the termination function of key in Brazil, 1975, 1979.)

Taken together then, the findings on sentence declination, paragraph and turn initiality, and turn finality point to multi-functional cues. Relative height and movement of pitch peak can mark sentence initiality, paragraph/topic/turn initiality, and prominence within the sentence. Height of tone units relative to each other (the downstepped contour) is strongly associated with turn finality, but may also be associated with topic finality.

There is yet **another** way in which a factor which is strictly speaking **outside** of the intonation system may enter into perception of the system. Fundamental frequency *range* is narrower in some kinds of speaking activity than others. Conversation is characterised by a narrower frequency range than either reading aloud or acting (Johns-Lewis, this volume); and reading aloud a dramatic dialogue produces a wider frequency range than reading aloud written prose text (Graddol; and Johns-Lewis, this volume). The narrowness of Fo range may **contribute** to the perception that conversation and reading aloud favour a greater proportion of level tones than other discourse modes (e.g. political oratory). (See remarks by Gussenhoven, this volume, on tone frequency.)

Finally, *pausing*, together with segmental lengthening, which contributes to the perception of sentence boundaries and paragraph/topic boundaries, undoubtedly contributes to the perception of intonational units. This is not to say that tone unit boundaries are marked by a pause. Rather, pauses coinciding with tone unit boundaries and simultaneously grammatical juncture or sentence boundaries will contribute to the perception of fluency and will produce something closer to the intonational canonical form. Hesitation pauses (those occurring at places **other** than major grammatical juncture) on the other hand frequently have the effect of disrupting intonational units (i.e. tone groups/units). Some descriptions not only allow tone-group internal pause, but accommodate the particular effect of such pause location. Gussenhoven (this volume) comments on the dramatic effect of pause-delay of tone-group prominence. Other descriptions seem uncertain as to the handling of pauses, sometimes requiring split tone groups, sometimes a proliferation of 'level' tones. (See Brazil, Coulthard and Johns, 1980, Appendix transcription.)

Drawing the threads of the argument about *prosody* and *intonation* together, then, it would seem that;

A   Some phonetic phenomena, *lengthening/drawl* and *sentence declination*, while outside of the traditional linguistic models of intonation (e.g. Halliday, 1967) are amenable to inclusion in abstract phonological models of sentence production, and are certainly relevant to representation of sentence intonation.

B   Some phonetic phenomena, *pause, tempo, and voice quality* do not appear at present to have a role in abstract phonological models of sentence production.

C Some phonetic phenomena, *pitch range* and *pitch downdrift* beyond the sentence are not currently included in abstract models of prosody, but are potential candidates if abstract models come to concern themselves with discourse phenomena such as topic marking, topic change, turn-finality and discourse mode.

It seems at least likely that as the scope of digital speech processing expands, regularities will be found in stretches of talk longer than the sentence which will be - potentially at least - amenable to theoretical representation in abstract models. If long term pitch characteristics can separate one discourse mode from another, perhaps it is not too speculative to suggest that some tempo phenomena (e.g. speech rate, and location/duration of pause) and the silence domain generally could be accommodated too. In other words, the scope of phonological theory might expand to accommodate newly perceived phonetic regularities.

The idea of abstract models concerning themselves not only with accent assignment rules, rhythmic structures and tone sequences (Liberman, 1975; Liberman and Prince, 1977; Selkirk, 1978, 1980; Hirst, 1977) but also with the phonetic realisation of whole texts is an attractive one - one which is bound to appeal to the many working on the linguistic characteristics of discourse.

2. The contributors

At the risk of repeating what has been said already, I should like to stress that the differences between contributors are not merely terminological. There are substantive differences on the status of empirical work. For Jassem, for example, descriptions of intonation are not proved true unless they are supported by the results of experiments, or measurement. For others, an equally legitimate approach is to begin with linguistic structures at the sentence level, and to either assign intonation contours and stresses 'in vitro', as it were, as Hirst does, or to describe linguistically significant choices made by speakers in operating the intonational system, as Gussenhoven does. This fundamental difference is expressed by the editors of an important recent volume of prosody as follows:

> On the one side of the dichotomy stand instrumental and experimental studies that seek to quantify acoustic features and investigate perceptual responses. On the other are descriptive and theoretical studies of prosodic structure and its relation to other aspects of grammar and phonology.

(Cutler and Ladd, 1983:1)

A further point to bear in mind is that the two approaches do not treat the same phenomena. Some prosodic phenomena (Category B referred to earlier) lie outside the activity of some practitioners in the field, while other prosodic phenomena (Category A) may be marginal to 'the intonation system as a set of linguistically significant choices' (i.e. to tone group boundaries, tone group structure, tone choice etc.). Others may be essentially concerned with the sentence as a domain, excluding therefore Category C.

The outlines that follow attempt to make common interests explicit and to locate contributions in the field generally.

Two contributions, **Hirst** and **Gussenhoven**, represent abstract accounts of intonational sturcture, and the difference in approach demonstrates the divergent meanings of the term 'model'. **Hirst** acknowledges a debt to Liberman (1975), Ladd (1980) and Pierrrehumbert (1980), a tradition continued by Selkirk (1980), Gårding (1983) and Nespor and Vogel (1983). Hirst proposes a phonological level of tonal melodies represented by two binary features [± high] and[± low]. Any pitch contour is representable as a combination of two features,

[+ high, − low] = H(igh)-tone

[− high, + low] =L(ow)-tone

[+ high, +low] =D(rop)-tone

[− high, − [low] = M(id)-tone

each combination forming a sequence of T-segments (L, M, H or D) corresponding to static or level tones. Phonetic realisation values of T-segments are determined contextually, the only relevant phonological values being distinguished by the two features [high] and [low]. The actual mapping of tones onto constituent syllables and foot segments is carried out by viewing Fo curves as a continuous function of time, which effectively ignores Fo perturbations brought about by intrinsic segmental voicing characteristics. The result is expressed as a series of target pitches from which actual Fo values in Hertz are produced. Measurement of Fo on a small corpus of short sentences read aloud suggests, firstly, that there is a positive correlation between the height of the first H-tone and the number of stress feet in the sentence, the effect being greatest in sentences with only one stress foot. This result is compatible with the finding by Grosjean (1983) that listeners can identify the amount of continuative material following sentence interruption, on the basis of prosodic characteristics which include the scaling of declination. The second trend to emerge in Hirst's corpus is a negative correlation between the height of the last H-tone and the number of stress feet in the sentence. These contradictory results are resolved by proposing a tendency to scale Fo values not downwards from a first fixed H-tone, nor upwards from a last fixed H-tone, but outwards away from some central value. A third result to emerge from his corpus is a strong correlation between the height of an H-tone (or D-tone) and the height of the following H-tone or D-tone. Two mechanisms are proposed for assigning Fo values: one makes use of a scale along which each pair of notes is separated by three semi-tones, and the other makes use of a scale on which each note is scaled down from a preceding value. In Hirst's model, then, detailed analysis of fundamental frequency values in short read aloud sentences contributes to the development of the phonological component whose input is linguistic structures. He shows how it is possible to describe intonation so as to represent both its hierarchical structure and its phonetic linearity.

Gussenhoven is concerned with the mapping of intonation units onto linguistic structures. His analytical framework is the British or 'consensus view' (after Ladd, 1980), which takes as the unit of analysis the tone group, split into nucleus, tail, head and pre-head and assumes a distinction between the fall (\), the rise (/), the fall rise (∨), the rise fall (∧), the level (−) and the stylised fall (=). He concentrates on the domains of the tail in tone groups, and identifies the semantic and syntactic categories of matter which are [-focus] (i.e. which fall within the tail or post-nuclear element). (The corpus consists of four instalments of British 'sitcom' television serials, comprising some 14,000 words.) The investigation highlights where the nuclear element does **not** fall, as a preliminary necessity to discovering the linguistic characteristics of where it does fall. (It should be noted that *focus* is a linguistic, not an acoustic category, [+ focus] being almost invariably reserved for what speakers consider to be the crux of their contribution to the conversation hence [+ new], while [− focus] goes with what speakers assume or want to be seen to be assuming (see Section 8.1). The Sentence Accent Assignment Rule (SAAR) is a mechanism for assigning [+ focus] marking to the domains of sentences, which consist of arguments, predicates and conditions. SAAR predicts that:

1) Conditions form a single focus domain, while arguments and predicates can fuse into one focus domain, and if this happens, SAAR assigns focus to the argument.

2) The last assigned sentence accent is the nucleus, accent being decided on the basis of focus markings and mode markings, and every [+ focus] domain acquiring an accent. There is no direct relationship between focus and accent such that what is [+ focus] is necessarily accented.

3) When accent is realised, there may be more than one accentable syllable, especially in arguments, switched on by SAAR if the whole domain is [+ focus].

4) Many adverbials are [− focus].

The analysis shows that [− focus] tails can be given semantic characterisation, and identifies expressions which are typically [− focus] (time-space markers, cohesion markers, softeners, vocatives, parentheticals/textual markers, comment clauses with epistemic verbs, and approximatives).

While Hirst focuses on the phonological specification of intonational contours, Gussenhoven uses an existing set of intonational contours (in the form of nuclear tone choices) as part of the phonetic realisation of accent rules, and investigates the semantic and syntactic input to a particular configuration, [− focus]. Thus, the two 'abstract' models are developing different facets of the phonological component, Hirst the phonological elements underlying intonational contours and Gussenhoven the interface between pre-defined phonological categories, and semantico-syntactic sentence configurations. The data bases of the two approaches are very different, Hirst working on the basis of a small number of sentences read aloud, while Gussenhoven examines a sizeable corpus of acted dramatic text.

The remaining papers in the volume involve experimentation and measurement as an approach to intonational and prosodic phenomena. Two contributions examine the acoustic cues that mark prominence. **Williams** is essentially concerned to show the difference between the acoustic basis of stress perception in Welsh and English. For Welsh speakers, the element considered stressed has no fundamental frequency change, shorter duration, lower envelope amplitude, greater mean amplitude and greater peak amplitude. For English speakers, on the other hand, the element considered stressed has pitch glide, longer duration, greater envelope amplitude, lower peak amplitude, and lower mean amplitude, which tallies well with what is known about stress Welsh, it is proposed, is that in English, pitch changes tend to coincide with rhythmically stressed syllables, which explains why, in perceptual experiments, pitch prominence is the best cue to prominence in a general sense, though it is never the only one. In Welsh, on the other hand, pitch prominence, which occurs on the ultimate syllable of the word, is not intimately connected with stress. Amplitude, usually greater in the penultimate syllable, marks the onset of the stress foot, and stress is essentially a rhythmic, not an intonational phenomenon. The prominence of the penultimate syllable is due, 'less to its inherent acoustic properties, than to its function as the keystone of the rhythmic unit'. The separation of the stress system and the intonation system in Welsh appears to be due to a historical development, the 'Old Welsh Accent Shift'. In consequence, and as a theoretical implication, Bolinger's system of pitch accent is best dispensed with for Welsh, since pitch prominence, stress, and acoustic prominence do not coincide.

Wells undertakes to examine the acoustic cues to *focus* in English, *focus* subsuming both 'contrastive information' and 'new information'. The experiment described first ascertains, in a controlled syntactic base, a four-term system of prominence, indicating that four degrees of focus are significant for listeners; then correlates the four experimentally identified degrees of focus with acoustic cues in phonological analysis, interfacing with the semantic level, the framework of analysis being Firthian. The acoustic cues that correlate best with prominence in English are reported as:

Pitch features : *maximum pitch range* and *kinetic tone*

Loudness features : *loudness peak* and *decrescendo*

Tempo : a *combination* of *pause, drawl* (segmental lengthening) and *rate*.

Wells proposes that the phonology of focus may be polysystemic, in that it is involved in the marking of other aspect of connected speech, namely sentence initial and sentence final position. In addition the same system may contribute to the phonological **undermarking** of the *verb*, and the phonological **overmarking** of the noun *noun*. Both Wells and Gussenhoven (see comments above on SAAR) independently point to the different status of nouns and verbs in the phonological systems of accent and focus.

The chapter by **Ladd, Scherer and Silverman** outlines existing approaches to the study of the intonational expression of speaker attitude, and suggests that their failure to produce conclusive results does not invalidate the theory that intonation conveys attitude. The two formally contrasted approaches involve, on the one hand, an assumption that some invariant acoustic form can be superimposed on otherwise neutral texts, and on the other hand, the belief that intonational meanings are that attitudes are conveyed through total context, and inference based on context. The techniques used to attack these questions involve, firstly, judgements of utterances removed from their original contexts, such that the only variable changed is context. Secondly, in a stimulus masking experiment, the authors attempt to discover what attitude judgements are made when specific features of the speech signal are removed. The results of the context-switching experiment indicate that even when contextual information is drastically reduced or absent, something in the non-segmental part of the speech signal directly conveys affective information.

The masking experiment shows that even when the non-segmental information is chopped up, run backwards and left unchanged, in the three different degraded signal conditions, affective information comes through. The authors argue that the real issue is not whether the signalling of attitude is indirect or direct, but whether intonation is a categorical or parametric phenomenon.

Does intonation involve the structured configuration of categories, or does it involve the interaction of multiple parameters? The latter is a characteristic of perceptual processing, whereas the former is in effect a grammar. The authors outline an experimental procedure to resolve the issue, involving listeners making judgements of intonational stimuli to listening tests are discussed, among them the problems of labelling and metalanguage. The importance of such experimentation is clear. Without it, the very existence of categorical linguistic distinctions of intonation must remain in doubt.

The chapter by **Jassem and Demenko** contributes to the 'categorical vs parametric' issue presented in Ladd, Scherer and Silverman. Given the multiplicity of sources of intonation variability (speaker attitude and emotion, discourse conditions, thematic accent placement, lexical and/or grammatical stress rules, segmental composition of utterance, length of linguistic domain for a contour, personal physiological features, personal pathological features, etc.), they question whether the functional units of intonation can be identified unless **all** of the effects of sources of variation can be accounted for. The experimental technique involves normalisation and equalisation of utterances for judgement. Personal effects are overcome by 'reducing the various voices to a common pitch, and by equalising individual voice ranges'. Tempo normalisation is achieved with linear and piecewise-linear adjustment. Linguistic effect is eliminated by rejecting all utterances which listeners fail to classify as 'linguistically the same as the prototype'. The assumption is that there **are** linguistically contrasting categories, and that only through the technique of successive approximation, altering one source of variation at a time, can the precise relationship between function and form be established.

A similar technique is used by **Maassen** in his investigation of the role of fundamental frequency in the perception of deaf speech. Maassen gives an overview of research on the question of why deaf speakers are difficult to understand. He argues that 'correlational' studies of the significance of different error types in intelligibility (consonant errors, vowel errors, suprasegmental errors, lexical stress etc.) fail because they cannot separate out acoustic parameters which are inter-dependent. An example is the relation between duration and spectrum of a vowel: vowels that are reduced in duration are also neutralised. The weakness of the correlational approach is that it cannot guarantee that correcting an error which 'correlates highly with intelligibility' will bring about improvement in intelligibility. The speech transformation method employed by Maassen avoids this drawback. By carrying out transformations on one parameter at a time (e.g. lengthening all stressed vowels; increasing loudness of stressed syllables, etc.), each feature, and various combinations of features, can be assessed for its role in intelligibility. Using this method, Maassen concludes that, although **temporal (i.e. durational) correction** is favoured in judgements of **quality, temporal distortion** (i.e. distortion of normal relative segment duration) does **not** affect intelligibility. Similarly, while normalising intonation contour can improve quality rating of utterances, fundamental frequency **alone** is not a significant factor in intelligibility. Improving the temporal organisation and pitch contour control of deaf speakers will, therefore, not bring about significant improvement in intelligibility, but is likely to improve its social acceptability.

Three papers can be grouped together as being concerned with prosodic features that function as cues in the management of spoken interaction: **French and Local, Cutler and Pearson** and **Local. French and Local** examine the phonetic characteristics of interruptions, and conclude that phonetic realisation is determined by whether the interruption is intended to be competitive for the turn or not. They identify two prosodic features in particular, pitch height and loudness, which are maximal when interruption is effective in taking over the speaking turn. In the tradition of Conversation Analysts, they argue that it is not sufficient to identify phonetic characteristics of successful interruptive speech. In order to show that speakers orient to these features, and that they are functionally real for conversational participants, they present evidence that once the turn is secured, interruptors drop the<h + f> combination. Further, turn occupants adopt phonetic modifications of their own (crescendo + deceleration) directly on the onset of<h + f> marked interruption, i.e. they **return** competition, or they yield by fading out. Finally, if a turn occupant hesitates at a non-completion point, and is interrupted, he regains the speaking turn by use of <f> only, since <h + f> would signal that he himself was an interruptor. French and Local conclude that conversational participants use and are sensitive to particular prosodic features, and combinations of features in the management of interruption.

Working, like French and Local, within the framework of Conversation Analysis, **Local** reports a study of regional variation in intonation. Two aspects of the variety in question, Tyneside, in the North East of England, are described: first, the nature of 'rises' and second the intonational exponence of 'doing understanding checks'. The phonetic characteristics of a particular type of rise in Tyneside are exemplified. Rises in the nuclear syllable, or if there is one, throughout the tail, involve continuous pitch change, whereas when the nuclear syllable is followed by one or more syllables (stressed or unstressed), the nuclear syllable has sustained level pitch (with crescendo loudness) from which the next syllable is stepped up to produce a second level pitch. The post-nuclear level pitch is especially obvious if the post-nuclear element is stressed. Having shown that the 'rise' in Tyneside is phonetically different from the 'rise' in the prestige British accent, Local argues that the function of the 'rise' is not equatable with the function of the 'rise' in the prestige accent.

Quirk et al (1972:1044) define the function of the rise as being 'to mark non-finality'. In the Tyneside speakers investigated, Local points out that the function of the 'rise' is not **non** = finality but **finality**. The behaviour of the interviewer shows that in no case is there an expectation that the interviewee has more to say. Further,level tones appear to have the same function as the prestige accent 'rise', namely utterance finality. Level tones can also be exponents of non-finality. Thus, it appears that:

1) the phonological inventory of Tyneside and the prestige variety are not in one to one correspondence: i.e. it is not the case that each merely realises the same phonological entity with a different phonetic form.

2) there are grounds for believing that phonetic forms associated with the prestige variety may have entirely different meanings in this regional variety.

This second point is developed in the discussion of 'doing understanding checks'. In understanding checks, interviewees repeat, or check the reputed regional item ('cree', 'bairn', etc.). A high fall with a mid point end in the checking repeat of the item signals that the interpretation of the item is uncertain. Where this occurs, the interviewer offers confirmation or a gloss. A high fall with a low end produces no confirmation/disconfirmation from the interviewer directly after the 'test word'. Thus, it appears that the end-point of fall has relevance to the system of delimination of finality, low end point indicating end-of-turn, mid end point indicating non-finality. Since at least two phonetic forms contribute to the realisation of finality (the rise, and the height of the end point of fall) it is clear that a) different phonetic forms can be exponnents of an underlyhing phonological cateogory and b) distinct phonological categories can share phonetic exponence. The polysystemic nature of the acoustic systems that realise focus is discussed in Wells, in relation to intonational phonology of the prestige accent of British English. Polysystemicity is apparent, as Local demonstrates, in regional variety of the language. Taken together, these two papers suggest strongly that it is misconceived to expect intonational meanings to be identical in all varieties of the language, and perhaps more importantly, erroneous to expect the sets of phonetic elements realising a phonological category to be mutually exclusive. The same phonetic entity can operate at different places in the linguistic system, and at different levels.

Cutler and Pearson, like French and Local, and Local, are concerned with the role of prosody in the management of interaction. They report on an experiment set up to investigate whether perceptually effective prosodic signals exist which mark turn finality. They required 10 speakers to read aloud short dialogues in which the same sentence occurred both turn-medially and turn-finally. In a text perception task, the individual sentences were presented, decontextualised, for judgement regarding finality/non-finality. The results of the experiment show that the correctness scores of judges were not different from chance performance. A significant prosodic effect was found, however, in those utterances that attracted finality ratings. **Turn-final** judgements were associated with **downstepped contours** on the final tone group, while **turn-medial** judgements were associated with **upstepped** contours on the final tone group of the utterance. The authors then examined the distribution of upstepped and downstepped contours across the corpus, and found a significant association between finality rating and choice of contour in the final tone group of the utterance. There is, then, experimental evidence for an aspect of intonational choice which has been described by Brazil (1975, 1979) namely the 'termination' function of key choice, low key termination in a series of tone units functioning to signal finality.

Two contributors concern themselves with the long term pitch characteristics of discourse, **Graddol** and **Johns-Lewis**. Both undertake the investigation of fundamental frequency beyond the sentence, and both show the effect of speaking task on long-term pitch trends. Graddol's subjects read aloud two kinds of text, expository semi-technical prose, and dialogue. Johns-Lewis's subjects were amateur actors who read aloud a short narrative, acted a dramatic text and conversed informally with the analyst. In both studies fundamental requency characteristics were assessed through digital extraction techniques, Graddol using time period between zero crossings as a basis, and Johns-Lewis using an existing frequency domain algorithm of the autocorrelation variety. Graddol reports that the dialogue has a higher mean than the prose text. He also finds that distributions seem to be flatter in the dialogue. The findings of Johns-Lewis are essentially the same, this paper arguing that conversation shows significantly less fluctuation around the mean Fo value than reading aloud, and acting significantly more. The mean Fo values show a heirarchy with acting highest, than reading aloud then conversation. Thus, the effect Graddol found that 'enacted more dramatic text' is higher in the fundamental frequency hierarchy than reading aloud is found in Johns-Lewis's results. An additional interesting finding in Graddol is the suggestion that the measures which most successfully distinguish between the sexes are the upper limit of range, the range itself and the degree of kurtosis. The implication of the differential use of pitch range is that females make greater use of their potential range than males, probably for psycho-social reasons to do with sex stereotyping. Graddol's work is undertaken within the framework of indexical and paralinguistic information inherent in voice pitch, while the point of departure for Johns-Lewis is the lack of a satisfactory base for discourse typology. The experimental work reported in these two papers suggests that long term pitch characteristics represent one prosodic dimension which varies with speaking task, and with sex of speaker, and that other prosodic dimensions may vary equally significantly across discourse modes and speaker categories.

Lieberman's paper is the only one to focus on the acquisition of intonation, and it does so by setting early fundamental frequency data in the context of biological, neurological and anatomical mechanisms. Pitch modulation emerges in infants long before systematic consonantal and vocalic distinctions are made, and Lieberman demonstrates that imitation of parental pitch contours begins as early as a few weeks old. He reports research which shows that the mother's fundamental frequency 'register' in addressing her infant is significantly higher than her average. Although infants imitate their parents' pitch contours, the anatomical structure of the infant's rib cage cannot produce long expiration at controlled subglottal air pressure. Early pitch modulation is thus structured by physiological mechanisms. The result is that the infant's intonation contour is shorter than the parent's while preserving overall shape of contour. The ability to match the absolute Fo of the mother (i.e. to produce vocal fold vibration at approximately her-lower-rate) does not emerge until three months. Lieberman describes one finding of his long-term study of the acquisition of intonation as being contradictory to the supposed universality of declination. Whereas Pierrehumbert (1979) claims that declination can be seen in the initial utterances of children, Lieberman does not find declination to be typical of children's early utterances: rather, a variety of contours is found, ranging from 'mainly flat with a sharp fall in Fo at the end' to 'rising then falling gradually' or 'gradual descent throughout'.

3. **Orientation**

Both abstract model building and measurement and experimentation are represented in this volume. The former category of activities in intonation and prosody have in common a tendency to disregard psychological processes, *prosodic* model building concentrating on the assignment of lexical stress, sentence stress and metrical organisation (Lieberman, 1975; Liberman and Prince, 1977; Selkirk, 1980), while *intonational* model building concentrates on delimiting the number and type of pitch categories (Hirst, Gussenhoven, this volume). (Lip service is often paid to the other physical parameters active in signalling 'intonational' categories, but abstract intonational models concentrate almost exclusively on pitch.)

Measurement and experimentation is concerned primarily with the relationship - and non-relationship - between physical parameters and perceptual phenomena. Nine of the papers in this volume are concerned with the perceptual role of specific prosodic acoustic cues - in stress/prominence perception (Wells, Williams), in signalling turn-competition (French and Local), turn-finality (Cutler and Pearson) and discoursal function (Local), attitudes and emotions (Ladd, Scherer and Silverman), speech intelligibility (Maassen), and language acquisition (Lieberman). Two focus on the long term physical characteristics of discourse (Graddol and Johns-Lewis) with potential for experimentation on perception (Johns-Lewis, forthcoming). One (Jassem and Demenko) concentrates on the pursuit of functional invariance and the 'core' set of acoustic cues for this.

The tendency is for model building to proceed without reference to psychological processing, as if there could be an optimal representation of categories which simply hooked in to psychological processing when the details of the latter are known. In measurement and experimentation, on the other hand, the problem may be one of placing a result in an explanatory framework, i.e. one of inferring processes which cannot be seen.

Clearly, the model builders and the experimenters/measurers are limited without each other. For experimenters/measurers, the ultimate goal is to reduce the multiplicity of correlations, between physical and perceptual phenomena, to something that is manageable in real time - to extract a workable model from the 'combinatorial explosion of possibilities' (Woods, 1982) that result from multiple correlations. Process models of cognitive activity (Rumelhart, 1977; de Beaugrande, 1980; Woods, 1982) stress the limited power of attending to the single domain, since interactive parallel processing necessarily implies integration, at some level, of multiple stimuli. For model builders, the goal of optimal representation of abstract categories becomes sterile unless ultimately linked to perception which must take place in the domain of real time.

Thus, the argument for communication between activities in the field of intonation and prosody is irresistible. Placing different approaches in the same volume will not necessarily break down the barriers; but it will sharpen the issues, make them more public, and perhaps increase the pressure for accountability to the complementary set of workers in the field.

(References given below are not included in the main Bibliography.)

de Beaugrande R (1980) *Text, Discourse and Process* London: Longman.

de Beaugrande R (1980) 'Design criteria for process models in reading.' *Reading Research Quarterly*, 16, 2, 261-315.

Brazil D C (1979) *Discourse Intonation II* English Language Research Monographs, Birmingham: University of Birmingham.

Buxton H (1983) 'Temporal predictability in the perception of English speech.' In Cutler A & Ladd D R (eds) *Prosody: Models and Measurements* Springer Verlag: Berlin, Heidelberg, New York, Tokyo, 111-121.

Cohen A & 'tHart J (1967) 'On the anatomy of intonation.' *Lingua*, 19, 177-192.

Fujisaki M, Hirose K, Ohta K (1979) 'Acoustic features of the fundamental frequency. Contours of declarative sentences.' Phoniatrics, University of Tokyo, 13, 163-172.

Gårding E (1983) 'A generative model of intonation.' In Cutler & Ladd (eds) *Prosody: Models and Measurements* Springer Verlag: Berlin, Heidelberg, New York, Tokyo, 11-25.

Grosjean F (1983) 'How long is the sentence? Prediction and prosody in the on-line processing of language.' *Linguistics*, 21, 501-529.

Hombert J M (1974) 'Universals of downdrift: their basis and significance for a theory of tone.' *Studies in African Linguistics* 5, 169-183.

Ladd D R (1983) 'Peak features and overall slope.' In Cutler & Ladd (eds) *Prosody, Models and Measurements* Springer Verlag: Berlin, Heidelberg, New York, Tokyo, 39-52.

Lehiste I (1970) *Suprasegmentals* MIT Press: Cambridge, Massachusetts, London.

Magno-Caldognetto E, Ferrero F E, Lavagnoli C & Vagges K 'Fo contours of statements, yes-no questions and wh-questions of two regional varieties of Italian.' *Journal of Italian Linguistics* 3, 57-68.

Rumelhart D (1977) 'Towards an interactive model of reading. In Dornič S (ed) *Attention and Performance VI* Hilldale, New Jersey: Lawrence Erlbaum.

Schaffer D (1984) 'The role of intonation as a cue to topic management in conversation.' *Journal of Phonetics*, 12(4), 327-344.

Selkirk E 0 (1980) 'The role of prosodic categories in English word stress.' *Linguistic Inquiry*, 11, 563-605.

Woods W (1980) 'Multiple theory formation in speech and reading.' In Spiro R J, Bruce B & Brewer W (eds) Hillsdale, New Jersey: Lawrence Erlbaum, 59-82.

LIST OF CONTRIBUTORS

Anne Cutler, MRC Applied Psychology Unit, 15 Chaucer Road, Cambridge CB2 2EF.

Grażyna Demenko, Acoustic Phonetics Research Unit, Noskowskiego 10, 61-704 Poznan, Poland.

Peter French, The College of Ripon & York St John, Lord Mayor's Walk, York YO3 7EX.

David Graddol, School of Education, The Open University, Walton Hall, Milton Keynes, MK7 6AA.

Carlos Gussenhoven, Katholieke Universiteit, Faculteit der Letteren, Erasmusplein 1, 6500 HD Nijmegen, Netherlands.

Daniel Hirst, Institut de Phonétique, 29 Avenue Robert Schumann, Aix-en-Provence, France.

Wiktor Jassem, Acoustic Phonetics Research Unit, Noskowskiego 10, 61-704 Poznan, Poland.

Catherine Johns-Lewis, Department of Modern Languages, University of Aston, Gosta Green, Birmingham B4 7ET.

D Robert Ladd, Department of Linguistics, University of Edinburgh, Adam Ferguson Building, George Square, Edinburgh E48 9LL.

Philip Lieberman, Department of Linguistics, Brown University, Providence, Rhode Island, 02912 USA.

John Local, Department of Language, University of York, Heslington, York YO1 5DD.

Ben Maassen, Department of Experimental Psychology, University of Nijmegen, Postbox 9104, 6500 HE Nijmegen, Netherlands.

Mark Pearson, Department of Experimental Psychology, Sussex University, Brighton BN1 9QG.

Klaus Scherer, Fachbereich Psychologie, Justus-Liebig-Universität Giessen, Otto Behaghel-Strasse 10, D-6300 Giessen, West Germany.

Kim Silverman, MRC Applied Psychology Unit, 15 Chaucer Road, Cambridge CB2 2EF.

William H G Wells, Department of Health Sciences (Speech Therapy), Faculty of Engineering and Science, Birmingham Polytechnic (North Centre), Perry Barr, Birmingham B42 2SU.

Briony Williams, Speech Research, IBM United Kingdom Limited, UK Scientific Centre, Athelstan House, St Clement Street, Winchester, Hampshire SO23 9DR.

ON EXTRACTING LINGUISTIC INFORMATION FROM Fo TRACES

Wiktor Jassem and Grażyna Demenko

1. Two Approaches

There are basically two philosophical approaches to objective phonetic data; metaphysical and empirical. In the former approach, (cf. Lass, 1976: 213ff), such data cannot be used either to verify or to falsify a phonological theory, which is arrived at deductively. The latter approach may methodologically be either heuristic or inductive. In practice, however, there is usually a combination of heuristics and induction. In any case, a theory (or a specific statement) is considered tenable to the extent that it is falsifiable in confrontation with objective data which may either confirm or disconfirm it.

In matters intonational, as with other phonetic/phonological problems, it is possible to take either one or the other position. As the choice is a question of philosophy and methodology and belongs to the metatheory of phonetics and phonology, we shall not discuss it here, but it is essential to mention the two possible positions right at the start and define ours, which is that of critical empiricism. We consequently take the specific view that (a) experimental data can be used to prove or disprove a hypothesis on intonation, and that (b) a description of intonation is not proved true unless it is supported by results of experiments.

2. Experiment, Theory and Practice

The literature relating to intonation and its main (only?) 'physical' exponent Fo is vast (cf. Léon and Martin, 1969; Léon, 1972d; Gibbon, 1976; Rossi et al, 1981) and a not inconsiderable part of it deals with the intonaton of 'RP', within British English. Essentially, the publications fall into three classes (a) experimental, (b) theoretical, and (c) didactic. Whilst, apart from reviews, there is no combination of all the three aspects in any one work, some combine two. The most extensive treatment of RP intonation to date (Kingdon, 1958; for instance) is both theoretical and didactic. Leben (1976) is, to take another example almost at random, experimental and theoretical. Students of English as a foreign language are, in one respect at least, more fortunate than those of other European 'conference' languages: an up-to-date intermediate or advanced course of English (less frequently, a beginners' course -unfortunately) is now almost certain to include intonation in the Exercises (or Drills).[1] This is a very good thing, of course, but it is, in a way, also a very strange thing. One would expect that a considerable measure of agreement among the specialists, at least about the most fundamental issues, should precede didactic applications of a theory. As we shall show, no such agreement exists. A variety of Kingdon's (1958) or O'Connor and Arnold's

(1973) systems is mostly used for teaching purposes. The fact that they have gained so much popularity in ELT (English Language Teaching) may be due to the high prestige of their authors, but it is more probable that their relatively wide acceptance in ELT courses reflects their inherent aptness at least with respect to native speakers' 'tacit knowledge', or 'competence', or 'intuition': the teachers are, after all, mostly native speakers of RP. But the fact remains that the theoretical basis of these systems is not indisputable and that they were evolved with very little, if any, experimental spadework.

In the few works in which an attempt is made to relate experiments to a theory of intonation (or a part of the theory), the relation of the results of the experiments to the theory is obscure. An Fo trace may, for example, be assumed to represent a 'full' or 'wide' (nuclear) tone. A picture shows some wriggling lines that seem to tend (perhaps quite strongly) to fall from something vaguely High to something just as vaguely Low. What exactly is High, what is Low or, indeed, what precisely is 'falling' (in view of the wriggles), one is not told.

3. Trends and Methods in Experimental 'Tonology'

It is impossible to review here, however sketchily, the various experimental methods used in investigating intonation, but in order to put our own methodology into proper perspective, we shall briefly mention some of the most typical kinds of experimental work.

3.1 Registration and interpretation of instrumentally obtained Fo traces

These have been obtained by analog or digital means. Various analog 'pitch meters' or 'pitch extractors' have been constructed as developments or modifications of Grützmacher and Lottermoser's Tonhöhenschreiber (Grützmacher and Lottermoser, 1937), including the Glottograph. In a number of papers, the Kay Electric Sonagraph has been used, one of the harmonics -usually a relative high one, e.g. the fifth or tenth - being traced from narrow-band spectrograms. Also, various kinds of Fo graphs used to be prepared on the basis of measurements of oscillograms of the (filtered or unfiltered) speech wave. A number of different algorithms for digital extractions of time-varying fundamental frequency in speech have been developed over the last 20 years or so, including Fourier, cepstrum and autocorrelation analysis. An excellent survey of both analog and digital pitch measurement methods is contained in Schroeder (1976) and more recently in Hess (1983).

3.2 Aural Analysis

The perception of time-varying pitch in speech has been involved in data-collecting in various ways, one of the earliest being in Jones (1909), where the intonation curves were obtained by picking up the needle of a gramophone in different points of every syllable, aurally comparing the sensation at the moment of interruption with the tone produced by tuning-forks, and selecting the closest match. Later, electrical oscillators were used for a similar purpose. Intonation curves as graphical representations of the auditory impressions were later obtained by Jones and others by carefully listening to recorded materials and making graphs unscaled either in time or in frequency.

3.3 Synthetic Speech

Synthetic speech has been used for intonation studies by several authors, e.g. by Uldall (1964) and Hadding and Studdert-Kennedy (1964). Special mention should be made of a relatively early but still relevant study by Hadding-Koch (1961), in which a very successful attempt was made to relate experimental data measurements and listening tests to linguistic entities.

4. Levels of Intonation Study

Intonation has been studied at three levels, the physical, the perceptual and the functional. The physical level of study includes extraction of fundamental frequency and time-varying overall intensity level (if this parameter is included in the definition), registration of Fo(t) and possibly I(t) and description of the data in statistical terms. Classification of the data in terms of linguistic entities is highly desirable. The results naturally depend on the accuracy of the instruments and the adequacy of analytical procedures. Perceptual studies have sometimes been regarded as in some way less trustworthy because of their subjective character. This standpoint, however, can engender some misunderstanding. General phonetics has to take into account all three aspects of speech activity, in its production as well as its reception: the neural, the physiological and the psychological. A psychological study of speech communication is not only perfectly legitimate, but is even an indispensable area of linguistic investigation. The study of speech perception is a rapidly developing field of research although relatively little has been done on the perception of pitch (and intensity) in running, natural speech by way of psychological experimentation. The early descriptions of English and French intonation by Klinghardt and Fourmestraux (1911), and Klinghardt and Klemm (1920) as well as the later ones contained, for example, in Jones *Outline of English Phonetics* (1975); Armstrong and Ward (1926); Coustenoble and Armstrong (1934) etc. were perceptual. They were not based on instrumental analysis and did little to structure the data into a system of functional units. Functional analysis of intonation in a non-tone language was pioneered by Palmer (1922), improved, among others, by Kingdon (1958), and brought to a high standard of theoretical abstraction by Hirst (1977), for example.

5. Representation of Intonation

At the *physical* level of description, there is little variation in the mode of representation. Fundamental frequency is recorded as a linear, logarithmic or hyperbolic function of time and the scale of the independent variable is almost invariably linear. At the level of *perception*, some of the earlier and just a few more recent descriptions use a continuous line which disregards voicelessness and syllabic structure (Jones, 1909; Jones, 1940; Hill, 1965). Mostly, the representation is in syllabic terms. The syllable is considered to be the sub-functional perceptual unit of pitch variation in speech, and each syllable is represented as having a level, falling, rising, rising-falling, falling-rising or rising-falling-rising pitch. Hardly anybody postulates falling-rising-falling syllabic intonation (probably such a pitch variation produces two syllabic peaks). Whether this is the way naive listeners perceive intonation sub-functionally has never been investigated. English is at present the only non-tone language whose intonation has been analysed in functional terms[2]. It is at this level of description that disagreement between the specialists is strongest. The distinction between tonality, tonicity and tone has been overtly or tacitly accepted by most authors, but there the consensus (if any) ends. A comparison of the different systems proposed for Standard English - British or American - would require separate monographic treatment, but some of the salient divergencies may be identified here:

(1) Tone-group as an indivisible entity vs. segmentation into its constituents (e.g. nuclear/pre-nuclear, tonic/pretonic, head/prehead, etc.).

(2) Primary distinction in terms of levels vs. configurations (or 'directions').

(3) Kinds of functionally distinct categories: are level tones, or rising-falling-rising tones functionally distinct or are they 'allotones'? If a fall-rise is an allotone, does it belong to one toneme together with a rise (Brazil, Coulthard and Johns, 1980) or a fall (Bailey, 1979)?

(4) Number of functionally distinct (sub) categories: e.g., *two* nuclear falls (O'Connor and Arnold, 1973); *three* (Jassem, 1952; Lindström, 1978; Jassem, 1983; *four* (Kingdon, 1958). For practically all authors the criterion of distinctiveness is semantic. But Crystal (1969: 282 ff.) has pointed out the vagueness of semantic formulations in intonation analysis. Discourse-pragmatic criteria have recently been tried (Brazil et al 1980) and at least one attempt at an a-semantic distributional approach has also been made (Jassem, 1978).

6. Sources of Data

The sources of data may be classified in various ways, but the main distinction, from the standpoint of methodology, is one between 'external' and 'internal'. When actual speech produced by people other than the observer is described, the source is external. A description of external data may be based on instantaneous impressions of transient speech stored in the listener's short-term memory and recorded by him graphically using some kind of pitch notation. A more reliable description is obtained by repeated listening to 'canned' speech, in fragments of various extent (individiual syllables, syllable sequences forming words, accentual groups, rhythm groups etc.). The 'internal source' is essentially the describer's linguistic long-term memory (or 'generating competence'). Authors using internal data do not usually say whether, before making a 'tonetic' notation, they externalise their 'inner speech'. But even supposing they do, and listen to it, such data must be considered 'internal', the long-term memory being the ultimate source. If, however, an author analyses, ex post, his own spontaneous speech recorded on tape, this is, in our sense, 'external' evidence.

Much relatively recent work is based on external data, usually in the form of canned speech (now almost invariably stored on audio tape). But some theoretical work is still given quasi-empirical support by quoting internal data (e.g. Bolinger, 1982). It has to be assumed that if an author does not indicate the source, it is 'internal'.

Experimental work is, by definition, based on external data.

7. From Fo Traces to Functional Units: Sources of Variation

Although few authors openly take the metaphysical position mentioned in Section 1, there is still no methodology, much less an algorithm, that would enable raw acoustic-phonetic data to be interpreted linguistically. This is of course true of Fo traces (curves) just as much as of multi- or two-dimensional representations of the dynamic spectrum correlating with the segmentals. But in one respect intonation is worse off. Although any language seems to allow more than one phonemicization at the segmental level, one interpretation can mostly be converted into another, even if different principles of functional analysis are applied.

This is not the case with intonation. None of the major systems proposed for British English intonation are mutually convertable beyond perhaps the most typical pitch patterns, mainly for reasons outlined in Section 5 above.

The explanation of the alleged impossibility of inductively passing from raw physical phonetic data to functional ('-emic') patterns is almost unanimously 'justified' or 'explained' by the apparent incompatability of the 'infinitely variable' and 'quasi-continuous' signal with its 'invariant' and 'essentially discrete' linguistic (structural, or functional) correlate - a common view recently expressed by Hammarberg (1982). It is alleged that this situation is the main stumbling block in Automatic Speech Recognition. But this situation is by no means unique or in any sense specific. Indeed, man's communication with his outside world depends crucially on his intellectual ability to categorise and to discretise incoming information of various kinds. And if other such abilities have successfully been simulated by computers, there is no reason to assume that this particular one, in one particular domain of phenomena, should not be amenable to computer simulation, and concomitantly, to logical-mathematical analysis and synthesis.

Our problem, then, is to look for a method of splitting up an Fo curve into fragments uniquely corresponding to some linear linguistic entities and assigning these fragments to the appropriate classes of some entities. This can be done by using statistical classification techniques used in pattern recognition. It is possible to apply either entirely inductive, or heuristic or mixed procedures. The choice largely depends on prior identification of the *sources of variation*. If these are found to be numerous and interactive, then strict induction may be too expensive computationally.

Very little systematic work has been done to uncover the various reasons why individual samples in an arbitrary ensemble of Fo traces may differ. A very important classification of the effects is made in Rossi et al (1981: 22 ff.) into:

(a) controlled linguistic and paralinguistic,
(b) uncontrolled inherent-deterministic, and
(c) random.

In a more detailed specification, the following variation sources are enumerated (ibid : 21) :

(a) the modality of the sentence phrase,
(b) the structure of the sentence phrase,
(c) the speaker's attitude,
(d) the quantity of information carried by the different parts of the utterance,
(e) the realisation of lexical and morphological stresses,
(f) the speaker's personal voice features,
(g) the socio-cultural characteristics and regional speech traits,
(h) the age and sex of the speaker, and
(i) the nature of the segmental units which constitute the signal and their concatenations.

In our experience (as well as that of other authors) we have identified a somewhat different and still more detailed set of variation sources, which we will now list with brief comments and/or examples.

(1) *Speaker's attitude, situational and/or discourse conditions*:
      (a) direction of pitch movement, e.g. / \Yes vs. / /Yes / vs. / ∨ Yes / etc.
      (b) height or width, e.g., / /Yes / vs. / ´Yes / etc.

(2) *Thematic accent placement*: I **didn't** see Ruth vs. I didn't **see** Ruth vs. I didn't see **Ruth** etc.

(3) *Lexical and/or grammatical stress realisation*: be**ll**ow vs. be**low**, im**port** vs. **im**port, etc.

(4) *Segmentally/lexically conditioned length of the curve and concomitant effects of the curve's gradients*: \one vs. \seven vs. \seventy, etc.

(5) *Free allotonic variation*: in long sequence of syllables in the **'tail'** of a rising nucleus, each syllable may be slightly higher than the preceding one, or any two or possibly three may have the same pitch as long as the last one of the whole series is higher than the first, etc.

(6) *Short-term or medium-term effects of emotional states* (only partially controlled, or uncontrolled, except when pretended, especially for artistic purposes), e.g. excessively high or excessively low pitch, tremble, etc.

(7) *Phsyiological long-term personal features*: individual mean pitch and range, other features of the statistical distribution of instantaneous Fo values (kurtosis, skewness).[3]

(8) *Pathological long-term voice features*: polyps, carcinoma of the vocal cords, etc.

(9) *Short-term pathological voice features*: hoarseness and other disturbances caused by a cold, etc.

(10) *Short-term changes of mean pitch*, e.g. low pitch for confidentiality or in parenthetical phrases.

(11) *Personal long-term speech tempo affecting the length of a curve and its gradients.*

(12) *Short-term changes in tempo* (increased tempo in repeated phrases, decreased tempo in contemplation, etc).

(13) *Effects of segmental features*: breaks in the Fo trace due to voicelessness, aperiodicity of glottal pulses due to segmental creakiness, local minima within voiced consonantal segments, etc.

(14) *Non-pathological irregularities in phonation* (non-segmental creakiness in final falls, sporadic aperiodicities, etc.)

(15) *Style*: greater differentiation of tones and greater range in artistic speech, oratory, etc.

(16) *Random.*

In natural spontaneous speech one is not likely to encounter, in proximity, two utterances (tone-groups) differing by an effect of exactly one source of variation. Even occasional repetitions in immediate succession by the same speaker will probably not differ just randomly. Such tone-groups, in normal speech, are almost certain to be affected by, for instance, change of tempo and register (height). Just to record samples of spontaneous speech, extract Fo from them and by applying strictly inductive methods obtain a description of the materials in linguistic terms is not a theoretical impossibility. This is precisely what a child's perceptual and intellectual processing mechanisms do during language acquisition. There is little doubt that in language acquisition and later in speech recognition by man, there are several stages of information reduction at the sensory and the substructural phonetic/tonetic level of processing pitch data. Maybe if we knew how this reduction is performed, we might be in a position to simulate that process and construct an algorithm for the extraction of linguistic information from a representative but random sample of speech data. Unfortunately, we know next to nothing about human processing of the Fo parameter in speech, so we are reduced to the laborious task of applying more general knowledge, formulating plausible hypotheses and testing them in a more roundabout way. We have to design the experiment, then, so as to deal, to start with, with as few variables at a time as possible. This can be done by elimination, normalisation or by rule - if the rule is known.

8. The Present Experiment

We are engaged in an attempt to describe the various sources of variation, i.e. to find how they affect the Fo trace individually and jointly. We are prepared to discover a new source of variation of which we have not been aware. We assume that the *linguistically relevant variations* (the 'distinctive features') that distinguish functional units of intonation cannot be identified experimentally unless we can account for all, or at least most of the remaining effects. We mainly use elimination and normalisation in our materials, which include samples of Standard Polish and Standard British English. The personal effects can successfully be normalised for by reducing the various voices to a common pitch and by equalising the individual voice ranges (see Jassem and Dobrogowska, 1980). For tempo, we are experimenting with linear and piecewise-linear normalisations (cf. Jassem and Demenko, 1981). A special design is being used to separate out the linguistic effect. We record prototype utterances containing what we hypothesise to be contrastive intonations. These are reproduced over earphones to the test subjects who are required to repeat the prototype utterances without attempting mimickry. The prototypes and the imitations are (re-)recorded alternately on a test tape which is submitted to a listening test by a panel of native listeners (separate, of course for the two languages). The judges are required to decide whether each imitation is what they would naturally (in natural speech-communication conditions) accept as being linguistically the same as the immediately preceding prototype. Imitations unanimously (or almost unanimously) judged as being the same as the prototype are assumed not to differ linguistically from it and from other imitations of the same prototype. Others are rejected either for a repeated imitation attempt or for scrapping. By then comparing normalised Fo traces of contrastive intonations we hope to be able to track linguistic distinctions.

The instrumentation which we are using is a hybrid system. It includes a Tonometer; a pitch extractor (or 'detector') devised by Kubzdela (1976); an extremely simple minicomputer (8K 8-bit-word memory, 2×10^{-5} s operation cycle); an interface designed in our laboratory; and an ordinary TV receiver. The special interface (called Memoskop) is able to produce on the screen of a commercially available TV receiver, a graphic representation of digital information stored internally or externally. An Fo trace is also obtained in the form of a printout together with the measurement of instantaneous pitch (in Hz) at time intervals that can be set to a variety of values (2 ms, 10 ms and 20 ms have mostly been used) or in the form of a graph on the TV screen, with variable time and frequency scales. Two or more traces can be overlaid on the display screen.

It is not possible, within the scope of this paper, to present the complete method which we are employing in analysing our materials, and some minor details of this method are still being improved on. But we shall now show, by way of a few examples, how we are attempting to deal with some of the sources of variation listed above.

Figures 1 to 7 are photographs taken from the TV screen. In these Figures, the marks on the time scale indicate intervals between 8 data points, the Fo values being here measured at $\Delta t = 10$ ms. The lowest mark on the frequency scale indicates 70 Hz in male voices and 140 Hz in female voices, and the distances between the marks on the vertical scale correspond to 20 Hz.

Figure 1 Does EVeryone here run a Rolls Royce? Two male voices.
No time normalistion.

In Figure 1, the two overlaid Fo traces are those of imitations by two male
voices of the prototype utterance *Does **EV***eryone here run a Rolls Royce?*
recorded on the commercial tape accompanying Halliday 1970 (p. 103 of the
text). According to Halliday's analysis, the utterance represents tone 2
described as 'pointed falling-rising'. It does not actually seem to correspond to
Halliday's description as the rise is obviously delayed, but what we want to
point out here is that whilst the two utterances are practically identical in
duration and the contours are very similar, there is a phase difference in the
incidence of the fall. There is, then a difference in timing which we assume to
be a random effect. But the entire black contour trace can also be seen strongly
to tend to be higher than the overlaid dotted trace. In order to make the two
more directly comparable by eliminating the phase difference, we apply
piecewise-linear time normalisation, after which the two curves come out as in
Figure 2.

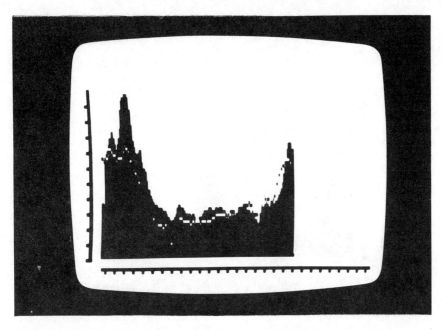

Figure 2 Does EVeryone here run a Rolls Royce? Two male voices. Piecewise linear time normalisation.

The falling fragments of the two curves are now exactly in phase. The final rises could also be brought into line, but this is a minor phase discrepancy of some 50 ms, and it has been judged not to justify the added computational cost involved in the adjustment. Even without this, the two traces show that one voice spoke the complete utterance at a consistently lower pitch than the other. A statistical analysis based on data from 25 utterances with various intonations produced by the two speakers showed, by a t-test, that indeed the respective long-term mean pitches were, at $p < 0.05$, significantly different (125 and 146 Hz). Note that the difference, at most points along the time scale, after time normalisation, are approximately proportional, so the absolute difference at the beginning of the full (or 'high') fall is greater (about 60 Hz) than that at the trough, where it does not exceed some 30 Hz. The evidence, then, for a hypothesis that the two traces represent liguistically identical intonations is strong.

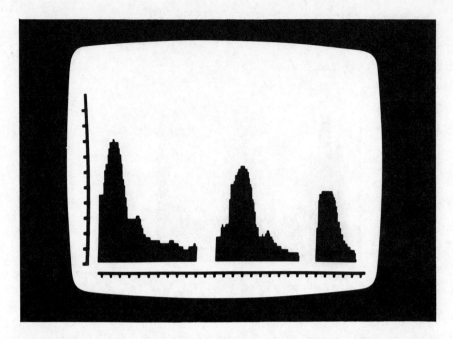

Figure 3 (1) GO home now. (2)GO home. (3)GO. Female voice. No smoothing.

Figure 3 depicts Fo traces of the utterances:

(1) *GO home now,*
(2) *GO home,* and
(3) *GO*

spoken by a female voice (Brazil et al, 1980: 43) and recorded on a commercial cassette. The three utterances are asumed by the authors to represent the same *type* of intonation, viz. a falling tonic (nucleus), the difference betwen the three being allegedly only due to lexical/segmental conditions. Actually, the peak can easily be seen to descend from (1) through (2) to (3). It cannot be assumed without further evidence that the three pitch patterns are in fact realisations of the same functional units of intonation. (1) and (2) here, as well as in the traces in Figures 1 and 2, show distinct local minima related to consonantal articulation (the resonants are known to have the weakest effect). But allowing for these local segmental influences, these traces show some slight irregularities which are unaccounted for and assumed random. A slight smoothing has consequently been performed.

12

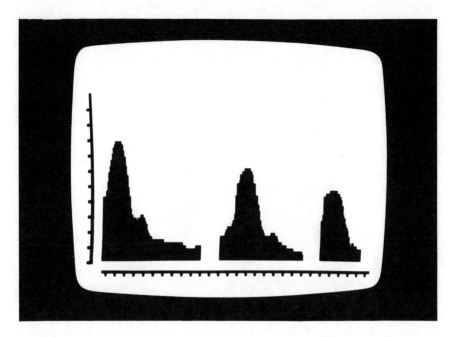

Figure 4. The same as in Fig.3, but curves slightly smoothed.

Each datum (except the first and the last two) represents the average of three succesive measurements. The curves are now less ruffled, as shown in Figure 4, but the local consonantal dips are preserved.

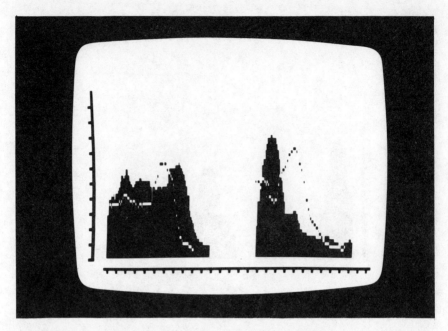

Figure 5   **(1) GO home NOW (left, black contour). (2) Go home NOW (left, dotted line). (3) GO home now (right, black contour). (4)Go HOME Now. (right dotted line). Female voice.**

In Figure 5 one female voice is saying:
(1) *GO home \ NOW,*
(2) *Go home \NOW,*
(3) *\ GO home now*, and
(4) *Go \HOME now*.

All the tonics (nuclei) are assumed to be falls (Brazil et al, 1980: 44). (1) and (2) reveal a slight difference in tempo. The pretonic (prenuclear) fragment is lower in the version with unstressed (unaccented) *go*, whilst the tonics (nuclei) are almost identical. (1/2), (3) and (4) are here compared to show the effect of nuclear accent placement on the pitch curve.

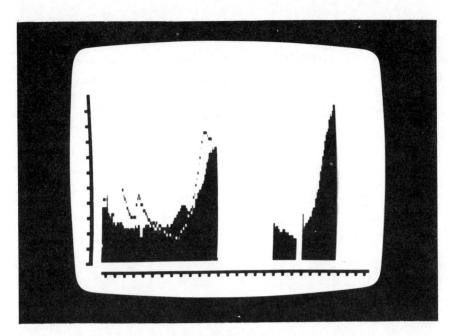

Figure 6 **(1) No-one here KNOWS you. (low rise, left black contour),
(2) Hasn't he any MANNERS? (high rise, left, dotted line). (3) Shall
we DANCE? (high rise, right, black contour). Male voice.**

Figure 6 represents the utterances:
(1) *No-one here KNOWS you* (Halliday 1970: 108 in the text), with a low
     rise,
(2) *Hasn't he any /MANNERS?* (Halliday 1970: 104) with a high rise, and
(3) *Shall we /DANCE?* (Halliday 1970: 104) with a high rise, spoken by one
     male voice imitating the prototypes. The two high rises indeed end higher
     than the low rise. But the difference between the low and the first high is
     about the same as that between the two highs. Is the difference between
     low and high, probably relevant functionally, a categorical one? Or would
     a fuzzy-sets approach be here more appropriate? Only large-scale
     experiments could give answers to a question of this kind.

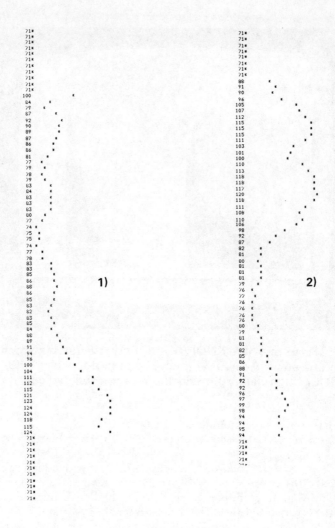

Figure 7 Do widzenia: (1)/dovi/dze ɲ a/, (2)/dovi,dze ɲ a/. Male voice

Figure 7 contains printouts of the Polish phrase *Do widzenia* ('Good bye') spoken by one male voice with two different final rises, a low one and a full one (low-to-high), with different pre-nuclear tones. The duration of the two phrases (unnormalised) is almost identical, and so are the consonantal effects. This is a case similar to the one in Figure 6, though simpler because of the elimination of two variables. But the main issue remains the same: are the differences representative of categorical or fuzzy (gradual) distinctions?

16

8. Conclusion

No-one probably believes that extracting functional units of intonation from Fo traces is a simple matter. But we hope to have shown that it is not an impossible proposition. We also trust that we have gone some little way towards indicating the procedures that may lead to a solution.

Footnotes

1.   *Haycraft and Creed (1973), for instance, intonation exercises in almost every Unit.*

2.   *An attempt at such an analysis of French was made by Thudicum (1926) and Polish intonation was described in function terms by Jassem (1962) and Steffen-Batogwa (1966).*

3.   *See Jassem (1971), and Graddol, this volume.*

PHONOLOGICAL AND ACOUSTIC PARAMETERS OF ENGLISH INTONATION

Daniel Hirst

1. Introduction: Models and Modules

Linguists, like all scientists, differ in the relative importance which they accord on the one hand to the description and classification of observable data, and, on the other hand, to attempts to develop a formal model, on the basis of which some (ultimately most, if not all) of the observed data becomes predictable and hence understandable. Although most accounts of intonation can be classified in the former category, I shall assume in this paper, without further argument, that the latter approach is at least as legitimate.

A model, in this sense, is nothing more than an abstraction from the complexity of reality and, as such, is simply our way of admitting that reality itself is too much for us. As the authors of a recent work on computer science put it:

> A deep philosophical assumption underlying modern science is that the complexity of reality can be understood by understanding a collection of models - some that describe macroscopic behaviour by ignoring detail, others that successively explain increasingly microscopic behaviour. Whether this simplifying assumption is entirely valid can be debated, but our limited intellectual capacity **forces** us to make it. Without this assumption, we could not cope with the complexity surrounding us.

(Wulf, Shaw, Hilfinger and Plon (1981: 3)).

This approach has proved particularly fruitful in linguistic research in recent years. One of the basic claims of the so-called 'Extended standard theory' of generative grammar, for instance, is that a grammar can be thought of as a number of interacting but autonomous sub-components or modules organised approximately as in (1.1):

(1.1)

"meanings" ⟨ - - SEMANTICS ⟨ - - SYNTAX - - ⟩ PHONOLOGY - - ⟩ "sound"

GRAMMAR

where a central syntactic component is interpreted by the phonology and semantics of the grammar (cf. Chomsky 1981). Phonetics and pragmatics, within such a framework, can be thought of as the interfaces mediating

19

between the abstract representations generated by the grammar and the concrete realities of sound and meaning, respectively, encountered in the 'real world'.

In this paper, I attempt to outline what I take to be some of the necessary characteristics of a model of intonation within a general linguistic framework organised as in (1.1). While this description is particularly concerned with British English, it is hoped that the general approach will prove applicable to the intonation systems of other languages. The model outlined here obviously owes a great deal to other recent formal descriptions of English intonation, (in particular Goldsmith 1974; Liberman, 1975; Leben, 1976; Ladd, 1980; Pierrehumbert, 1981), although primarily for reasons of space and time the emphasis here is on the presentation of the model itself rather than on a comparison with the way in which the same facts have been treated in other frameworks.

2. Phonological Parameters

Assuming the general linguistic model outlined above, the phonological representation is in some way derived from the surface syntactic represent-ation. In this section I shall not be concerned with the actual derivation (for some discussion cf. Selkirk, 1978; Hirst, 1983c), only with the **form** of the phonological representations.

Recent work on the nature of phonological representations suggests that an appropriate form for such representations is a hierarchical structure, each node of which corresponds to a phonological category (such as syllable, foot, phrase, etc.), and which serves to link up two distinct levels of segments: the traditional segments of linear phonology, which I shall refer to here as P-segments, as well as a separate level of tones which I shall refer to as T-segments.[1]

Segments at each level can be defined by a distinct and restricted set of distinctive features. Specifically, I assume that tonal melodies (following Woo, 1969) can always be represented as a sequence of T-segments corresponding to static, level tones.[2] I shall assume, as I have argued elsewhere (Hirst, 1980 and 1983b), that T-segments in English can be defined by two binary features: [high] and [low]. Although there are obviously a great number of *phonetic* values for pitch-height which need to be specified for an adequate description of English intonation, the claim behind the analysis I propose is that these values are determined contextually, and that the only *phonologically* relevant values are those distinguished by the two features [high] and [low]. If we take the feature [+ low] to define a lowering of pitch and the feature [+ high] to define a (slightly smaller) raising of pitch, the following combinations are possible:

$$[+high, -low] = H(igh)\text{-tone}$$
$$[-high, +low] = L(ow)\text{-tone}$$
$$[+high, +low] = D(rop)\text{-tone}$$
$$[-high, -low] = M(id)\text{-tone}$$

where an H-tone will be realised on a relatively high pitch, an L-tone on a relatively low pitch and a D-tone on a pitch level just slightly lower than that of a preceding H-tone. The status of the M-tone is less clear. I assume in the following discussion that the initial tone-value found at the beginning of sentences and typically situated towards the middle of the speaker's pitch-range is in fact an L-tone. An alternative analysis would be to take this initial tone to be an M-tone, thus increasing the tonal inventory to four tonal segments instead of three.

A reasonable constraint on the input to the phonetic component might be summed up by saying that representations at this level must be "pronounce-able". A possible form for such a constraint could be to allow a representation at this level to consist of a sequence of "chunks" consituting an exhaustive segmentation of the prosodic structure, where each chunk consists of one foot (F) which must dominate at least one syllable (S) and one T-segment, and where each syllable must dominate at least one P-segment. Thus:

(2.1) Chunking constraint
Surface-representations must conform to the following template:

$$\underset{F_1}{\left[\begin{array}{l} \underset{S_1 \qquad \ 1}{[\text{P-segment}\ ]} \\[2ex] \underset{\qquad \ \ \ 1}{\text{T-segment}} \end{array}\right]}$$

where, following standard conventions the notation X_1 is shorthand for a sequence of one or more occurrences of the symbol X.

The neutral, unmarked intonation for both falling and rising patterns in British English has been described as a "descending scale" (Armstrong and Ward, 1926: 4) "a series of gently descending stresses" (Pike, 1945: 106), "une suite descendante" (Faure, 1948: 123) to cite but a few early accounts. In terms of T-segments as outlined above, this can be represented as a sequence

21

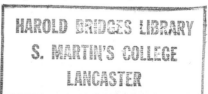

[H D D ...]³, so that a sentence like:

(2.2)
[Would you like a-] [nother glass of] [whisky]

assuming that it is divided into stress-feet as in (2.2), could be represented as either:

(2.3)a
[Would you like a-] [nother glass of] [whisky]
[L   H   ][D   ][D L]

(2.3)b.
[Would you like a-] [nother glass of] [whisky]
[L   H   ][D   ][L H]

depending on whether the final *nuclear* foot is realised as a rise or a fall.

Examination of fundamental frequency curves shows that T-segments are apparently of two types depending on whether they seem to be timed to coincide (approximately) with:

a) the middle of a phonological category (here the foot)
b) the boundary of a phonological category (here the phrase)

We can account for this distinction if we introduce these tones at different levels in the grammar, so that the boundary tones are originally directly dominated by the category phrase, and the other tones are directly dominated by the category Foot. The chunking constraint (2.1) can then be assumed to account for the linearisation converting such an abstract representation to a pronounceable sequence of categories.

The possible phrase contours can now be specified as, for example:

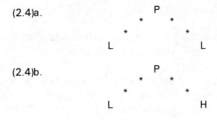

(2.4)a.   P
                         *   *
                      *   *
                   L   L

(2.4)b.   P
                         *   *
                      *   *
                   L   H

which will account for the basic division of intonation contours into two
tunes: falling and rising (Tune 1 and Tune 2 in the terminology of Armstrong
and Ward, (1926)).

Sentence (2.2) could now, consequently, be represented as either:

(2.5)a.
[[Would you like a] [nother glass of] [whisky]]
   [H   ][D   ][D   ]
   [L   L   ]

OR

(2.5)b.
[[Would you like a] [nother glass of] [whisky]]
   [H   ][D   ][L   ]
   [L   H   ]

The representations (2.5) are identical except for the final foot where the
choice of tone depends on the choice of the final boundary tone. Note, though,
that in both cases the linearised version of the final foot (as in (2.3)) specifies a
fall from a D-tone to an L-tone. Since there is nothing to prevent two tones
from being assigned to the same category in the underlying representation, we
could analyse the final foot of both sentences as containing the sequence [D
L] so that (2.5) would be replaced by:

(2.6)a.
[[Would you like a-] [nother glass of] [whisky]]
   [H   ][D   ][D L]
   [L   L   ]

(2.6)b.
[[Would you like a-] [nother glass of] [whisky]]
   [H   ][D   ][D L]
   [L   H   ]

(2.6)b
where the only difference between the two representations is now in the final
boundary tone. This is of course a highly desirable result since it means that we
can characterise a discrete difference between two contours as the result of a
single binary choice between (2.4)a and (2.4)b.

If we now look at the possible tonal combinations for each foot, we find:

        (2.7)a.   F

                                   H   L

for phrases containing only a single foot, otherwise we find:

        (2.7)b.   F
                                   |
                                  H

(2.7)b for the first foot,

        (2.7)c.   F
                             *   *
                       *   *
                  D   L

(2.7)c for the final foot, and (2.7)d

        (2.7)d.   F
                                 |
                                  D

for any intermediate feet. It is noteworthy that the occurrence of a D-tone is restricted in that it can only occur after an H-tone. This is precisely the distribution of downstepped high tones found in a number of African tone-languages (for an account of Anderson, 1978: 141-2) which, as Anderson points out:

> "usually results from the loss of a low-tone element (either historically or synchronically) between two highs; when the low tone has conditioned the downdrift of the following high, and is then lost, it results in the appearance of a third, potentially contrastive, tonal value following a high tone, in addition to 'high' and 'low'"

(op. cit. p.142)

If we adopt a similar account for the origin of the D-tones in English, this would result in an underlying form:

                       (2.8)
                       [[Would you like a-] [nother glass of] [whisky]]
                       [H   L   ][H   L   ][H L]
                       [L   **   ]

(where .... is either H or L). This would then be converted by a downstep-rule into the intermediate forms (2.6) and finally linearised into the surface forms like (2.3) except that the final foot can be taken to be [D L L] and [D L H] respectively. Note furthermore that if the downstep-rule is taken to be optional, both (2.8) and (2.6) would be available as near-surface forms, thus accounting for O'Connor and Arnold's (1961) distinction betwen stepping and sliding heads. O'Connor and Arnold describe the sliding head as follows:

> "the pattern of the accented syllables is exactly that found in the stepping head, the first high, the second lower, and so on, but the unaccented syllables are treated differently: instead of being said on the same pitch as the previous accented syllable, they form a descending sequence." (p.20)

Interestingly, Pike (1945) proposes what seems very much like O'Connor and Arnold's sliding head as the unmarked pattern for American English, pointing out that "in usage (and meaning?)" this corresponds to the British "series of gently descending stresses" (p.106). This means simply that the dialectal difference between British and American usage can be characterised as a difference of interpretation of the optional downstep rule, the application of which appears to be the unmarked case in British and the marked case in American. In both cases we can assume that T-segments are assigned to the category foot in conformity with the foot template:

(2.9)

which covers all the possibilities listed above.

Besides the two unmarked patterns, many linguists have pointed out the existence of 'marked' or 'emphatic' variants of the two tunes. I have proposed (Hirst, 1977 Ch. 8) an analysis in which a feature of 'emphasis' (covering both emphasis for intensity and emphasis for contrast) can contribute to the intonation of a sentence, being specifically intended to account for high-falling and falling-rising intonation patterns. Although the abstract feature I proposed was not assumed to have any specific phonetic exponent, an analysis of the effect of this feature on the overall intonation pattern is interesting. The essential difference between a low-falling nucleus and a high-falling nucleus is the relative height of the starting point of the fall with respect to the preceding stressed syllable (if any, otherwise with respect to the speaker's normal voice range): the low-fall beginning at a level on or just below that of the last stressed syllable and the high fall generally starting clearly above this level. In the case of rising patterns, the unmarked rise drops from a level at, or just below, that of the preceding stressed syllable, and then rises to a relatively high level at the end of the phrase, whereas the marked rise drops from a level distinctly higher than that of the last stressed syllable before rising to a relatively high level at the end of the phrase.

Schematically:

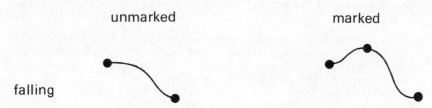

A possible represenation for the four different final feet might be as follows:

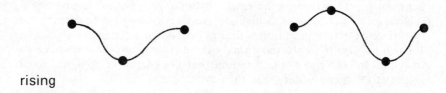

assuming that in a sequence [D + H] or [H + H], the second tone is actually higher than the first.

The final tone of the marked pattern corresponds evidently to the boundary-tone, as discussed above for the unmarked pattern. The difference, consequently, is that the marked pattern in both cases contains an extra H-tone. Remembering that the initial D-tone has been analysed as deriving from an underlying H-tone preceded by an H-L sequence, by means of the downstep rule, the marked and unmarked feet before the operation of this rule, correspond respectively to:

$$[\,H\,L\,]\,[\,H\,H\,L\,]$$

Suppose now we set up an underlying form where the initial H-tone of the marked foot is in fact outside the final foot, constituting perhaps a foot in its own right, but a foot of a rather special kind since it contains only the T-segment consituted by the H-tone and no P-segments. This is in contradiction with the chunking constraint (2.1), but as we saw above this constraint can be assumed to apply only at the input to the phonetic component so that it will in fact have the effect of deriving the surface representation from the more abstract underlying form. This analysis then implies that we set up an underlying emphatic morpheme consisting of a "floating" H-tone. Such an analysis is by no means exceptional, floating tones have been proposed to simplify the analysis of a number of complex phenomena encountered in the analysis of tone-languages. A well-documented example is found in Bambara where the definite marker behaves like a floating L-tone, affecting the surface manifestation of the surrounding tones (cf. Bird, 1966).

In conclusion, then, while of course we are far from a complete description of English intonation, a "core" system for British English can be derived rather naturally from a small number of interacting principles, the "chunking" constraint (2.1), the downstep rule, the phrase templates (2.4) and the foot template (2.9), together with the possibility of an emphatic morpheme, consisting of a floating H-tone. Such a simple system can of course be extended in a number of directions, by increasing the number of phrase or foot templates, or by the introduction of other conditions. I shall not pursue these possibilities here. Instead, I shall try to outline the way in which the prosodic representation described in this section determines the actual acoustic parameters of intonation patterns.

3. Phonetic and Acoustic Parameters

The output of the phonetic model can be taken to be a set of physiological and/or acoustic parameters which vary as a function of time. In this section I briefly sketch the way in which we get from the sort of representation described above to the specific physical parameters. If we restrict our attention to acoustic parameters, we shall particularly be concerned with segmental duration, fundamental frequency (Fo) and intensity since the other parameters can be assumed to be determined by the actual P-segments of the utterance.

The measurable Fo curve of an utterance can be thought of as an interaction between the intrinsic characteristics of the P-segments and the continuously evolving tension of the vocal-folds. During voiceless segments, for example, there is no detectable Fo value although it can be shown (Hirst, 1981 a,b) that vocal-fold tension continues to change throughout the duration of the segment, irrespective of the voiced/voiceless nature of the segment in question. This means that we can in fact ignore such perturbations of the underlying pitch-curve and model Fo curves (at a first approximation) as a continuous function of time.

These continuous functions can be thought of as an interpolation between a sequence of target-points.[4]

A minimal curve, in this sense, would be defined by two points constituting either a rise or a fall. The typical form for such a contour, assuming that we ignore segmental disturbancies, is an s-shaped curve linking the maximum and minimum values:

27

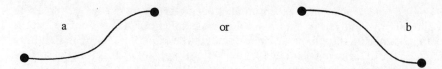

a　　　　　　　　or　　　　　　　　b

There are, of course, an infinite variety of ways of generating curves like (3.1) from a specification of the initial and final values. I have shown (Hirst, 1981a) that an extremely close approximation to natural Fo curves can be obtained by using a quadratic spline function.[5] This function in fact requires three parameters for each target-point, two of which can be determined from the inflection-point of the curve, (the relative position of which with respect to the two adjacent target-points is probably a speaker-dependent parameter). Measurements with my own productions show a tendency for the inflection-point to be closer to the higher of the two tones. This is consistent with Ohala and Ewan's well-known result that active lowering of pitch is faster than active raising of pitch (cf. Ohala and Ewan, 1973, Sundberg, 1979).

If we can predict the shape of the curve between successive target-points of an utterance, this means that an appropriate phonetic representation of the Fo curve would be the sequence of target-points itself, a sequence of pairs $<$ti, hi$>$ for example, where ti represents a time-value in seconds and hi a fundamental frequency value in Hertz.

The role of the phonetic component will thus be to derive such a sequence from the phonological representation sketched in Section 2. This can be broken down into two distinct tasks:

(3.2)　　　a) Deriving the time value (ti) of the tonal segment
　　　　　　b) Deriving the Fo value (hi) of the tonal segment.

It seems reasonable to suppose that ti will be a function of the time value of the beginning and of the end of the stress-foot in which the T-segment occurs, as well as of the number of T-segments in the stress-foot and the position of the T-segment in that sequence. Representing these parameters respectively as ta, tb, ns and ps, a first approximation to (3.2a) would be:

(3.3)　　　ti = ta + (ps/(ns + 1)).(tb - ta)

Thus for example the second (ps = 2) of three tones (ns = 3) occuring in a stress-foot, the beginning of which is situated at 2.345 secs (= ta) and the end of which is situated at 2.560 secs (= tb), will be assigned a time-value

ti = 2.345 + (2/(3 + 1)).(2.560 — 2.345) = 2.4525

(3.3) as it stands needs a slight modification so that the first and last T-segments of a phrase are timed to coincide with the beginning of the first stress-foot and the end of the last stress-foot respectively. A further defect of (3.3) is that it does not take into account the *nature* of the tones, implying that within a given stress-foot, the time-interval between for instance H and L will be the same as that between L and L or H and H. A cursory examination of actual Fo curves suffices to show that this is not correct. Rather, the time-interval between two T-segments seems to be related in some way to the pitch difference between the two target-points. In fact, if the quadratic spline-function model is correct, assuming a constant acceleration/deceleration of pitch-change, we should expect to find that the square of the time-interval between two points is proportional to the absolute difference in Fo.

Let us define the "pitch-distance" PD between two values as the square-root of the absolute difference in Hz. Thus the PD between 100 and 200 is 10. Now let us define CPD, the cumulative pitch-distance, for a value in a sequence of values, as the sum of the PDs for consecutive values up to and including the value itself. Thus for the sequence [135 200 100] the CPD for 135 is 0, that for 200 is 8.062 and that for 100 is 18.062.

Let us finally refer to the CPD of the boundary at the end of the phrase, as TPD, the Total Pitch Distance of the phrase. We can now propose the following approximation to (3.2a):

(3.4) $t_i = t_a + (CPD_i/TPD)(t_b - t_a)$

where CPD_i and TPD are calculated as outlined above and where t_a and t_b represent respectively the beginning of the first stress-foot and the end of the last stress-foot.

Table 1 gives an example of the actual and estimated timing of the T-segments (mean values for 3 repetitions) for the sequence /mə ma mə ma/ pronounced echoing the intonation of the phrase "a cup of tea?" and "a cup of tea ...!" with an unmarked and marked rising intonation pattern respectively.

29

P-segments	[mə	[ma	mə]	[m	a	]]
Foot boundaries	0	65		350		690
T-segments		[L	H]	[D	L	H]
Hi (Hz)		129	219	184	95	176
Ti (ms)		85	350	430	550	690
Estimated Ti		65	240	350	524	690

P-segments	[mə	[ma		mə]	[m		a	]]
Foot-boundaries	0	70			375			760
T-segments		[L	H	L]	[H	H	L	H]
Hi (Hz)		152	209	114	149	172	86	166
Ti (ms)		65	225	370	450	510	650	760
Estimated Ti		70	183	328	416	488	626	760

Table 1	Estimated and measured time-values (Ti) for T-segments for unmarked and marked rising intonation patterns. The values given are mean values for three repetitions of each sentence.

As can be seen from Table 1, the approximation given by (3.4) is quite good. Note, however, that (3.4) assumes that the Fo values of the target-points are given, but not the time-values of the foot boundaries, which can now be assumed to be determined in part as a function of the tonal constituents of the foot.

Let us now turn to (3.2b) which, as we have just seen, appears in fact to be determined before (3.2a). I shall not attempt to present here anything like a complete model for the determination of Fo values from a prosodic representation, the following remarks are merely intended as an outline of work in progress.

Measurements on a fairly small corpus of short sentences read aloud out of context suggest the following tendencies:

(3.6)   (i) a positive correlation between the height of the first H-tone and the number of stress-feet in the sentence.
(ii) a negative correlation between the height of the last H-tone (excluding boundary tones) and the number of stress-feet in the sentence.

(3.6)(i) and (ii) appear at first sight almost contradictory. One might have supposed that either the first H-tone would be given a fixed interpretation and the others scaled down from it, or that the last would be fixed and the others scaled upwards. In fact, the tendency would seem to be for the extreme values to be scaled away from a central value. It seems probable, however, that the sort of pre-programming that a speaker can afford when he is reading sentences aloud is not necessarily available to him in normal conditions of spontaneous speech. This is obviously a subject for further research. It is worth noting that the largest effect of the correlation mentioned in (3.6)(i) is that between sentences containing only one single stress-foot (mean value 165 Hz for 16 sentences) and sentences containing more than one stress foot (mean value 196 Hz for 16 sentences). Rather than link the pitch-value of the first H-tone to the number of stress-feet in the sentence, we can account for this tendency by assuming that the difference is due to an all-or-nothing effect, sentences containing only one foot being assigned a pitch-value H1 and sentences containing more than one stress-foot being assigned a pitch value H2. The interval separating H1 and H2 in the case of the recordings in question is $196/165 = 1.188$ corresponding approximately to three semi-tones, a minor third or (looked at another way) a quarter of an octave. This interval is one which, as I have pointed out elsewhere (cf. Hirst, 1981b; cf. also Liberman, 1975), frequently turns up in the measurement of Fo values of target-points. The value 165 Hz is itself approximately an octave above the average end point for these sentences. Suppose that we take literally the suggestion that 1/4 octave is a basic pitch interval. This would imply that the speaker's pitch-range is divided into a number of discrete quantal levels, each separated from the lower one by 1/4 octave. If we represent the lowest of these values as 1 and successively higher values as 2, 3 etc., the pitch-assignment rule mentioned above will not state that H1 = 5 and H2 = 6. It seems likely, though, that even this is far too specific. It is well-known that some speakers use a much wider pitch-range than others, and that speakers can vary their pitch-range for various expressive purposes. Suppose instead that our pitch assignment rule merely states that H1 and H2 are assigned a positive integer value n such that n is greater than 2. This would imply that the observed difference between the mean value of H1 and H2 is not determined by the grammar at all and corresponds simply to a general tendency to start longer sentences higher. If this is true we should expect occasionally to find H1 assigned the value 6 or greater and H2 the value 5 or less, which does in fact seem to be the case.

In addition to (3.6), there is a strong correlation between the height of an H-tone or D-tone and the height of the following H-tone or D-tone. This correlation is even stronger when it is estimated on a log scale rather than a linear scale. This means that the descending scale can be modelled very simply as a recursive function of the form:

(3.7) $\ln(Hi) = aO + a1.\ln(Hi-1)$

which is assymptotically declining to a limit determined by $aO/(1-al)$. For the corpus mentioned earlier the regression values for aO and a1 worked out at 2.155 and 0.568 respectively.

In summary, then, it seems that there are two distinct mechanisms for determining the Fo value of a T-segment. The first of these makes use of an "absolute" quantal scale along which each consecutive pair of notes is separated by 1/4 octave (3 semi-tones). The descending series observed in a sequence of D-tones, however, does not seem to use the same absolute scale, but rather makes use of relative steps down from the preceding value - thus giving the possibility of an undetermined upper limit on the number of steps in a given sequence.

Footnotes:

1.   *For a useful summary of much recent work on phonological representations of van der Hulst and Smith (1982). For a more detailed justification of the specific representation I assume here cf. Hirst (1983a, b), where I show that an n-ary tree with each node corresponding to a category symbol is under certain natural assumptions isomorphic to the binary-branching trees of "metrical phonology".*

2.   *Static level tones as distinct from the complex dynamic tones (such as rise, rise-fall etc.) that have sometimes been proposed since Wang, 1967. In fact, the tonal segments I propose inthis model correspond to idealised pitch points rather than actual steady-states, as will be clearer from the discussion of pitch-targets in Section 3.*

3.   *P Schachter (cited by Stewart, 1971) has pointed out the tonal similarity of English stressed syllable sequences and sequences of downstepped high tones in African tone-languages such as Twi. Schachter suggests the possibility of using the Twi notation system for marking English tones and gives the example:*

        H´e ! c´ame ! h´ome th´is ! m^orn`ing

        where´marks a high tone,`marks a low tone and ! represents a downstep.

4.   *Another approach is to think of the continuous curves as filtered step-functions cf. Ohman, 1967; Fujisaki and Sudo, 1969. See Hirst (1981a) for a discussion of this and various other models.*

5.   *A spline-function of degree n is a continuous sequence of polynomial functions, the derivatives of which up to and including degree n-1 are everywhere continuous.*

AN ACOUSTIC STUDY OF SOME FEATURES OF WELSH PROSODY

Briony Williams

1. English Stress

This paper concentrates on the acoustic aspects of stress in Welsh. Most work to date on the acoustic correlates of stress has been done on English. So that the unusual nature of Welsh stress may be appreciated, a summary follows of the main findings about English stress from the acoustic point of view.

There is a fair degree of consensus as to the acoustic correlates of stress in English. The primary cue to stress is a change in fundamental frequency (Fo) within a syllable. The next most important cue is a step change in Fo between a stressed syllable and a neighbouring syllable, the stressed syllable usually having higher Fo. Also important is the fact that the stressed syllable usually has longer duration and greater amplitude, though the relative importance of these two cues is uncertain; for Lieberman (1960), peak amplitude is a more reliable cue than duration, while for Fry (1958), the opposite is the case. Fry also notes that, in the case of changes in Fo within a syllable, the actual shape and extent of the pitch curve are immaterial; what matters is its occurrence. Similarly, in the case of a difference in Fo between two syllables, Fry observes that the amount of difference in Fo is insignificant; this is the so-called 'all-or-none' effect. Lieberman (op. cit.) discovered 'trading effects' between Fo cues and amplitude cues; within certain limits, changes in Fo that fit with perceived stress may compensate for amplitude changes that do not fit with perceived stress, and vice-versa. Lieberman also noted that the integral of the amplitude with respect to time, as against simple peak amplitude, to some extent improves the degree of correlation with perceptual stress judgements.

Lieberman gives a 'flow chart' to represent his method of locating stressed syllables in pairs of syllables, from acoustic cues alone (Fig. 1).

The predictions made by this algorithm agreed with the perceptual stress judgements 99% of the time, for his data. It should be noted that the algorithm is framed in relative, not absolute, terms, and is suitable only for comparing two syllables. Variation along all three acoustic dimensions occurs to such an extent that it is at best unwise, at worst impossible, to give a yes/no stress judgement for an isolated syllable, based on absolute values alone. This point may be seen as significant when considered in relation to the 'metrical' theory of stress, the basic tenet of which is that stress is essentially a relative concept, only indirectly related to observable facts. More will be said later on this theory.

35

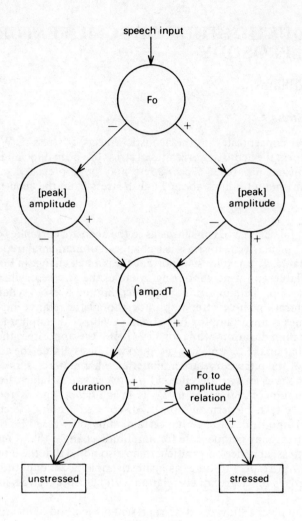

(after P. Lieberman, JASA 32 (1960): 451-454)

Figure 1   Program for mechanical recognition of stressed syllable

Referring again to Lieberman's flow chart, it will be noted that the Fo criterion at the top of the flow chart corresponds to the traditional notion of 'pitch-prominence'. A pitch-prominent syllable is one that contains a pitch glide, or is significantly higher or lower in pitch than a neighbouring syllable. The overall effect of a pitch-prominent syllable is to break away from an established intonation contour and/or to begin a new intonation contour. In English, most of the stressed syllables are also pitch-prominent. I hope to show that this is not necessarily the case in Welsh.

2. Prepausal Welsh Words

As a preliminary investigation of the acoustic correlates of stress in Welsh, recordings were made of a native (South) Welsh speaker reading a list of Welsh words and sentences. This speech, obviously not spontaneous, would be likely to show maximal exploitation of intonational and stress cues. Thus the results gained from examining these words would provide, it was hoped, a clear indication of the general tendencies in the realisation of stress in Welsh. Sound-spectograms were made of the isolated words, and of the word at the end of each sentence, with a frequency range of 80-8000 Hz. For each utterance, both wide-band and narrow-band spectograms were made, as well as an amplitude display.

Various measurements were then made from these spectograms, viz.; duration of each segment, peak and mean amplitude of vowels, Fo at the beginning of each vowel(in many cases the Fo nearer the end could not easily be ascertained), and the integral of the amplitude with respect to time (or 'envelope amplitude', measured as accurately as was possible by hand and eye).

Two English speakers then listened (independently) to the words and made stress judgements. In a few cases, one or both listeners found it impossible to decide which syllable sounded stressed, and these words were not counted in the subsequent analysis. The first listener's judgements are shown in Figure 2.

This histogram represents the acoustic properties of those vowels judged stressed by this speaker. The values are given as percentages, since the number of cases varied for some acoustic parameters, as mentioned above. The figures along the horizontal axis refer to the acoustic parameters, as follows:-

1. shorter duration of vowel
2. Fo change (within vowel) of less than 10 Hz
    (and therefore scarcely perceptible)
3. lower envelope amplitude within vowel
4. higher Fo at start of vowel
5. greater mean amplitude of vowel
6. greater peak amplitude of vowel
7. lower peak amplitude of vowel
8. lower mean amplitude of vowel
9. lower Fo at start of vowel
10. Fo change (within vowel) greater than 10 Hz
    (this was often very much greater than 10 Hz)
11. greater envelope amplitude within vowel
12. longer duration of vowel

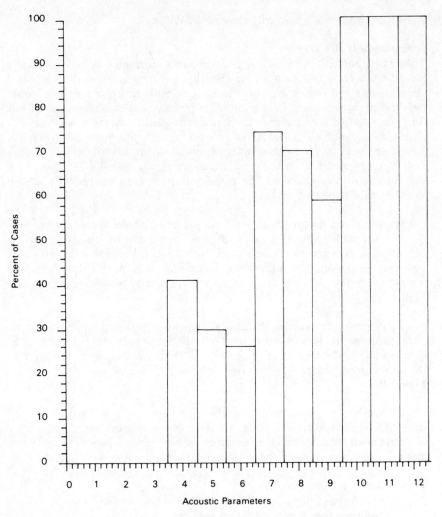

Figure 2 Vowels judged stressed by first English Speaker

Where the vowel has a greater or lesser degree of amplitude, etc., this is in comparison with the other syllable(s) of the same word. The total number of words was twenty; this, of course, was not enought to give a detailed account of stress in Welsh, but was sufficient to make plain the main trends. It will be noted that each acoustic cue has its converse (greater/lower, longer/shorter, etc.); although in nearly all cases the value for a cue is easily deduceable from that of its complement, the few cases of equality between two vowels in one or other of the dimensions made it necessary to include converse cues as well.

In Figure 2, the vowels judged stressed by this English speaker had, in every case, a pitch glide, longer duration, and greater envelope amplitude. Most cases also had lower peak and mean amplitude. These results fit in roughly with Lieberman's findings for stress perception in English by native speakers.

The corresponding results for the second English speaker are shown in Figure 3.

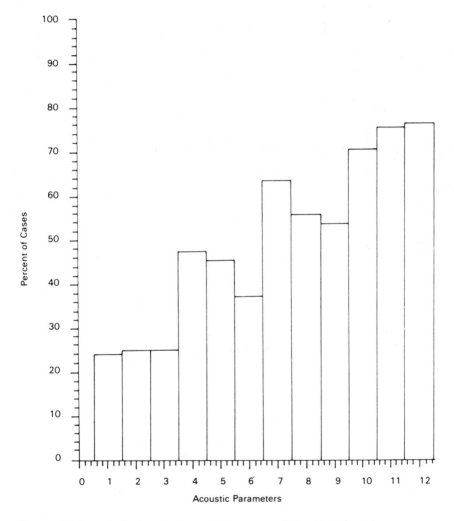

Figure 3 Vowels judged stressed by second English Speaker

While less clear-cut, these findings nevertheless tally with the first speaker's judgements and with the general pattern of stress perception in English.

The results for a Welsh speaker (Figure 4) do not, however, fit this pattern.

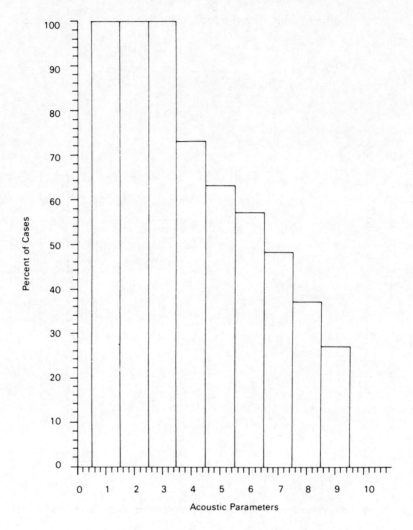

Figure 4 Vowels judged stressed by a Welsh Speaker

In each case, the vowel considered stressed by a Welsh speaker always had no Fo change at all, shorter duration, and lower envelope amplitude. It usually also had greater mean and peak amplitude. (Regularly-stressed words only were considered). A comparison of these histograms will reveal that the trend of the English speakers' judgements is in almost exactly the opposite direction to that of the trend of Welsh judgements.

In Welsh polysyllables, it is always the penultimate syllable that is stressed, except in a few irregular cases, most of which have the stress on the final syllable. In practically every word measured, however, the final and supposedly unstressed vowel had longer duration, a pitch glide, and greater envelope amplitude. This was the syllable typically chosen as stressed by the English listeners, which tallies well with what is known about stress perception in English.

3. Continuous Welsh Speech

These results had been obtained from isolated words and sentences, read from a list. To find out whether they held for continuous speech, recordings were made of Welsh speakers in various situations (at the 1981 National Eisteddfod at Machynlleth). As before, spectograms were made of some of the intelligible utterances, and measurements were taken. English listeners' judgements could not be tested, since it would have been impossible for a non-Welsh-speaking English speaker to divide the utterances into words and syllables.

The acoustic properties of stressed syllables in these utterances are represented in Figure 5, in the same format as before.

The number of words concerned is forty-six. Only non-prepausal and regularly stressed words are represented, since prepausal and irregularly-stressed words deviate markedly from this pattern, due to factors that have nothing to do with stress. The pattern is not as clear-cut as in the previous set of measurements, but the same trend is unmistakably present. In most cases, the stressed vowel had shorter duration, and greater peak and mean amplitude. There was only one major difference between these measurements and those from the list. This was that the results from spontaneous speech indicated that the envelope amplitude of the vowel, and a step-up in pitch, were not at all reliable as cues to stress (or rather, to the lack of it), while mean and peak amplitude gained a little in reliability as cues to the presence of stress. By far the most consistent cue was the shorter duration of the stressed vowel compared to the vowel of the unstressed final syllable. Since duration appeared to be an important factor, lengths of different types of vowels and consonants were examined.

41

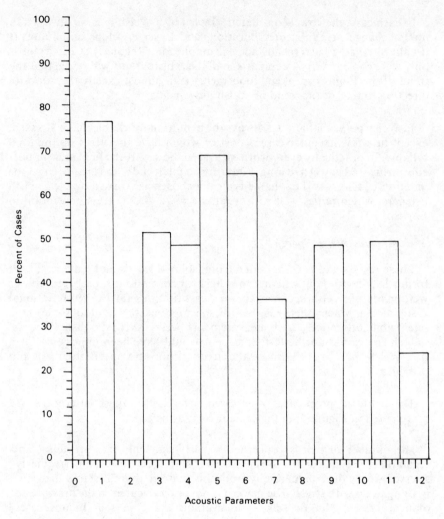

Figure 5   Judgements of stressed vowels in Welsh continuous speech by Welsh Speakers

4. Length of Segments

4.1 Vowels

Prepausal vowels were found to be significantly longer than non-prepausal vowels (at the 0.01 level; n = 221). The mean length of prepausal vowels was 129 msec, that of non-prepausal vowels was 78 msec. A significant difference in length was also found between vowels that were phonologically long and short (at the 0.01 level; n = 221). The mean length of phonologically long vowels was 123 msec, that of phonologically short vowels was 69 msec. Since long vowels may only occur in stressed syllables in Welsh, stressed and unstressed *short* vowels only were compared, to discover what effect stress had on vowel length. Any difference in length between non-prepausal short stressed and unstressed vowels was found to be not significant, statistically speaking. This finding contrasts with the highly significant length difference found for phonologically long and short vowels.

4.2 Consonants

The consonants (total no. 176) were divided into four categories: after stressed vowel, after unstressed vowel, before stressed vowel, and before unstressed vowel. The only significant length difference found within these categories was the greater length of consonants after stressed vowels compared to consonants after unstressed vowels. The mean consonant lengths were 94 msec and 81 msec respectively, a difference of 13 msec at a significance level of 0.05 (these results are tabulated in Figure 6).

Mean consonant lengths

after stressed vowels: after unstressed vowels

94 msec   81 msec

significance level = 0.05

Figure 6 Mean consonant lengths

This finding agrees with the 'extra duration' of the post-stress consonant observed for short vowels and in stressed monosyllables in three Welsh dialects in a recent auditory study (Jones, R.O. , 1967).

5. Evidence for Penultimate Stress

Given the lack of acoustic prominence of the supposedly stressed penult in Welsh, one may be forgiven for wondering what evidence there is that this syllable is, in fact, stressed. The obvious argument is that Welsh speakers, and traditional grammar-books, agree that it is. Also, in Welsh songs, the penult is the syllable that occurs on the beat of the music. The most recent sound changes in Welsh have been changes that reduce the vowels or consonants of final syllables and unstressed monosyllables, while leaving intact the vowels of the penult and of stressed monosyllables. Diphthongs have become monophthongs in final syllables (e.g. au>o in the eleventh century, as in *matawc* > *matoc*), and 'h' has been lost in certain words before the final syllable only (e.g. *brenin* 'king', but *brenhines* 'queen'). So it seems the penult must still be regarded as stressed; it is the standard notion of the *realisation* of stress that needs to be reconsidered.

6. Interval Hearing

Some of the spontaneous Welsh utterances are schematically represented visually in Figure 7, which is an attempt to translate into diagrammatic terms the acoustic pattern of the utterances.

Each string represents one utterance, corresponding to a phrase or represent short sentence. The blocks vowels; the filled-in blocks are stressed vowels, the blank blocks are unstressed vowels. The lines represent consonantal stretches, segmented by short vertical lines. The key at the top represents a stressed vowel, a consonantal stretch, and an unstressed vowel, all of equal duration. The diagram demonstrates the tendency for the consonantal stretches after a stressed vowel to be longer than those after an unstressed vowel; a tendency which is present but, naturally, not apparent in all cases.

In the late 1970's, an experiment was carried out by Alan Bell with speakers of various languages (Bell, 1977). The subjects made stress judgements while listening to sequences of pure tones. These sequences each varied along a particular acoustic dimension, i.e. duration, fundamental frequency, or amplitude. For example, in one sequence every third tone had higher Fo, while in another every third tone was lengthened, all other factors remaining constant. Bell found that the accent placement system of each listener's native language had no significant influence on the listener's perception of stress patterns. The factor deciding perceived stress was prominence in any acoustic dimension. All the listeners showed a preference for marking their perceptions of the tones as being in groups of three with initial accent, this accented tone being the one which had been made more acoustically prominent. This result fits in well with what we know about stress in English and other European languages.

There was a major exception, however, in the case of the tone sequence where every third tone had greater duration. In 48% of cases, there was a tendency to hear groups of three with medial, not initial, accent, with the long tone in the middle - as against 36% for initial accent and 16% for final accent. Bell's attempted explanation is in terms of 'interval hearing'. Because the distances between tone onsets were kept constant, there was a shorter interval than normal between the offset of the lengthened tone and the onset of the following tone. Bell argues that the lengthened tone and the following tone would tend to be perceived within a single rhythmic group by some listeners. The tone before the lengthened tone was separated from it by a comparatively long gap, and so was more conspicuous in one sense, not forming part of this rhythmic group. The perceived prominence of the isolated tone would then derive not from any intrinsic prominence it might have, but from the fact that it is 'picked out' from the surrounding syllables in this way.

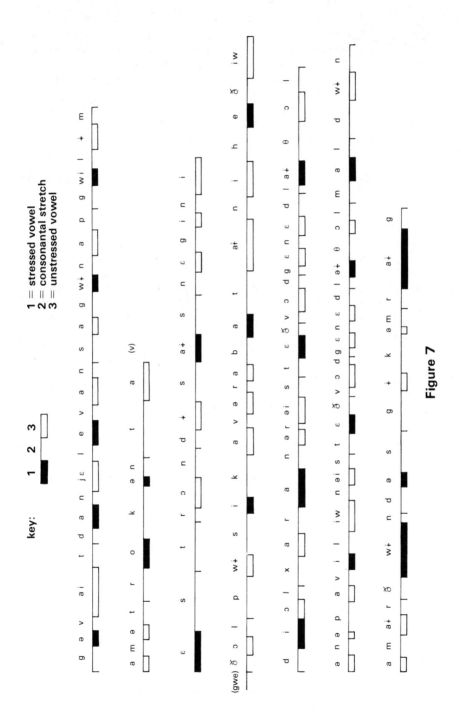

Figure 7

45

It could be that Welsh speakers perceive an 'interval pattern' of this kind, while English speakers perceive a 'length pattern', where the longest item is the stressed one. The finding of greater duration for post-stress consonants would support such a view, since this is a device whereby a stressed vowel is isolated from the following vowels.

The utterances represented in Figure 7 suggest that there is indeed a tendency in Welsh for stressed vowels to become temporally isolated in this way - by the greater number of surrounding consonants, as well as by the greater length of following consonants. It should be noted that these utterances were chosen as being typical of the utterances examined, and so are not all the best examples of this tendency.

7. Foot Measurements

The next stage of investigation was to look at temporal phenomena in a wider domain than that of the syllable - that is, rhythmic phenomena. Using the recorded spontaneous sentences and phrases, the stretches between the onset of each stressed vowel were measured, these stretches being referred to as 'feet'. Two different kinds of measurement were carried out, corresponding to two different hypotheses. Under the first hypothesis, penultimate syllables, usually the stressed syllable in Welsh, were counted as stressed for the purposes of foot demarcation. Under the second hypothesis, it was final syllables that were counted as stressed. The resulting feet could be termed a 'Welsh speaker's foot' and an 'English speaker's foot' respectively, as shown schematically in Figure 8. Stressed monosyllables counted as stressed under both hypotheses.

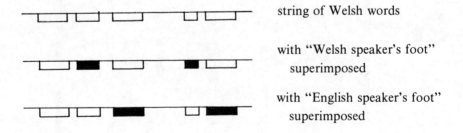

string of Welsh words

with "Welsh speaker's foot" superimposed

with "English speaker's foot" superimposed

Figure 8 Foot demarcation

The results using the 'Welsh speaker's foot' showed a slight tendency for stressed syllables to occur at apporoximately equal intervals. Although the length of the foot was partly determined by the number of syllables in the foot, there was also a tendency for the length of each syllable to be negatively correlated to the number of syllables per foot. This means that the more syllables there were in a foot, the shorter each syllable would become (on the whole), so that the interval between stressed syllables was not as long as it would have been were the length of the foot solely determined by the number of syllables in it.

However, this was not the case for the measurements based on the 'English speaker's foot', which counted the more acoustically prominent final syllable as stressed. Here, an important influence on foot length was the number of syllables per foot, as it was for the 'Welsh speaker's foot'. The negative correlation between syllable length and number of syllables per foot was less marked than with the 'Welsh speaker's foot', and also had a much lower degree of significance, as may be seen from the table in Figure 9.

Correlation of:	"Welsh Speaker's Foot"		"English Speaker's Foot"	
	coeff.	significance	coeff.	significance
Length of foot: no. of syllables in foot	0.58	0.0001	0.59	0.0001
		n = 53		n = 54
Length of syllable: No. of syllables in foot	-0.51	0.0001	-0.39	0.0033
		n = 53		n = 54

Figure 9 Correlation coefficients (product-moment) (non-prepausal feet only)

This table of product-moment correlation coefficients applies to non-prepausal feet only; in the case of prepausal feet, the 'Welsh speaker's foot' showed a much greater tendency towards isochrony, while the 'English speaker's foot' showed no such tendency at all. So the non-prepausal feet, although less isochronous than prepausal feet, nevertheless show a distinct advantage for the 'Welsh speaker's foot' in respect of isochrony.

The result is that, if the penult is counted as stressed, a greater tendency towards isochrony is seen than if the more intrinsically prominent final syllable is counted as stressed. The prominence of the penult seems to be due less to its inherent acoustic properties than to its function as the keystone of the rhythmic unit, which may be seen as vital to the realisation of stress in Welsh.

Psychological experiments have shown that listeners tend to superimpose a rhythmic structure on sound sequences even where no such structure exists physically (see Bell (1977) for summary of findings in this field). It is possible that Welsh speakers, when hearing an utterance that merely *tends* towards isochrony on the objective level, would normalise the rhythm subjectively on the basis of what regularity already existed. Thus isochrony would indeed be present, but mostly on a subjective level. This notion goes against the accepted orthodoxy that stress is a simple matter of direct mapping onto intrinsic acoustic properties such as Fo change, greater duration, and greater amplitude. Although these intrinsic properties may have a part to play, the realisation of stress in Welsh depends far more on rhythmic and perceptual phenomena; since, as Fred Householder put it, '... people hear things that aren't there' (Householder, 1957).

8. The Old Welsh Accent Shift

In any attempt to explain the strange behaviour of stress in Welsh, it is important to consider a historical development, the 'Old Welsh Accent Shift'. This change, taking place in the late eleventh century, shifted word stress in Welsh from the final to the penultimate syllable, where it has remained ever since; while stressed monosyllables remained stressed.

Before the shift, sound changes took place in final syllables and stressed monosyllables, such as the diphthongisation of long open *o* to *au* in the late fifth and early sixth centuries (e.g. British *Carataco*s > Old Welsh *Caratauc*). These changes affected vowel quality rather than vowel quantity. After the accent shift, sound changes occurred in penults and stressed monosyllables, and mostly affected vowel and consonant quantity; for example, *au* monophthongised to (short) *o* in final syllables (e.g. Middle Welsh *Caradawc* > Modern Welsh *Caradog*), and final -nn, -rr, became simplified to -n, -r, in Middle Welsh; i.e. between the twelfth and late fourteenth centuries (for full details of sound changes, see Jackson, 1953).

One Welsh scholar has taken the view that, before the accent shift, the accent had both a 'stress element' and a 'pitch element', as he calls them (Jones D M, 1949). At the time of the accent shift, he writes, only the stress element shifted to the penult, while the pitch element remained on the final syllable. This view is supported by the common observation that, at least for words in non-nuclear position, the unstressed final syllable very often has higher pitch than the preceding stressed syllable. The utterances in this study mostly conformed to this pattern, which is also described in Watkins (1953) and Thomas C H (1967). Another Welsh scholar has suggested recently that it may be necessary to recognise two different types of 'accent realisation' in Welsh (Thomas A, 1979). These would be; rhythmic stress on the penult, and pitch-prominence on the final syllable. Such an interpretation would fit the findings of this study, in that the penult seems to function as the vital element in the rhythmic unit, while the ultima often has higher Fo and is more acoustically prominent. There could be some justification for regarding the ultima as 'stressed' in a certain sense, as it is the only syllable immune to the morphological process of vowel reduction known as 'vowel mutation' in Welsh, whereby certain high vowels are reduced to schwa.

9. Theoretical considerations

The findings of this acoustic study of stress in Welsh are at variance with some theories of stress that have been based on stress in English. Such theories could be characterised by the terms 'stress-as-loudness' and 'stress-as-accent', represented respectively by Trager and Smith on one hand, and by Bolinger on the other.

9.1. 'Stress-as-loudness': Trager and Smith

In the first formulation of their theory, Trager and Smith wrote as follows:

'Stress is assumed to be manifested by loudness, each level being louder than the next lower level.'
(Trager and Smith, 1951)

They distinguished four 'phonemes of stress', namely; primary ///, secondary /∧/, tertiary /\/ and weak /∨/. Primary stress corresponded to sentence-stress or 'nuclear stress', while weak stress corresponded to unstressed or 'O' in Chomsky and Halle's system. Stress and pitch were seen as separate elements within the suprasegmental system. Not much more was said about stress by Trager and Smith, and this.attitude is characteristic of the view of stress taken by scholars before Bolinger formulated his theory of pitch accent.

Subsequent phonetic experiments into the acoustic correlates of stress showed that intensity was by no means the most reliable cue to stress (see the summary of Lieberman's experiment in Section 1 of this article; see also Fry (1958) for a similar view). The work on Welsh stress described earlier in this article also shows intensity to be a less than reliable cue to stress. Thus the early, 'stress-as-loudness' view can no longer be justifiably held.

9.2 'Stress-as-accent': Bolinger

Bolinger formulated his theory of pitch accent in an attempt to take account of the experimental work on stress, which showed pitch change to be by far the most reliable cue to stress in English. In common with all other scholars at that time, he was working under the assumption that there existed inherent cues to stress contained within each stressed syllable and within no unstressed syllable. His innovation was the identification of 'accent' as a candidate for this inherent cue.

Bolinger distinguished between 'stress' and 'accent'. His 'stress' is merely the *potential* for accent, a lexical abstraction that is part of the unchanging properties of a word. His 'accent' is the realisation of this potential for prominence, on a particular syllable in a particular case. This realisation manifests itself in the form of pitch prominence or pitch change, which can take one of three forms (accents A, B, and C).

Accent A shows a marked pitch *drop* during or immediately after the accented syllable. Accent B, on the other hand, shows a marked pitch *rise*, either during or immediately after the accented syllable, or from the preceding syllable to the prominent one. Accent C shows a marked pitch *drop* from the preceding syllable to the accented syllable. There seems to be an inconsistency in his description of accent A, when he asserts first that 'It is neither skipped down to nor skipped up from' and a sentence or so later; 'Or it may be approached from a relative level and skipped up from' (Bolinger, 1958). In any case, it is not clear why accents A and C are held to be separate accents, while the analogous (rising) accents are subsumed into the one accent B.

Bolinger's system seems to apply reasonably well to English, since in this language major pitch changes tend to co-occur with stressed (or 'accented') syllables. In Welsh however, as has been seen earlier in this article, the syllables regarded as unstressed contain many of the pitch glides present, and are ofter higher in pitch than the preceding stressed syllable. In the case of Welsh words spoken in isolation, this leads to the unstressed syllable very often being pitch-prominent. Thus Bolinger's system will describe this syllable as 'accented', contrary to the usual view of stress placement in Welsh. In the case of continuous speech, the stressed penults are often pitch-prominent by virtue of beginning a new contour (they are usually too short to contain a glide), and usually step down in pitch rather than up. However, Bolinger's system will not work even here, since not all stressed syllables are pitch-prominent; thus many stressed syllables will not count as 'accented' despite having relatively high amplitude, a phonologically long vowel, etc. Also, not all pitch-prominent syllables are stressed, since pitch glides often occur on the long, unstressed, final syllables of words. Thus Bolinger's system of pitch accent cannot be applied to Welsh. Another theory must be found for Welsh that will 'rescue' the traditional notion of stress as marking prominence of some kind distinct from pitch change, for otherwise the situation in Welsh could be reduced to the level of 'stress is what you make it'.

9.3 'Stress-as-rhythm-: Liberman

Such a theory could be the 'metrical' theory of stress proposed by M. Liberman (see Liberman (1975) for the first formulation, and Liberman and Prince (1977) for its application to word stress in English). This theory separates stress and pitch phenomena, and views stress as a relational, not absolute, concept, with rhythm underlying the perception of stress.

The 'metrical' or 'prosodic' structure of a sentence or word is seen as a binary-branching tree with the elements 'strong' and 'weak' as the branches at

50

each node. Thus the relative prominence of syllables within a word will be preserved even when the word is embedded within a compound, or used within a sentence. Similarly, 'strong/weak' relationships will be preserved when compound nouns or adjectival phrases are used within a sentence, so that the (compound) noun phrase 'English teacher' ('English'=strong, 'teacher'=weak) and the adjectival phrase 'English teacher' ('English'=weak, 'teacher'=strong) are distinguished from each other in an identical fashion however deeply the phrase may be embedded in the sentence.

The metrical structure of the sentence (loosely based on the surface syntactic structure) is reduced to a 'metrical grid' which gives a different type of patterning of the syllables. The metrical grid is the basis for determining the rhythm of the sentence, which in turn determines which are the stressed syllables. Intonational phenomena are then superimposed on the structure defined by the metrical tree and metrical grid, and play no part in identifying the stressed syllables (though major intonational phenomena may of course be associated with stressed syllables). It is the rhythm of the sentence that is seen as underlying the perception of its stress.

Liberman claims that sequentially-ordered events of any kind are not perceived merely as a linear sequence, but have an organisation imposed on them by the hearer, according to perceived cues which are often very indirect. Thus, given this view, measurements of fundamental frequency, duration etc.,

> '... should not be interpreted as demonstrating the acoustic correlates of a particular stress peak, but rather as indicating the sorts of acoustic features which induce us to hear an overall rhythmic organisation which includes the particular stress peak.'
> (Ladd, 1980: 26)

It is also noted by Liberman that major pitch changes tend to occur at rhythmically stressed syllables in English. This explains why, in perceptual experiments with English speakers, pitch-prominence is consistently the best cue to 'prominence' in a general sense - but never the only one. In Welsh, pitch-prominence seems to be only loosely connected with perceived prominence, which makes even clearer the connection shown between stress and rhythm.

The conclusion must be that, in Welsh at least, pitch movement is not intimately connected with stress; such a connection belongs to rhythm. Thus intonational phenomena are essentially distinct from stress phenomena in Welsh, and require quite different descriptive systems. It is also possible that this approach would clarify some current puzzles if applied to stress and intonation in English - this is the view taken in Ladd (1980). However, the arguments for this would be based more on considerations of theoretical economy and generality, while in Welsh there is also concrete acoustic evidence that stress is based on rhythm and that it is essentially distinct from intonational phonomena.

AN EXPERIMENTAL APPROACH TO THE INTERPRETATION OF FOCUS IN SPOKEN ENGLISH

W H G Wells

1. Information Focus

The notion of information focus has frequently been invoked in the literature, notably by Halliday (1967:204). This paper reports an experiment which was run with the aim of providing an empirically-derived basis for a definition of focus, in terms of its semantic reality for the native speaker and in terms of its phonological and syntactic exponents in the grammar of English [1]. This is a desirable goal, since previous discussions of information focus and related concepts such as new/given information, contrastive focus and emphasis, have been vitiated by a priori assumptions about these loosely defined semantic categories and their exponents in phonological systems of stress (as in the American notion of sentence stress) or intonation (as with Halliday's tonicity). To take a recent example, Brown, Currie and Kenworthy (1980) limit their field of investigation by restricting what they admit into the field of intonation: they first identify a phonological system of pitch, then explain contrasts in meaning expounded by that system in terms of a number of semantic systems that are not otherwise defined, and which, incidentally, include "given/new/contrastive information structure", subsumed here under the term 'focus'.

In the experiment reported here, the reverse procedure is adopted, in the belief that a more comprehensive account of information structure is possible if we hypothesise that there **is** a system of focus, find out what categories of focus (if any) are meaningful for native speakers, then correlate the resulting categories of focus with liguistic features. What these features might be is not prejudiced by having recourse to phonological systems that are set up independently of the focus system. Instead, a very wide range of potentially relevant features is examined. The experimental hypothesis was that some or all of a specified set of linguistic features are associated with perceived focus, and that those features interrelate systematically with different categories of focus. The framework in which the subsequent analysis is presented is that of Firthian prosodic analysis (Firth, 1949 and 1957). In the context of intonation studies, this entails setting up a mediating category of phonological analysis (see Sections 9.3 and 9.4 below).

2. Experimental Design

In order to obtain spontaneously uttered sentences which contained a variety of locations and degrees of focus, and yet which were reasonably controlled with regard to other intonational and syntactic variables, a technique devised by Currie (1978) was used. Three native speakers of British

English[2] were invited to take part in a game in which each had to study a list of characters from a story, and a list of the principal actions in the story, presented in random order, and then attempt to work out what happened. The player was allowed to ask the experimenter questions, to which the latter could reply "yes" or "no".

3. The Data

From the three conversations thus recorded, 23 sentences were selected, removed from their original context, and presented in random order to the experimental subjects, 30 undergraduates in their first term at the Department of Language, York University. The subjects received the following instruct-ions: "On your tape you will hear 25 sentences, separated by a short pause. The same sentences are printed on the sheet in front of you. Listen to each sentence once only and draw a line under the part which, in your view, the speaker is focussing on as particularly important, e.g. "Did the princess kill the soldier?" If you think two elements are equally important, put a line under each, e.g. "Did the princess kill the soldier?" If you think two elements are important but one is more important than the other, use numbers to indicate this: 1-most important; 2- less important; 3- less important still. Use as many numbers as you require, e.g. "Did the[1] princess[2] kill the soldier?"

4. The Experimental Sentences

Before discussing the results of the experiment, some comments on the selection of the data are in order. When choosing test sentences, the following criteria were employed:

1) All are polar questions. This was so that irrelevant syntactic and intonational variation would be excluded, making inter-sentence compar-ison in terms of focus more reliable.

2) Almost half the sentences are cleft constructions (11/23). This was to test whether clefting is crucially involved in the perception of focus.

3) A proportion of the sentences should be identifiably contrastive. The notion of contrastivity is often referred to in discussions of information structure (e.g. Halliday, 1967; Chafe, 1970; Brown et al, 1980), and quite specific phonetic exponents have been proposed for it, e.g. by Chafe. It is therefore interesting, as part of the experimental investigation of focus, to attempt to determine the linguistics exponents of contrastivity, and specifically, to determine whether there is justification for treating 'contrastive' as a distinct category, rather than as part of a more general category of 'new'. However, it is notoriously difficult to define with any precision what constitutes a 'contrastive' context. So, for the purpose of selecting 'contrastive' sentences from the original data, the following ad hoc definition was used: a sentence is contrastive if it is identical to the

sentence immediately preceding, except for the replacement of one semantic variable by a new item, e.g.

> S1: Did the witch steal the tinderbox?
> S2: Did the princess steal the tinderbox?
> or Was it the princess who stole the tinderbox?

By this definition, 7/23 sentences were contrastive.

4) Other criteria used in choosing sentences were: the sentence must be free from interfering noise and be clearly audible, for the purposes of instrumental analysis; all three speakers should be represented; the sentences should represent varying degrees of syntactic complexity and of length.

5. The Intonational Domain under Investigation

It will be noted that the sentence is taken as the domain for the investigation of focus rather than, say, the tone group. This is because the sentence can be readily defined in terms of syntactic criteria which are not crucially involved in focus, whereas the tone group has traditionally been defined at least partially in terms of tonic placement, and the tonic is crucially involved in focus. It will also be noted that the 23 sentences were presented to the subjects out of context. It is clear that contextual factors play a vital role in determining the placement of focus by the speaker, and also, though this is at present even less well understood, in determining how the listener interprets the focus structure of a sentence. If we wish to examine the interaction between sentence and discourse context with a view to discovering general principles which relate the two, we must first establish whether there are any linguistic features whose presence indicates focus to the listener regardless of discourse context. Having done that, we could then investigate how, and under what circumstances, discourse factors can override the presence of these sentence-internal features, so that the listener assigns focus to a different item. The procedure in this experiment was therefore to collect spontaneous data uttered in a meaningful context, so that the speaker would be subject to contextual influences, but to present the data out of context to the listener, who would therefore be wholly reliant on sentence-internal features when assigning focus.

6. Judgements Regarding Focus

The 30 subjects had no apparent difficulties in assigning focus according to the instructions. All 30 subjects made use of a unique focus category (i.e. one constituent focussed, the rest of the sentence not focussed); all subjects also employed a distinction between primary and secondary focus (in addition to no focus); 24 subjects used equal focus; 15 subjects made use of a tertiary focus category. The following scale was used to score the amount of focus assigned to each constituent by the subjects; primary focus - 3; secondary focus - 2;

tertiary focus - 1; no focus - 0. The scores for each focussed constituent in each sentence were then totalled, and the focussed constituents sorted into groups according to the number of points they had been assigned. Six groups were used, on the grounds that the subjects' responses seemed to reflect a readiness to perceive several different types of focussed constituent: those which bear the only focus in the sentence; those which clearly bear the primary focus, though other constituents in the sentence bear lesser degrees of focus; those for which the attribution of primary focus is not clear; those which receive secondary focus but are not clearly distinguished from the primary constituent; those which are clearly given secondary focus; and those which receive tertiary focus. Constituents were allocated to groups as follows:

Group 1:   unique/primary focus: 35-70 points clear of the next focussed constituent.

Group 2:   clear/primary: 35-70 points clear of next focussed constituent.

Group 3:   unclear primary: 1-35 points clear of next focussed constituent.

Group 4:   unclear secondary: 1-35 below primary focussed constituent.

Group 5:   clear secondary: 35-70 below primary focussed constituent.

Group 6:   tertiary focus (or lower): below two other focussed constituents, whilst receing at least 20 points.

All constituents receiving less than 20 points were classified as zero focus. This grouping was necessarily rather arbitrary, but it was hoped that the criteria would be sufficiently broad to reveal any general differences between different degrees of focus with regard to the distribution of the specified linguistic features.

7. Features of Focus Constituents

Each focus constituent was analysed in terms of linguistic features whose presence, it was hypothesised, might be associated with focus. The first five are features of pitch:

(1)   PITCH PEAK. It has been suggested (e.g. in Currie, 1978) that maximum pitch height is one of the phonetic manifestations of tonic prominence, which in turn has been associated with information focus, e.g. by Halliday (1967:203). Pitch is here defined as the highest point of the pitch contour of the sentence. The possibility of there being more than one peak is not disallowed.

56

(2) MAXIMUM PITCH RANGE. Currie (1978) mentions maximum pitch movement as one of the phonetic features that linguists have associated with tonic prominence. The feature is defined here as the range of pitch spanned by the focus constituent (not just the pitch range of the kinetic tone).

(3) PITCH OBTRUSION (a). This is defined as a step up or down in pitch immediately preceding the focus constituent, such that the previous direction of the pitch contour is interrupted. This seems intuitively to be a potential means of marking a constituent as perceptually prominent, thence focussed; cf. Bolinger, who associates pitch prominence with information focus, defining prominence as "a rapid and relatively wide departure from a smooth or undulating contour" (Bolinger, 1958:112).

(4) PITCH OBTRUSION (b). This is defined as a step up or down in pitch immediately following the focussed constituent, such that the previous direction of the pitch contour is interrupted. The comment on (3) applies equally here.

(5) KINETIC TONE. Pitch movement has been associated with information focus by many linguists, e.g. Bolinger (1958) and Halliday in his definition of the tonic as exponent of information focus. In this experiment, two questions were asked: firstly, are particular tones associated with focus in general or with particular grades of focus; and secondly, is the distinction between kinetic and level tone relevant to focus? Pitch features were allocated to focus constituents by auditory analysis in conjunction with instrumental analysis using a Frøkjaer-Jensen pitch-meter, from which mingograph tracings were obtained. For the purposes of this investigation, it was thought reasonable to assume that Fo correlates reliably with perceived pitch, since the experiment is concerned not with precise and absolute correspondences between particular Fo's and particular perceived pitches, but with the *relative* pitch height and pitch movement of particular constituents, in relation to the rest of the sentence. Using this method of instrumental analysis, it is not always possible to obtain a clear reading of pitch for each syllable, particularly when it is unstressed and spoken at speed. The consequences of this are not too serious for the present study, as there is invariably at least one syllable per constituent for which a clear reading can be obtained.

(6) LOUDNESS PEAK. This is the third of the phonetic maxima used by Currie (1978) in her experiments. Loudness has been associated with stress and, by extension with focus, particularly in the American concept of 'sentence-stress'. The loudness peak is defined here as the highest point on the intensity curve obtained by playing the recorded sentence through a Frøkjaer-Jensen intensity meter.

(7) CRESCENDO. This is defined here as a step up in perceived loudness from the constituent preceding the focus constituent to the focus constituent.

(8) DECRESCENDO. This is defined as a step down in perceived loudness from the focus constituent to the constituent following.

Features (7) and (8), like feature (6), were chosen on the basis of a hypothesis that perceived prominence resulting from the relative loudness of the focus constituent might be a cue to the perception of focus. As with pitch, the loudness features were allocated to focus constituents by means of auditory analysis in conjunction with instrumental readings.

The remaining phonetic features belong to the temporal dimension of the utterance. These were assigned on the basis of auditory analysis alone.

(9) PRECEDING PAUSE. This is defined as a perceptible pause immediately before the focus constituent.

(10) FOLLOWING PAUSE. As (9), after the focus constituent.

(11) DRAWL. This is defined as abnormal sustension of a syllable or syllables within the focus constituent.

(12) PRECEDING DRAWL. As (11), but on the syllable immediately preceding the focus constituent.

(13) FOLLOWING DRAWL. As (12), but on the syllable immediately following the focus constituent.

Although little work has been done on the co-occurrence of pausing and drawling with focus or emphasis, it seems a plausible hypothesis that the presence of these features might serve to mark off a part of the utterance as prominent. This is not to deny that these features may also serve as exponents of other systems, e.g. hesitation, as Crystal observes with regard to 'drawled' (1969:154).

(14) PRECEDING ALLEGRO. This is defined as increased tempo, relative to the speaker's norm, on the section of the utterance immediately preceding the focus constituent.

(15) FOLLOWING ALLEGRO. As (14), immediately following the focus constituent.

(16) ALLEGRO. AS (14) and (15), but **on** the constituent.

These three features were selected on the basis of the intuition that parts of the utterance delivered at a faster rate than normal might be interpreted as being relatively less prominent, and thence less focussed (Feature (16)), whereas a constituent might be perceived as prominent, and by extension focussed, if adjacent constituents are uttered at a faster rate: (14) and (15).

Finally, one syntactic feature was considered:

(17) CLEFTING. The data elicitation procedure had been set up in the hope of eliciting both cleft and non-cleft sentences containing varying degrees of focus, with a view to determining whether the clefting of a constituent serves as a focussing device and if so, whether it interacts systematically with other means of expounding focus.

8. Results

8.1 Features in focus

Table 1 presents, for each focus group 1-6, the proportion of constituents in that group which bear the feature (æ) and which do not bear it (-), the proportion being presented as a figure out of 10 in order to make comparison easier between the groups, which contain different numbers of constituents. For example, for feature (1), we see that in Group 1 (unique focus), containing six constituents, the proportion bearing the pitch peak is 8.4 to 1.6, whilst in Group 6 (tertiary focus) the proportion is 4 to 6. The purpose of Table 1 is to indicate firstly those features which co-occur regularly with focus, irrespective of the of the 'amount' of focus involved, and secondly those features whose occurrence varies systematically with the amount of focus involved.

(1) We can see that although PITCH PEAK coincides frequently with unique and primary focus (Groups 1-3), it is not an invariable cue. We see quite a high occurrence in Group 6. Moreover, there are 15 instances of pitch peak on a zero focus item (though this group is not included in Table 1). In fact, out of 36 instances of PITCH PEAK recorded, 17 occur with unique or primary focus constituents and 19 with secondary, tertiary or zero focus. The implication is that PITCH PEAK does not function solely to expound main focus.

(2) MAXIMUM PITCH RANGE presents a more regular and systematic correlation with degrees of focus, as represented by the focus groups, with the proportion dropping gradually through the groups. There are 11 instances of this feature in the zero focus group. Out of a total of 40 occurrences, 20 are in the top three groups. Once again, the feature cannot be associated uniquely with the exponence of main focus, but the relationship appears quite systematic.

TABLE 1

Feature	1 Pitch Peak		2 Max. Pitch Range		3 Pitch Obtrusion (a)		
Group	+	-	+	-	+	-	M
1(n=6)	8.4	1.6	10.0	0	5.0	5.0	1.5
2(n=8)	6.3	3.7	8.7	1.3	6.3	3.7	0.6
3(n=9)	7.7	2.3	7.7	2.3	7.7	2.3	1.9
4(n=10)	2.0	8.0	5.0	5.0	7.0	3.0	0.7
5(n=7)	0	10.0	4.3	5.7	7.1	2.9	0.7
6(n=5)	4.0	6.0	2.5	7.5	6.0	4.0	0.6

Feature	4 Pitch Obtrustion (b)			5(a) Tone Type				5(b) Kinetic vs Level		
Group	+	-	M	/				-	Kinetic	Level
1	8.3	1.7	2.9	6.7	3.3	0	0	0	10.0	0
2	2.9	7.1	0.3	10.0	0	0	0	0	10.0	0
3	7.5	2.5	0.5	6.7	1.1	1.1	1.1	0	10.0	0
4	8.3	1.7	1.4	8.0	0	0	1.0	1.0	9.0	1.0
5	4.0	6.0	0.4	4.4	0	0	2.8	2.8	7.2	2.8
6	5.0	5.0	0.5	8.0	0	0	2.0	0	10.0	0

Feature	6 Loudness Peak		7 Crescendo		8 Decresendo			
Group	+	-	+	-	M	+	-	M
1	10.0	0	10.0	0	+5.0	10.0	0	-8.5
2	5.0	5.0	5.0	5.0	+0.5	7.1	2.9	-3.6
3	5.5	4.5	6.6	3.4	+1.6	8.7	1.3	-4.5
4	0	10.0	3.0	7.0	-1.1	8.3	1.7	-2.6
5	0	10.0	5.7	4.3	-0.2	10.0	0	-1.8
6	0	10.0	0	10.0	-3.2	7.5	2.5	-1.0

Feature	9 Preceding Pause		10 Following Pause		11 Drawl	
Group	+	-	+	-	+	-
1	3.4	6.6	1.6	8.4	3.4	6.6
2	0	10.0	2.8	7.2	4.3	5.7
3	4.5	5.5	1.3	8.7	1.2	8.8
4	0	10.0	0	10.0	1.0	9.0
5	1.5	8.5	2.0	8.0	0	10.0
6	0	10.0	0	10.0	0	10.0

Feature	12 Preceding Drawl		13 Following Drawl		14 Preceding Allegro	
Group	+	-	+	-	+	-
1	3.4	6.6	0	10.0	1.6	8.4
2	0	10.0	0	10.0	0	10.0
3	1.2	8.8	0	10.0	1.2	8.8
4	1.0	9.0	0	10.0	1.0	9.0
5	1.5	8.5	0	10.0	1.5	8.5
6	0	10.0	0	10.0	0	10.0

Feature	15 Following Allegro		16 Allegro		17 Cleft	
Group	+	-	+	-	+	-
1	5.0	5.0	1.6	8.4	3.3	6.7
2	1.5	8.5	0	10.0	6.3	3.7
3	0	10.0	1.2	8.8	3.3	6.7
4	0	10.0	2.0	8.9	1.0	9.0
5	2.0	8.0	0	10.0	0	10.0
6	0	10.0	2.0	8.0	0	10.0

(3)   and (4). Both PITCH OBTRUSION features co-occur frequently with focus in all groups. There is no obvious systematic variation between groups, except in the mean amount of obtrusion (Column M). (The units used in the M column are the steps in the calibrated scale of the pitchmeter.)

(5)   KINETIC TONE co-occurs very regularly with focus, non-kinetic (level) tones only appearing in very small proportions in the lower groups, though very frequently in the zero focus group (39, where n). However, it does not appear that distinctions **between** different grades of focus are realised by kinetic tone, as the distribution of the various tone types seems to be random.

(6)   Table 1 indicates that unique focus (Group 1)   invariably co-occurs with LOUDNESS PEAK, and that non-primary focus never does (Groups 4-6), though in fact there are 7 instances in the zero focus group. Generally, LOUDNESS PEAK is the most reliable cue to primary/unique focus.

(7)   Unique focus co-occurs with CRESCENDO, and tertiary focus with a drop in loudness, onto the focus constituent. However, there are also 26 instances of CRESCENDO in the zero focus group. The figures for the mean in column M   (given in units of the calibrated scale of the intensity meter) suggest more persuasively a systematic relationship between focus and the loudness of the preceding constituent.

(8)   There is a high co-occurrence of DECRESCENDO with focus in all groups, which suggests that this may be a reliable cue to the presence of focus. This is reinforced by the figures for the mean, which decrease fairly regularly through the groups. However, there are 23 instances of DECRESCENDO in the zero focus groups, which suggests that this may be to do with a general tendency for English sentences to decrease in loudness as they progress.

(9)   and (10). There is a tendency for PAUSE adjacent to the focus constituent to co-occur with the higher, rather than the lower, groups, but the proportion is small for each feature.

(11),(12) and (13). Feature (13) FOLLOWING DRAWL does not co-occur at all with focus and so can be discounted. DRAWL and PRECEDING DRAWL, like the PAUSE features, tend to occur with unique and primary focus, rather than the lower groups, but again the proportion is small.

(14) (15) and (16). The number of constituents affected by each of the ALLEGRO features is small. It is noteworthy, however, that in the zero

focus group there are no instances of PRECEDING ALLEGRO, only one of FOLLOWING ALLEGRO, and 22 of ALLEGRO, which suggests that although these features occur relatively infrequently, when they do occur they influence the perception of focus.

8.2 Feature Groupings

In Table 1, we saw that some features co-occur regularly with focus in all groups (e.g. 5,8) or their co-occurrence varies systematically with amount of focus (e.g. 2,6). However, in the case of other features, the number of occasions on which the particular feature occurs is too small for that feature to be a plausible diagnostic for focus. For this reason, in Table 2, certain related features of the same phonetic dimension are combined in order to create composite features whose distribution is proportionately wider, and which therefore offer a potentially more reliable correlation with focus in the analysis that follows.

Feature	3/4 Pitch Obtrusion			9/10/11/12 Pause/Drawl			14/15/16 Tempo Prominence		
Group	+	-	M	+	-	M	+	0	-
1	8.3	1.7	2.0	6.7	3.3	1.2	6.6	1.7	1.7
2	6.3	3.7	0.6	6.3	3.7	0.6	1.3	8.7	0
3	8.8	1.2	0.9	4.5	5.5	0.8	2.3	6.6	1.1
4	5.0	5.0	0.5	2.0	8.0	0.2	1.0	7.0	2.0
5	5.7	4.3	0.6	2.9	7.1	0.4	2.9	7.1	0
6	10.0	0	1.0	0	10.0	0	0	8.0	2.0

Table 2 Distribution of composite features in focus groups.

8.3 Restructuring Feature Groupings

At this point it is convenient to restructure the original grouping of the data for analysis. Firstly, it will be recalled that for the purpose of selecting sentences for analysis, an ad hoc definition of contrastivity was used: a sentence is contrastive if it is identical to the sentence immediately preceding, except for the replacement of one semantic variable by a new item. It is interesting to note that of the seven contrastive constituents thus defined that were included in the analysis, five are in Group 1, the others in Group 2. This means that only one Group 1 constituent is not contrastive, by this very strict definition. There therefore seems to be some justification for designating the top focus group 'Contrastive'. Secondly, although the focus constituents were sorted into six groups plus the zero group for the purpose of analysis, it will be recalled that the subjects themselves made use of four grades: unique, primary, secondary, zero, with half the subjects using a further, tertiary grade. In the light of this behaviour, it is interesting to note that in Table 1, the distinction between Groups 2 and 3 (both primary focus) and the distinction between Groups 4 and 5 (both secondary focus) are not made as regularly as the other distinctions between adjacent groups: see e.g. Features 1, 3,4, 6,7,8. As the next step in the attempt to set up linguistically valid categories of focus, it was therefore decided to combine Groups 2 and 3 into one category 'primary focus' and likewise Groups 4 and 5 into one category 'secondary focus', for the subsequent analysis.

9. Analysis of Results

9.1 Feature Correlations

Once it had been established that a number of phonetic features co-occur with perceived focus, statistical tests were carried out to determine which of these features, and which combinations of features, correlate most reliably with focus. The advantage of such tests is that they enable us to identify those features which are most significant for the perception of focus because they co-occur **only** with focussed items and because their co-occurrence varies systematically with the degree of perceived focus, as opposed to those features which co-occur with focus but also co-occur with unfocussed constituents, i.e. whose association with perceived focus is not significant.

Table 3 presents two sets of correlation coefficients. The ITEM column represents the correlation of the specified features with all the constituents analysed in the data (45 focus plus 78 non-focus), ranked in order of focus by using the raw score of focus points assigned by the subjects, within the focus grades established above. The GROUP column represents the correlation of the features with the focus groups only (4 focus groups plus 1 non-focus group); here, no account is taken of variation within each group.

Dimension	Features	Item	Group
Pitch	1 Pitch peak	0.240	0.368
	2 Max. Pitch Range	0.562	0.592
	3/4 Pitch Obtrusion	0.319	0.254
	5 Kinetic Tone	0.449	0.394
	1+2+3/4+5	0.565	0.575
	1+2	0.485	0.579
	2+5	0.590	0.575
	2+3/4	0.538	0.515
	3/4+5	0.476	0.401
	2+3/4+5	0.583	0.543
Loudness	6 Loudness Peak	0.295	0.445
	7 Crescendo	0.017	0.230
	8 Decrescendo	0.470	0.363
	6+7+8	0.344	0.455
	6+7	0.157	0.367
	6+8	0.475	0.484
	7+8	0.322	0.395
Tempo	9/10/11/12 Pause/Drawl	0.249	0.308
	14/15/16 Tempo Marking	0.230	0.399
	9/10/11/12 + 14/15/16	0.301	0.454
Mixed	1+2+6	0.483	0.612
	2+6+14/15/16	0.487	0.647
	2+5+6+8+9/10/11/12+14/15/16	0.569	0.674
	1+2+5+6+8+9/10/11/12+14/15/16	0.592	0.679
	1+2+6+8+9/10/11/12+14/15/16	0.552	0.666
	1+2+6+8	0.581	0.645

Note: N =123   Significance at 5%: 0.174

Table 3   Correlation coefficients: Features and feature combinations against focus

Table 3 calls for some comment. Firstly, of the three phonetic dimensions of pitch, loudness and tempo that were considered, it is pitch features that in general correlate best with focus; and of the pitch features involved, MAXIMUM PITCH RANGE and KINETIC TONE give the best correlation. In the loudness dimension, LOUDNESS PEAK and DECRESCENDO correlate best with focus, with CRESCENDO correlating quite poorly. In the tempo dimension, the combination of all tempo, pause and drawl features correlates rather better than the individual features PAUSE/DRAWL and TEMPO MARKING.

Turning to the mixed sets of features, we can see that these generally correlate much better than the separate phonetic dimensions, especially with the focus *groups* which have been proposed, and which are our chief interest. It is evident that the most satisfactory statement of the exponency of focus categories can be obtained only by reference to systems of pitch, of loudness and of tempo in combination.

9.2 Non-phonetic Features

Before stating the exponency of our focus categories, let us turn to the single non-phonetic feature referred to in the analysis, CLEFT. It seems reasonable to suppose that if a constituent is focussed by means of syntactic clefting, there is correspondingly less need for the presence of phonetic signals in order to mark that constituent as focussed. It is therefore interesting to compare cleft with non-cleft constiuents in each focus group where both occur, to see whether the syntactic difference is associated with any marked difference in the distribution of phonetic features. Table 4 shows the mean number of phonetic focus features, taken from the set of mixed features that shows the best correlation in Table 3 , for cleft vs non-cleft constituents.

Group	Cleft	Non-cleft
Contrastive	6.0	6.0
Primary	4.8	4.3
Secondary	3.0	2.6

Table 4

Table 4 indicates that cleft constituents are no less marked for focus phonetically than their non-cleft equivalents -if anything they are slightly more marked. We may conclude that clefting is not in a commutational relationship with the phonetic features that indicate focus. We are now in a position to state the system of focus in English in phonological terms.

9.3 Focus Categories

The purpose of phonological statement is to link phonetic events to categories established at other linguistic levels, e.g. lexical and grammatical. To quote one prosodic analyst: "... it is by means of the silent and unpronounceable abstractions of phonology that one can relate the ever changing phonetic detail of the speech stream to the grammatical statement." (Carnochan, 1960). In the present instance, we have seen that there are grounds for treating focus as such a category: the native speaker subjects responded to the notion of focus in the experimental situation, and there is no reason to think that they do not do something very similar in everyday linguistic interaction. Within the broad notion of focus, we saw that all subjects had recourse to a category of unique focus and to a distinction between primary and secondary focus. It is appropriate to set up four focus categories:

1. CONSTRASTIVE (unique focus)
2. MAIN (primary focus)
3. SUBSIDIARY (secondary and tertiary focus)
4. ZERO (no focus)

The phonetic analysis of the experimental data indicated that the following seven features are involved in the perception of focus:

PITCH PEAK (P1); MAXIMUM PITCH RANGE (P2); KINETIC TONE (P3); LOUDNESS PEAK (L1); DECRESCENDO (L2); TEMPO MARKING (T1); PAUSE/DRAWL (T2).

(For ease of reference, the bracketed symbols will be used in the subsequent discussion).

The mean number of these features present in each of the four focus grades is as follows:

1. CONTRASTIVE	6.0
2. MAIN	4.5
3. SUBSIDIARY	2.4
4. ZERO	1.4

A phonological system of Prominence can be established, corresponding to the four focus grades:

CONTRASTIVE	Maximal Prominence
MAIN	Major Prominence
SUBSIDIARY	Minor Prominence
ZERO	Minimal Prominence

The exponents of the Prominence system are as follows:

Maximal	P1; P2; P3; L1; L2; T1 or T2.
Major	P3; L2; at least one of P1 and P2; at least one of L1, T1, T2.
Minor	P3; L2.
Minimal	P3 or L2 or zero.

9.4 Focus Categories and Phonological Categories

The claim of the present statement is that any constituent bearing a specified configuration of phonetic events will be susceptible to interpretation by the listener as belonging to the appropriate focus category. (1) and (2) below illustrate the case where the focus categories, as established on the basis of the experimental subjects' responses, are matched exactly by the corresponding phonological categories, established on the basis of the phonetic exponents listed above. (In the examples that follow, the experimentally-derived focus category of the constituent is given above the orthographic transcription, the zero category being indicated by a blank. The phonological category of the constituent is given below the transcription, and below that, the phonetic exponents).

66

(1)

	CONTRAST				
Did	the queen	ask	the soldier	to bring	the tinderbox?
MINIMAL	MAXIMAL	MINIMAL	MINIMAL	MINIMAL	MINIMAL
ø	P1, P2 P3, L1 L2, T2	ø	L2	P3	L2

(2)

	MAIN	SUBSID	SUBSID
Did	the lady-in-waiting	follow	the princess
MINIMAL	MAJOR	MINOR	MINOR
P3	P1, P3, L1, L2, T2	P1, P3, L1, T2	P3, T2

SUBSID
to the soldier's door?
MINOR
P2, P3, L2

9.5 Phonetic Features of Constituents

However, the great majority of the experimental sentences (19/23) contain at least one constituent that is, in terms of the focus system, phonologically overspecified: in these cases, the phonetic features of the constituents in question locate it in a phonological category that corresponds to a higher focus category than the one to which it has been assigned on the basis of the experimental subjects' responses. Far from being problematic for the present analysis, which claims only that the presence of a specified configuration of phonetic features renders a constituent susceptible to interpretation as belonging to the corresponding focus category, this result is what one would expect, since it is clear that the phonetic features serving as exponents of focus in the present system may also have other functions in English. Some of these possible functions will be discussed below.

9.6 Phonological Function of Features

In the nineteen sentences mentioned, there are 32 constituents that are phonologically overspecified. Of these, 27 are overspecified by just one grade, i.e. MAIN focus receives MAJOR prominence, SUBSIDIARY focus receives

MAJOR prominence, or ZERO focus receives MINOR prominence. Of the five constituents that are overspecified by more than one grade, three occur in *sentence-initial* position. (3) is an example:

		SUBSIDIARY		MAIN	
(3)	Was it	the soldier	who cut	the witch's	head off?
	MAJOR	MINOR	MINIMAL	MAJOR	MINIMAL
	P1, P3 L1, L2	P1, P3, L2		P2, P3 L2, T2	L2

Sentence (3)   In these three sentences, the considerable phonetic prominence of the sentence-initial auxiliary piece does not elicit any focus attribution from the experimental subjects. This suggests that some of the phonetic features assigned here to the phonological system of Prominence expounding focus may also be used to mark sentence beginnings, presumably under certain contextual conditions which remain to be specified. In this respect, the distribution of certain phonetic features, assigned here to the exponence of MAXIMAL and MAJOR prominence, is suggestive. PITCH PEAK occurs on fifteen constituents belonging to the ZERO focus category; ten of these are sentence-initial auxiliaries. LOUDNESS PEAK occurs on eight constituents in the ZERO focus group, seven of which are sentence-initial auxiliaries. MAXIMUM PITCH RANGE occurs on eleven constituents in the ZERO focus group, one of which is a sentence-initial auxiliary. The distribution suggests that PITCH PEAK and LOUDNESS PEAK, but not MAXIMUM PITCH RANGE, are involved in a system operating at sentence-initial position which is distinct from focus. This in turn implies that if the speaker wishes to mark a sentence-initial auxiliary as focussed (i.e. to question the polarity of the sentence) he may have to use a configuration of phonetic features that differs from the configuration he would use at other places in the sentence. It is therefore necessary to admit the possibility that the phonology of focus is *polysystemic* in respect of the place of the constituent in the sentence. Relevant observations about the role of high pitch and loudness at the beginning of sentences have been made by a number of contributors to this volume. (e.g. French and Local, Lieberman, Cutler and Pearson).

9.7 Phonological Function and Sentence Final Position

Turning to sentence-final position, we find that of the 32 phonologically overspecified constituents in the corpus of 23 sentences, 11 are sentence-final: in almost half the sentences of the corpus, the final constituent has more phonetic prominence than its focus value warrants in terms of the present system. Furthermore, only five of the 23 sentences have MINIMAL prominence on the final constituent. All 18 remaining final constituents have the

68

feature KINETIC TONE, and 7 have MAXIMUM PITCH RANGE, where only one has PITCH PEAK and none has LOUDNESS PEAK. There is an association of pitch-movement features with sentence final position which, in conjunction with the frequent phonological over-specification in this position, suggests the function of dynamic pitch movement at the end of the sentence may be principally one of delimitation. The suggestions made in this and the preceding paragraph as to the delimitative function of phonetic features must remain tentative, since it is only the focus function that has been analysed systematically in the present study. If further investigations should bear out these suggestions, there are no theoretical objections, within the theory of prosodic phonology, to a description in which there is partial overlap of the exponents of systems (e.g. focus) and structures (e.g. sentence):

"The use made of the phonic material in the phonetic description of exponents does not require that the phonic details variously allotted should be mutually exclusive. The description of the phonetic characterisics of elements and categories of structure is relevant to that order, which is a different order from the order of units and terms in systems... There can be no question of 'residue' in the phonic material after any particular abstraction for a particular purpose has been made. All the phonic material is still available for further abstractions for a different order in separate analyses."

(Firth 1957: 15)

We can envisage a description in which some phonetic features are shared by a phonological system of focus such as one set up here and by elements which help to delimit the sentence.

9.8 Focus in Contrastive Constituents

17 of the 32 phonologically overspecified constituents are neither initial nor final in the sentence. Only three of these are instances where MAIN focus is overspecified by MAXIMAL prominence, and they are of particular interest with regard to the notion of contrastive focus. It will be recalled that for the initial investigation of the semantic notion of contrastivity, a very strict ad hoc definition was used: a constituent in a sentence was designated contrastive if the sentence was identical to the immediately preceding sentence except for the semantic variable expressed by that constituent. (See Section 4.) In Section 8.3, it was noted that in the top focus group, which had been determined on the basis of intra-sentence difference in number of focus points assigned, five out of the six constituents were contrastive by the original definition. This top group was labelled 'Contrastive' on the basis of the strong correlation between contextual contrastivity and the phonetic features characterising Group 1 . It is therefore interesting to note that the two constituents which are contrastive by the original definition but which appear in Group 2 (Main Focus) rather than Group 1, are in fact two of the three instances in the data where a Main Focus constituent is phonologically

overspecified, i.e. Maximal. In both sentences (4) and (5), the most focussed constituent received very nearly the maximum number of focus points possible (89/90 and 87/90 respectively) but did not fall into Group 1 because another constituent in the sentence was also assigned a significant number of focus points.

		MAIN		SUBSID
(4)	Was it	the shoemaker's boy	who put	the crosses
	MINIMAL	MAXIMAL	MINIMAL	MINOR
	P1, P3	P1, P2, P3 L1, L2, T2	P3	P3, L2

on all the doors	in the town?
MINIMAL	MINIMAL
L2	L2

		MAIN		SUBSID
(5)	Was it	the lady-in-waiting	who put	crosses
	MINIMAL	MAXIMAL	MINIMAL	MINOR
	P1	P1, P2, P3 L1, L2, T2	∅	P3, L2

on all the doors	in the town?
MINIMAL	MINOR
L2	P3, L2

Sentences (4) and (5) provide support for the hypothesis that a constituent can be clearly marked by the speaker as contrastive and yet not be the only focussed constituent in the sentence: other constituents may also be focussed, as with 'the crosses' in (4) and 'crosses' in (5). We thus have persuasive evidence that Maximal Prominence, as defined here, is the exponent of semantic contrast in this variety of English.

9.9 Non-contrastive Medial Constituents

However, in the third sentence where a Main Focus constituent is phonologically overspecified in the way just described, the constituent is not contrastive by the contextual definition, nor did it receive a particularly high number of focus points (52/90). Furthermore, there are fourteen other phonologically overspecified medial constituents in the data that cannot readily be accounted for by contrastivity or by delimitative systems. Still more problematic for the present analysis are the eight constituents in the data whose focus grade is phonologically **under**specified, i.e. when a constituent is assigned a certain degree of focus by the experimental subjects but is not accompanied by the minimum configuration of phonetic features that, according to this analysis, must be present for that degree of focus to be assigned. Although the present analysis is clearly inadequate in this respect, it is likely that further refinement will enable some of these exceptions to be accounted for. In the discussion of phonological over-specification, it was suggested that the analysis might be improved if we allow a polysystemic phonology, in which constituents in sentence-initial and sentence-final position may require different phonological statements from those elsewhere in the sentence. In a similar way, it is possible that some of the instances of phonological underspecification may be accounted for if we admit a polysystemic system of Prominence according to which different classes of syntactic constituent may require different phonological statements.[3] Some of the most obvious instances of phonological underspecification suggest that this may be so. For example, there are only 2/23 sentences in which the most focussed item is a verb rather than a NP, and in both cases this consituent is underspecified phonologically.

			CONTRAST	
(6)	Was	the witch	helping	the soldier ?
	MINIM	MIMIM	MAJOR	MIMIMAL
	P1, P3	P1	P2, P3, L1, L2, T1	L2

		MAIN	SUBSIDIARY
(7) Was	the king	asked	by the soldier
MINIMAL	MINOR	MINOR	MINOR
L1, L2	P1, P3, L2	P2, P3, T2	L2, T1

if he could smoke one last pipe	before he was hanged?
MINOR	MINIMAL
P2, L2	L2

It is possible that if a verb is to be interpreted as having a given degree of focus, it will be less phonetically marked than a NP. This seems plausible, since there are likely to be more NP's than verbs in a sentence in competition for focus assignment: a relatively slight departure from phonetic expectation could be enough to signal that the verb has some prominence. This is certainly the impression gained from listening to (6) and (7), and also (8), where, by feature counting, the subject NP is grossly overspecified in terms of focus. The auditory impression, however, is that the verb 'tie' is just as prominent as 'the lady-in-waiting': it is as if the prominent verb attracts the focus off the preceding NP.

A further plausible explanation for some of the problematic cases is that there is a trading relationship between the delimitative systems hypothesised in Sections 11.6 and 11.7 and the focus system: if certain features are 'used up' by a delimitative system (e.g. PITCH PEAK or LOUDNESS PEAK at the beginning of the sentence), they are not available to mark focus. Thus in (6), the PITCH PEAK feature is associated with the initial auxiliary but not with the focussed constituent. The same is true of LOUDNESS PEAK in (7) and (9). The latter is a particularly interesting example, since the main focus constituent here is not specified as having Major Prominence, as it lacks one of the three features LOUDNESS PEAK, TEMPO PROMINENCE and PAUSE/DRAWL. At the same time, it has **both** major pitch features (P1 and P2) even though only one is required for Major Prominence.

72

		SUBSID	SUBSIDIARY
(8) Did	the lady-in-waiting	tie	a leaking bag of flour
MINIMAL	MAXIMAL	MINOR	MINIMAL
ø	P1, P2, P3 L1, L2, T2	P3, L2	L2

MAIN
onto the princess?
MINOR
P3, L2

MAIN			SUBSID
(9) Was it	the princess	who married	the soldier?
MINOR	MINOR	MINIMAL	MINOR
P3, L1, L2	P1, P2, P3, L2	ø	P3, L2

10. Conclusions

The following conclusions may be drawn from the experiment reported here:

(1) Native English speakers respond in a systematic fashion to the notion of focus (as 'relative importance'), under experimental conditions. There is no reason to believe that they do not operate with a similar notion in their everyday language use. The experimental reponses indicate that English speakers regularly operate with up to four degress of focus. Thus there is psycholinguistic justification for undertaking a linguistic investigation of the notion of focus and for hypothesising four categories of focus (Sections 6 and 8.3).

(2) In English, focus is a phonological phenomemon. The comparison of cleft with non-cleft sentences indicates that syntactic structure is not crucially involved in the interpretation of focus (Section 9.2).

(3)   The semantic system of focus is realised by a four-term phonological system of prominence, the exponents of which are features of pitch, loudness and tempo (Section 9.3). If a constituent is to be interpreted by the listener as having a certain degree of semantic focus, that constituent will be marked by a specified configuration of phonetic features serving as the exponents of the corresponding phonological category.

(4)   In English, a constituent can be identified as contrastive on purely phonological grounds. This is highly desirable, since a satisfactory definition of contrast in contextual terms has hitherto proved elusive, and the mentalistic definitions which have been employed as a result readily lead to circulatory statements in the description.[4]

(5)   Exceptions to (3) might be accounted for by further refinement of this description, specifically by hypothesising:

(i)   phonological systems of sentence delimitation, and trading relationships between these systems and the system of prominence (Sections 9.6 and 9.7).

(ii)   that the phonology of prominence is poly-systematic: different phonological systems are to be stated for different syntactic classes e.g. nominal phrases and verbs (Section 9.9).

The present approach to the semantics and phonology of focus offers a number of theoretical advantages over other investigations of intonation and semantics.

(a)   The semantic categories used are grounded in the observed behaviour of naive native speakers, rather than the intuitions of the linguist. It is only by adhering rigorously to this principle that intonational studies can achieve the sophistication that has been attained at other levels of phonological analysis.

(b)   The phonetic analysis is not limited a priori to any particular phonetic dimension or phonological category (e.g. pitch or stress): phonetic selectivity is not allowed to prejudice phonological statement.

(c)   The phonological statement, whilst linking categories to exponents, does not bind the two together inextricably. It may be that another variety of English, or a related language, has the same four focus categories realised by a four-term phonological system of prominence, but with slightly different phonetic exponents. The present description, unlike some current approaches to intonation, would permit a straightforward comparative statement.[5]

(d) Although the data used was somewhat artificial and restricted, the present description does offer a precise tool for analysing focus in more naturally occurring modes of speech. There can no longer be any justification for devising ad hoc definitions of information focus and relating them to putative linguistic correlates, as a foundation for a theory of information structure.

(e) Now that the phonetic correlates of focus have been established empirically, it is possible to study the interaction of focus and context. To this end, it is intended to repeat the experiment, this time presenting the sentences **in context** to the subjects, to determine whether there is a significant difference in the assignment of focus to constituents. On the basis of the data thus obtained, it may be possible to identify circumstances under which the phonological specification of focus can be 'over ridden' by sentence-external factors. In this way we might gain some empirically-based insights into the interaction of discourse factors with sentence grammar and sentence phonology.

Footnotes:

1. *The work reported here could not have been carried out without the guidance and support of John Local. Thanks are also due to Patrick Griffiths and John Kelly for suggesting improvements to an earlier version.*

2. *Two females, in their twenties; one male, in his thirties. All speak non-localised varieties of English.*

3. *cf. Kelly (1974:104): "The linguist often has to separate out for individual treatment various lexical and grammatical categories, and he always has to bear in mind that it may prove necessary to do this."*

4. *cf. Wells (ms), where this problem is treated in detail.*

5. *cf. Kelly (1974:107): "It is...desirable - ideally - that the phonological statement arrived at for a particular language should be relatable in the simplest possible way to those made for languages known to be of the same family or group, and, if possible, to the statement posited for the earlier stages of the history of that language or, indeed, of the group as a whole."*

THE INTONATION OF 'GEORGE AND MILDRED': POST-NUCLEAR GENERALISATIONS

Carlos Gussenhoven

1.0 INTRODUCTION

1.1 Preliminary Comments

A general reference point for the treatment of English intonation as attempted in this article is the 'British' traditon of intonation contour analysis begun by Palmer (1922), an introduction to which is perhaps most readily available in J D O'Connor and G F Arnold (1973) *Intonation of Colloquial English* (2nd edition, Longman).[1] An important unit of analysis in this tradition is the intonation contour associated with the stretch of speech known as the 'tone group'. This contour is split into four parts: the *nucleus,* a one syllable stretch with which the last major intonation movement is associated, the *tail,* which is the stretch following the nucleus, the *head,* which is the stretch preceding the nucleus counting from the first accented syllable onwards, and the *prehead,* any stretch preceding the head. The nucleus is the only obligatory element, tone groups being minimally one syllable long. In the following example, taken from O'Connor and Arnold (1973: 13), *I* is the prehead, *want to be absolutely* the head, *sure* the nucleus, and *about it* the tail.

|| I *want* to be *absolutely sure* about it. ||

O' Connor and Arnold (1973: 13)

This article concentrates on the stretches of intonation contours formed by the *nucleus and the tail.* In spite of the fact that this stretch is talked about as if consisting of two parts, the British tradition views it as a holistic 'bit' of the contour, each such bit providing an instance of a *nuclear tone.* Examples of nuclear tones are the fall, the rise, the fall-rise, the rise-fall, and the level tone. If there is no tail (and the stretch is only one syllable long), the nuclear tone will run its full course on that syllable; if there is a tail, the nuclear tone will expand so as to cover the whole stretch. (Details of mapping vary from tone to tone. For instance, the fall is usually virtually completed on the nuclear syllable, while the rise may be literally stretched out from the nucleus to the last syllable of the tail).

Observe that in the above there is no suggestion that the nucleus is necessarily the most prominent syllable of the tone group (where 'prominent' is used in some loose sense of 'subjectively most striking'), or that it is necessarily the syllable with which the largest pitch movement is associated. We can encourage a child who is just learning to write by saying *Write it down!* with a generally falling contour from beginning to end, causing the (high-pitched) *write* to be subjectively the most prominent syllable, and the syllable with which the largest pitch movement is associated (assuming *it* is already rather low in pitch). Yet, it is the auditorily less striking hump on *down* that we would perceive as marking the nuclear syllable, recognising it as a well-formed instance of the (low) fall. That is, the utterance would not be interpreted as an injunction to **WRITE** it down, as opposed to *jot, clumsily note, press* etc. it down.

The 'British' approach represented above, which we should now perhaps refer to as the 'consensus view' of intonation analysis, (Ladd, 1980) implies that quite long sections of contours may have to be seen as holistic units. After all, there is no theoretical limit to the length of the tail. It also implies that pitch movements that are quite far apart may have to be seen as belonging to the same unit, the same nuclear tone. This will happen when a fall-rise is used, and there is a long tail. In this situation, the fall-element will be mapped onto the nuclear syllable, while the rise-element will be mapped onto the last syllable of the tail, irrespective of whether it is accentable. This situation is illustrated in (2), where *true* is the nucleus.

(2)   It's **true** as a matter of fact

However, it is precisely with regard to the implication above that opinions differ in the literature. For the pattern in (2), for example, interpretations have been proposed in the literature that range from one nucleus, via a compound bi-nucleus or two nuclei, to a sequence of tones from different tonal paradigms, one nuclear and the other non-nuclear (for reference see Section 7). In this article the one-nucleus interpretation is defended against these alternative analyses.

1.2 The Aims of the Investigation

Our aim in undertaking a corpus-based analysis of tails, of which this article is a report, was twofold.

First, the analysis was intended to yield part of the answer to the question where speakers place their nuclei. If we know where these nuclei are **not** placed, we also know at least part of the answer of where they **are** placed. As such, the article is intended as a contribution to the discussion of the location of the sentence stress, or 'nucleus' in English.

The second aim, whose attainment should in a sense precede that of the first, was to try and gather evidence concerning the identity of the nucleus and the domain over which the nuclear tone is assigned. This evidence is extracted from the analysis by exploiting the circularity inherent in a classification of tails. The circularity is, of course, that we are generalising over phenomena, in our case 'tails', that we are at least partly free to define as we please, in our case so as to maximise our ability to generalise. Clearly, if of a number of possible interpretations of what should be considered 'tail', one admits of more powerful generalisations than the others, it will have to be preferred to them, other things being equal. In particular, this line of argument is brought to bear on the interpretation of falling-rising intonation patterns of the type exemplified in (2). The question of the interpretation of pitch movements in terms of nucleus and tail is of far-reaching importance. It immediately affects one's definition of the nuclear tones, and as such essentially concerns the segmentation of utterances into the basic units of analysis. Different interpretations will inevitably lead to different statements about the paradigmatic and syntagmatic properties of the intonational system, and with it, most probably, too, about the semantics of that system.

Our procedure is as follows: we will begin by assuming that one of the interpretations proposed in the literature is the correct one, and apply it. We will then evaluate the resultant description in terms of the extent to which the generalisations produced by it would have to be given up, if we were to adopt one of the other interpretations suggested in the literature. Before doing so, however, we will describe the corpus on which the investigation was based and characterise it by means of a few general statistics.

1.3 The Corpus

The corpus consists of four instalments of British television serials, together comprising some 14,000 words.[2] Three of these, or 11,550 words, are instalments of the serial 'George and Mildred'. These are *Days of Beer and Rosie* (DBR), *Finders Keepers?* (FK), and *On the Second Day of Christmas* (SC). A fourth instalment of 'George and Mildred' could not, for technical reasons, be made available, and was replaced with one taken from 'Roath' (R). The origin of the examples given below is indicated by the initials of the instalment concerned (see above), while examples that are made up for the purposes of exposition are followed by [*]. Only George (G) and Mildred (M) are specified as speakers of the examples. 'O' is used to indicate that the example was spoken by some other actor in the George and Mildred data. The language of both serials can be characterised as familiar-style Standard English.

1.4 Motivation

The motivation for choosing quasi-spontaneous rather than real spontaneous speech as the basis of our analysis is partly that the latter frequently contains 'mushy' material like false starts, repetitions and vocalisations of various sorts, towards which our analysis was not directed. In material of the kind represented in our corpus, by contrast, we can be sure that all utterances are intended to be well-formed, in that they may be expected to have made a closely-vetted pass through the filter of the actors' linguistic competence. As such, our material is the natural, direct spoken counterpart of written language, which has usually undergone a similar degree of monitoring on the part of the producer.

A second reason for choosing this corpus was that it was hoped that the significance of the intonational features to be studied was more clearly brought out in it than in other types of corpus, in so far as it may be expected that they are used to create particular 'comedy' effects, which might make it easier to determine just what their significance is. It may at this point be relevant to observe that, apart from punctutation marks, the scripts of the G and M instalments contain no prosodic indications of any kind, and that the actors - George and Mildred more so than the others - frequently deviate from their text, and are clearly allowed to improvise on their script to a certain extent. The script of the Roath instalment, by contrast, occasionally contains capitalisations, suggesting particular prosodic 'readings'.

1.5 Transcription

The material was transcribed orthographically, with nuclear tones and tone group boundaries indicated. No systematic attempt was made to indicate pitch range, rhythm or any other features. The analysis was carried out by the author on an auditory basis. This was not out of a cavalier attitude towards instrumental registrations of periodicity, but because recognition of nuclear tones on the basis of periodicity tracings is still beyond the power of man or machine. The transcription was checked some eight months after it had first been done. Changes of opinion were few and far between, and most frequently concerned decisions about the inclusion of short introductory vocalisations like *well*, *yeah*, *oh*, which were often spoken rapidly and lacked an easily interpretable 'tone'. Another area of uncertainty was the division into tone groups. On a number of occasions, stretches that had been regarded as single tone groups with a pre-nuclear and a nuclear accent were re-analysed as two tone groups in the second analysis. Second thoughts about which was the nuclear syllable and which tone was used were rare in other instances. In a few cases more detailed information about general contour range or tone variants was noted. All counted, changes accounted for less than 5% of the data, and did not concern the examples cited in this article.

The following tones were distinguished in the transcription: the fall ($\backslash$), the rise ($/$), the fall-rise ($\vee$), the level tone (—), the rise-fall ($\wedge$), and the stylised fall (—). As was said above, no distinction between high tones and low tones was made, although in some cases certain tone variants were noted. These refinements have been ignored in the representation of the examples in this paper.

The following comments should be made:

1. The fall-rise was considered a unitary tone, marking a single syllable as nuclear, also when the fall-element and the rise-element were quite far apart, as in

(3) G: I think Geor∨**GIN**a would have been a better name
           [DBR]

(4) G: Nothing to∨ **DO** with you, in fact
           [DBR]

in which the rise-elements are on *name* and *fact*, respectively. It should be noted therefore, that what Crystal (1969, 1975), Crystal and Davy (1969, 1975) Svartvik and Quirk (1980) may regard as a compound (binuclear) fall-plus-rise, or what Brazil (1978), Brazil, Coulthard and Johns (1980) may regard as a sequence of two tone groups, one with a fall and one with a rise, or what Bing (1979) may regard as a nuclear fall followed by a non-nuclear boundary tone, has here been analysed as a single tone group with a mono-nuclear fall-rise.

2. There is no rise-plus-fall in the analysis: sequences of such pitch movements are either instances of unitary rise-falls (as in most, if not all other analyses), as in

(5) O: For handing in my ∧**CRED**it card
           [FK]

or as a sequence of two tone groups, one with a rise and one with a fall, as in

(6) O: As I was saying to ╲**ANN** ╱ oil and
           ╱**WA**Ter ╱ simply don't ╲**MIX** [FK]

3. The stylised fall (Ladd, 1978), earlier also called the 'spoken chant' (Pike, 1945: 71), or 'call contour' (e.g. Gibbon, 1976: 276), as in

(7) M: ⁻**MOR**ning George [FK]

occurred sufficiently frequently for it to be marked separately.

4. As was implied earlier, the fact that these tone categories were distinguished in the analysis must not be taken to mean that it is proposed that 'English has six tones'.

2.0 Some Statistical Data

Bearing potential differences of analysis in mind, it may be interesting to compare some general statistical data with data obtained by other researchers. Crystal (1969), for example, while noting that length of tone group is a stylistic variable, gives 5 as the mean number of words per tone group in his corpus. In DBR it is 4.5, to which the comment should perhaps be added that the number of one-syllable tone groups, such as vocatives or interjections like *oh, yeah, right,* etc., seems rather high in our material generally. The incidence of nuclear tone-types, in particular, can only be compared across researchers with considerable caution, in view of the different treatments of 'compound tones'. Table 1 gives the percentages obtained by Davy (1968, cited in Crystal 1969: 225) for conversational style and reading style separately, as well as the fequencies in the G and M data. The Davy data have been adjusted so as to make a comparison more meaningful: the percentages for the fall-rise (11.1 and 7.4) and the fall-plus-rise (5.5 and 5.1) have been added together, and those given for the rise-plus-fall (0.6 and 0.4) have been divided between the rise and the fall.

	\	v	/	—	∧	⹀	
Reading	50.5	16.6	24.9	5.5	2.1	-	
Conversation	58.9	12.5	16.3	8.0	4.2	-	
G & M	61.8	18.7	15.3	3.3	0.4	0.4	N=2411

Table 1   Proportions of nuclear tones in (a) reading style, (b) conversational style and (c) 'George and Mildred'. The data for (a) and (b) are from Davy (1968).

The proportions in the G and M data are extremely stable. Table 2 gives the percentages for the three instalments separately. None of the differences are significant.

	\	V	/	—	∧	=	
FK	62.4	17.8	14.5	4.1	0.6	0.3	N=777
DBR	62.0	18.8	14.0	4.1	0.5	0.6	N=870
SC	61.3	19.2	17.6	1.7	0.1	0.1	N=764

Table 2 Proportions of nuclear tones in three instalments of 'George and Mildred',

It would appear that the shift observed by Davy from the rise in favour of the fall between reading and conversation is reflected in the G and M data. The G and M data is distinct from conversational style, it would seem, in that the incidence of fall-rises is higher, and those of rise-falls and level tones lower. I will refrain from ad hoc explanations of these findings.[3]

If we want to see if nuclear tone choice is exploited in any way to assist in creating particular effects in the material under investigation, it would obviously be better to look for patterns in the speech of individual characters. If we take George and Mildred separately, for example, it appears that in both instalments George uses significantly fewer falls than does Mildred, and uses significantly more fall-rises than does Mildred. The differences are even more striking if we count only those nuclei that occurred in situations in which the two actors are by themselves, without other actors either taking part in the conversation or being present as listeners. The figures are given in Table 3. The probability levels are based on χ^2 tests for the frequencies obtained for the combined data.

		\	V	/	—	∧	≈	
FK	George	60.8	22.2	13.1	3.3	0.6	-	N=153
	Mildred	66.4	11.2	17.6	4.0	-	-	N=125
DBR	George	50.6	30.3	14.8	3.7	-	-	N=162
	Mildred	75.0	13.0	10.3	1.7	-	-	N=116
SC	George	58.3	27.1	6.3	8.3	-	-	N=48
	Mildred	71.2	19.2	6.8	2.7	-	-	N=73
		$p<.01$	$p<.01$	n.s.	n.s.	n.s.	n.s.	

Table 3 Proportions of nuclear tones for George and Mildred separately in mutual interaction in three instalments.

It is reasonable to assume that the observed frequency differences are related to the particular characters the two actors are supposed to portray, with Mildred being the more assertive of the two and George more often than not playing the 'hen-pecked' husband.[4] It should be stressed that these data are in no way intended to serve as pointers towards any male-female distribution differences in actual speech. More probably, they are the result of the unconscious exploitation of the actors of social/sexual stereotypes. Correlations between nuclear tone-frequency profiles and social roles have not, as far as I know, been researched, although Crystal (1974: 85) notes that complex tones, i.e. fall-rise and rise-fall types, may be more frequent in a 'simpering' speaker than in other speakers. It may be further observed that, contrary to what is sometimes suggested, no evidence was found that the rise was more frequent in the speech of actors portraying non-assertive characters than in that of other actors.

3.0 Classifying Tails

Ours is not the first attempt to see if any generalisation can be made with respect to what sort of material typically goes into post-nuclear stretches. Apart from numerous incidental observations, there are three more or less systematic listings of final non-nuclear items in English: Crystal (1975: 25-8), Bing (1979: Ch 2) and Firbas (1980). The classification offered below differs considerably from Crystal's. In part, these differences are due to differences of interpretation in the area of the nuclear tones themselves: 'compound tones' do not figure in the present analysis, but do in Crystal's. In other respects, the present analysis may be seen to be more complete than Crystal's, and to offer generalisations that go beyond it. Bing discusses linguistic expressions that fall in one of our categories. There are many similarities and some differences between her list and ours in that category. More important, there are theoretical differences between the two anlyses that concern the intonational status of the linguistic expressions in it. It will be argued that Bing's proposal to reserve a special, separate domain for these expressions must be rejected. Our analysis agrees best with that given by Firbas (1980). Our main disagreement here concerns the status of post-nuclear predicates.

3.1 Three Categories of Tail

A discussion of tails cannot be undertaken without some clarification of the theoretical status of the nucleus. It is assumed that the location of the nucleus is the major surface realisation of two binary variables, focus and mode. The variable 'mode', which specifies whether or not the focus of the sentence is meant as a counterassertion, is not relevant to our discussion here, and can therefore be ignored. Focus, however, is relevant. It is seen as a binary variable, obligatory marking all or part of a sentence as [+ focus] (to all intents and purposes equivalent to Halliday's 'new' (1967: 204)). If only part of a sentence is so marked the rest is said to be [–focus] (similarly equivalent to Halliday's 'given'). Accent assignment rules take the sentence with its focus and mode markings as their input, and assign accents accordingly. The advantage of this approach is that it makes it possible to divorce the significance of the nucleus from the word it happens to be assigned to, and instead see the nucleus as manifesting focus on linguistic material including more than just the nuclear word (or, in rarer cases, not necessarily including the nuclear word itself). It thus rids us of explanations in terms of ill-defined notions of 'salience' or 'importance' of the words that are seen as potential candidates for the nucleus in a given utterance.

There is only one accent assignment rule we need consider here, which I refer to as the Sentence Accent Assignment Rule, or SAAR. For the purposes of SAAR, sentence constituents should be allocated to *arguments* (subject, objects), *predicates* and *conditions* (most adverbials).[5] SAAR operates over *focus domains,* that is, it assigns an accent to each [+ focus] focus domain. A condition forms a focus domain by itself, but an argument and a predicate may fuse into a single focus domain: in it, SAAR assigns the accent to the argument. Thus, if in *I met Jane in London* everything except *I* is [+ focus], two accents are assigned: one to *Jane,* the argument in the focus domain *met Jane,* and one to *in London,* a condition. If we alter the focus distribution so as to leave *Jane* [– focus], again two accents are assigned, one to *met,* which now forms a focus domain by itself, and one to *in London,* the condition. The last of these assigned sentence accents in a tone group is the nucleus.

Given the word order of English, the number of sentences that have the predicate in final position is statistically smaller than the number that have an argument in final position, and the all-pervasive operation of the rule is therefore less than obvious. A clear example of a structure where it is apparent, is the subject + intransitive predicate construction. An example is (8), where *I've got* is [– focus]:

(8)   I've got me\SON coming round to dinner
                [DBR]

Here, *coming round to dinner* should be seen as a single predicate that combines with the argument *me son* into a single focus domain. Note that although adverbials like *in London, at the airport* regularly function as conditions, and thus require their own focus domain when they are [+ focus], such expressions can also function as predicates, in which case SAAR treats them as such, as illustrated in (9):

(9)   My LUGGage is still at the airport [*]

It may further be noted that, particularly in arguments, there is frequently more than one accentable syllable. Thus, *an elderly person* or *electrification* will have both accentable syllables 'switched on' by SAAR if these arguments are (entirely) [+ focus]. Finally, note that many adverbials, of which *still* in (9) is an example, are typically treated as [– focus]. These adverbials are accounted for in Section 5.

Obviously, a classification of tails will have to distinguish between tails that are [+ focus,] but are not assigned an accent given the operation of SAAR, and those that are [– focus]. Also, a distinction should be made between expressions that are typically [– focus], even on first introduction, and items that are [– focus] because they have explicitly or implicitly been introduced into the discourse model. The three main categories therefore are:

           Category I: [+ focus] tails

           Category II: typically [– focus] expressions

           Category III: pragmatically [– focus] expressions

This division interestingly reflects the three general factors that are involved in the determination of the location of the nucleus. Category I might be said to be grammatical in nature insofar as arguments are typically expressed in NP's and predicates typically in VP's (in the sense of Quirk et al, 1972). Category II could be said to be semantic in nature insofar as the class of expressions in it can be given a semantic characterisation. Category III is more clearly pragmatic in nature, in that expessions in it refer to entities that the speaker assumes are available in the discourse model by virtue of prior introduction.

4.0 Category I: [+ Focus] Tails

Apart from the frequent, but relatively trivial case of [+focus] parts of compounds, nearly all items in this category concern instances of the operation of SAAR. Rules responsible for the assignment of accents in compounded constituents, such as *problem* in (10) and *book* in (11), may create tails that consist of [+ focus] subconstituents:

(10) O: You are the man with the sewage $\vee$ BACKflow
            problem? [DBR]

(11) G: I've still got me $\setminus$RATion book. [DBR]

These compound rules will not concern us here.

There were two other types of [+ focus] tails that did not concern full-focus argument + predicate combinations. One resulted from the use of verbs like *to KILL oneself, to CUT oneself.* When [+focus], these verbs have the accent on the verbal element, as in

(12)   I must stop $\setminus$TALKing to myself [R]

They are discussed further in Section 8.2.2. The other case concerned the occurrence of an adverb of 'proper functioning' (e.g. *right, well, properly).* As is shown in Gussenhoven (forthcoming, a), these adverbs, unlike other adverbs, are treated as unaccented parts of predicates.

(13) O: But one doesn't want one's /SON | mixing with
            /PEOPLE | who can't $\setminus$SPEAK properly [FK]

The remainder of this section is devoted to the types of full-focus argument + predicate combination that occurred in the corpus. Rather than necessitate a reformulation of SAAR, these structures demonstrate that SAAR expresses a significant linguistic generalisation.

When seen from the point of view of syntactic structure, there were four structures that had the right sort of word order for the operation of SAAR to be apparent. These are discussed below. A fifth type, though unattested in the corpus, has been added for the sake of completeness.

4.1 Type 1: Subject + Intransitive Verb / (Be) Complement

This may be said to be the basic type. It is the structure that led Schmerling in 1976 to postulate her principle II, which said that 'news sentences', i.e. sentences in which everything is 'new information', received accents on their arguments rather than their predicates. Examples in the corpus are numerous.

(14) G:	...with his \HAIR all wet
(15) M:	The \FLAGS would have been out
(16) G:	Her \SON's turned up [all DBR]
(17) O:	(I'm scared to∨ PRESS the red one) I have a feeling the \KITCHen will blast off [SC]
(18) G:	Do you think the ∨ TURkey will be unfrozen yet? [SC]

4.2 Type 2: Transitive Verb + Object + Verbal Particle

In this type the predicate consists of a phrasal or phrasal-prepositional verb, with the verbal particle (*out, at, to* etc.) moved to a postion after the object. While the operation of SAAR is not evident in e.g. *I'll put on the KETTle,* it is in *I'll put the KETTle on.* Although *put* in the latter sentence has a certain degree of (rhythmical) stress, it is not stress that derives from SAAR, which would of course select the particle if only the predicate was [+ focus], and it was assigned an accent, as in *Stop fiddling about with the KETTle. Put it ON.* Examples of this type are:

(19) M:	Keep your \ VOICE down
(20) M:	Are you going to bring the \ PRAM in?
(21) O:	I'll put the ∨ KETTle on [all DBR]
(22) O:	If you don't change those ∨ WIRES over.... [SC]

As a subtype in this category we may include object + predicate combinations that contain an object complement. For example, in *to paint the door green, door* is the argument. This status of *green,* an object complement, is interesting: it would seem that, for the purposes of SAAR, such object complements, particularly when adjectival, are part of the predicate. Thus, if such structures are entirely [+ focus], and the accent goes to the object (the argument), the object complement is left in the tail, like the verbal particle discussed above. Note that **within** the predicate it is the object complement that is the accentable part (cf *to paint (it) GREEN).* In (23), the context is included:

(23) Tristram: Where does most of our \COFFee come from?
Mildred: (...) Bra\ZIL!
Tristram: (slowly, to co-occur with his spelling of the word)
Bra\ZIL... ⎯RUBber!
Mildred: That'll be Ma\LAYa dear
Tristram: \No. I've spelt Bra\ZIL wrong
[DBR]

4.3 Type 3: WH-Movement in Questions

This category comprises utterances in which an element is moved to the beginning of the clause by the syntactic rule of WH-movement, and in which as a result the predicate is left in right most position. It should be noted that the queried element in WH-questions is always a separate [+ focus] focus domain and is, for that reason, always assigned an accent, in addition to any accents assigned to other [+ focus] focus domains in the tone group. This is not only plausible from a pragmatic point of view (the speaker is after all crucially interested in the queried bit of information), but is also apparent from the 'untransformed' versions of such structures, which naturally have the nucleus on the WH-word if it is final *(You like WHAT?, Most of your coffee comes from WHERE?* etc...). These 'untransformed' sentences, incidentally, are in fact much more frequent than may be thought, and regularly occur in (low-brow) TV quiz programmes. Additional evidence for the view that WH-words must be assumed to have a focus domain to themselves lies in the fact that when they occur exclusively with a single predicate, the WH-word and the predicate do not fuse into a single focus domain. Rather, both are assigned an accent, as in (24) and (25), in both of which *what* has a (pre-nuclear) SAAR accent.

(24) M: What are you\DOing? [FK]
(25) M: /SO...What's so /SPECial about it? [FK]

If we did not postulate separate focus domains for the two elements, SAAR would obviously apply incorrectly so as to assign the nucleus to the WH-word: WH-words are arguments, and as such would be candidates for merging with predicates, leading to *WHAT are you doing* for (24). Thus focus boundaries surrounding the WH-words prevent this from being generated.

Examples illustrating final unaccented predicates in this type are:

(26) O: How's the \HOMEwork coming on? [DBR]
(27) O: I wonder what \IT means (spoken when O interrupted his reading of a letter after 'It finally \HAPpened')
[DBR]
(28) O: Where does most of our \COFFee come from?
[DBR]

(29) O: Did Mr Roper find out who that ∨ CREDit card
belonged to? [FK]

Type 3 is the first type of tail to be commented on in Crystal (1975: 25).
There it says that the nucleus is placed on the word that is governed by the
question word, as in *What TIME does your watch say, Whose CAT's in the
doorway, Isn't it wonderful how NICE she looks.* This formulation of course
misses the generalisation expressed by SAAR. More significantly, it would
seem to make incorrect predictions by tying the nucleus to the head of the NP
in which the WH-word is a modifier and ignoring the fact that there may be
more arguments later in the utterance. That is, *What COUNtries does most of
our coffee come from,* with a nucleus location as predicted by Crystal's
formulation, is not in fact well-formed unless at least *our coffee* is
[–focus]. SAAR, conversely, does account for Crystal's examples, if *your watch*
in the first and *she* in the second example are taken to be [– focus]. The first
question is equivalent to *What TIME is it:* the fact that the time is to be read off
from the hearer's watch is taken for granted by the speaker. Similarly, *she* in
the second example is [– focus], its referent being assumed by the speaker to be
available in the discourse model.

4.4 Type 4: [–Focus] Post-Verbal Argument

If, in an SVO or SVAdv structure, the final (accentable) element is [-
focus], the nucleus goes to the pre-verbal subject by SAAR (the next
argument up), rather than to the predicate. In the following examples, *it, you*
and *me* are [- focus] arguments:

(30) M: Let's hope \GEORGE doesn't see it
(31) O: (Imagine you're in a ∨ PUB) and a perfect ∨ STRANGer
comes up to you....
(32) O: Mrs \ ROPer has been helping me
[all DBR]

In this category we should include as a subtype relative clauses in which
what would have been a post-verbal element is relativised. Like the
construction discussed under Type 3 above, relativisation also involves WH-
movement. It is intonationally distinct from WH-movement in WH-questions, in that the element that is moved is [–focus] rather than [+ focus]. That
is, the fact that the relative is **moved** has no consequence for the location of the
nucleus, since it is not assigned an accent anyway. Perhaps more correctly, we
should say that it is a **condition** of relativisation that the item to be relativised is
[– focus]. An example is:

(33) O: That's what \ GOERing said [DBR]

Example (33) concerns an utterance in which the verb is arguably non-salient from a pragmatic point of view. It is, however, not the case that it is this non-salience that accounts for its not being nuclear. The nucleus location would be preserved if we replaced *said* with the semantically weightier *died,* and we could have the following well-formed exchange:

(34) A: Shall we meet in ∨ X?
              That's where ＼ GOERing died [*]

(Note, incidentally, that *how* in the last of Crystal's examples quoted in 3.3 is not a question word, but an independent relative pronoun, being equivalent to *the way in which* in the same way that *what* is equivalent to *the thing which,* cf Quirk et al, 1972: 730, 864).

4.5 Type 5: Subject + Passive Verb

Although utterances in this category were expected to be rather liberally represented, there was not a single example in the corpus in which a passive verb phrase was tone-group final and the preceding subject was [+ focus]. Passive constructions generally are surprisingly infrequent: in DBR the total number was six. The two of these that had the predicate in final position had a [– focus] subject:

(35) M: He'll have it towed a＼WAY [DBR]
(36) (O: I'm ∨ SORry | you're an arrogant little
              ＼TWERP)
G: Apology ac＼CEPted [DBR]

(Note that in (36) the accent on *twerp* serves to support the 'comedy' effect achieved by the deletion of *I said that,* and that the [–focus] treatment of *apology* by George enhances this effect.) Subject + passive verb constructions that are entirely [+ focus] can easily be supplied from other sources:

(37)   CLASSes have been cancelled (Bing, 1979: 176)

4.6 Exceptions to SAAR

Prosodic data are often viewed in a less absolute light than syntactic data. Rules of syntax are generally - and rightly - seen as being absolute statements about syntactic well-formedness. The fact that speakers may on occasion choose not to apply the rule should no be seen as 'invalidating' that rule in any way. The utterance *Here's the CAR...the gentleman says that the car is STOLen* cannot serve as evidence that RELATIVISATION is not a true rule of English syntax. And the fact that speakers may be heard to say *Helsinki is the capital of WHICH country* does not mean that WH-MOVEMENT in questions is not a 'rule' of English, but rather indicates that there may be an area of pragmatic research into why speakers do or do not employ the options available to them. In the area of prosody, by contrast, it is sometimes expected that the rules that one postulates should actually predict speakers' options rather than specify surface structures that are the result of these options. Clearly, just as speakers may or may not employ certain syntactic options available to them, so they may freely exploit the set of prosodic options available to them. The view taken here is that we should first of all concentrate on the structure of this set of options and their effect on surface structure, and only secondarily investigate the reasons for their employment. As an example of such an apparent exception, consider (38), in which *my dad* is treated as [−focus] by the speaker:

(38) O: I was just curious to see what my dad \LOOKED
               like [DBR]

In the context, George, much to his dismay, was taken by the speaker to be his father. After a volley of disclaimers on George's part, the speaker expresses his surprise at George's reaction, and then utters (38). The fact that *my dad* was [−focus] by the speaker considerably added to George's discomfort, as it underscored the fact that his parental status was being taken for granted. It would of course have been **possible** for the speaker to have explained his visit with... *my* \DAD looked like, but the option he did employ was natural enough. In the circumstances, full focus (i.e. including *my dad*) would have made the reason for his visit sound somewhat more casual, and would have suggested that he was not so much interested in *George* as his father, as in his father, whoever that might be. Thus, the issue here is not whether SAAR is a rule of English (which it is), but what the speaker's motivation was for choosing the focus distribution he did choose.

It is stressed that there are different types of apparent counter example to SAAR, some of them occurring in our corpus. These can be given structural explanations, i.e. can be analysed as resulting from the employment of linguistic options that prevent the pattern of accented argument + unaccented predicate from surfacing, such as topicalised arguments, which require a focus domain to themselves,[6] independent permutation of argument and predicate, the use of non-eventive sentences, etc... For these analyses, see Gussenhoven (1983).

Somewhat surprisingly, there were two genuine exceptions to SAAR in the corpus, both of them in DBR. Both concern what I would like to call 'idiomatic' nucleus placements. The first is:

(39)   Stranger things have \HAPpened [DBR]

SAAR requires the nucleus on *stranger* (assuming that *things* is [−focus]).The utterance would seem to be peculiar to English, and is possibly a quotation. Note that related languages have the nucleus on the equivalent of *stranger: Es sind schon MERKwurdigere Sachen passiert!* (German), *Er ziji wel GEKkere dingen gebeurd* (Dutch). A possible explanation of the nucleus location in (39) was suggested to me by Gill Brown, who observed that (39) has a fuller version 'Stranger things have happened at sea'. When speakers left off *at sea,* they may have placed the nucleus on *happened* not unlike the way in which a teacher drilling the Lord's prayer might say: *Our father who* \ART (...) in\HEAVen. Good\LAD.

The second exception represents an instance of conventionalised usage in the world of broadcasting. It is also exceptional in that the 'nuclear tone' is not part of the paradigm of tones normally employed in English.

(40)   Germany CALLing Germany CALLing [DBR]

(with raised larynx and strong nasalisation to imitate transmission distortion, and *Germany* with mid level pitch and *calling* a little lower, but also level)

Although similar to what Ladd (1978) call the 'stylised fall' (which would seem to have a greater step down from the first to the second 'level', from *Germany* to *calling* if *Germany* has the nucleus) and similar to a level nuclear tone (Crystal, 1969: 215), it would appear to be different from either. Note, incidentally, that this is not the normal usage in telephone conversation:

(41)   Ummmm...this is Philip\ROATH speaking [R]

Both exceptions, I would suggest, only bring out the correctness of the generalisation expressed by SAAR.

5.0 Category II: Typically [−Focus] Expressions

Category II comprises expressions that can be given a semantic characterisation. It could be argued that this group should really be seen as a subgroup of Category III, insofar as the expressions concerned refer to aspects that are somehow inherently present in the discourse model, like time, or the relationship with the interlocutor. The bulk of the expressions fall into three classes:

1. time-space markers

2. cohesion markers

3. hearer-appeal markers.

The justification for treating them as a category separate from Category III is that they have an orientating function in common: the propositions to which they are appended are anchored by them to points in, respectively, the outside world ('time-space'), the surrounding discourse ('cohesion'), and some set of possible affective interpretations available to the hearer ('hearer-appeal'). An example of a time-space marker is *this morning;* cohesion markers include expressions like *as a matter of fact, for example,* while *mind you, you know* are examples of hearer-appeal markers.

In addition to these three classes, two further classes have been included in this group:

4. textual markers

5. approximatives

The first of these, the textual markers, comprises comment clauses like *to be prefectly frank, I believe* (Quirk et al, 1972: 778) and reporting sentences, like *he said* (Quirk et al, 1972: 785), also called 'direct speech markers' (Crystal, 1975: 25). While this class can similarly be said to have an orientating function, specifying the status of the 'text' they are appended to, they are virtually absent from our corpus. The final class is that of the approximatives (e.g. *or something, and all that*). It is unlike the others in not having a similar orientating function. It is, however, semantically easily identifiable, and should as such be included in Category II.

At the risk of labouring the obvious, it is pointed out that, in many cases, expressions in Category II can themselves be [+ focus], without their lexical meaning being different in any way. Their membership of Category II expressions is based on their occurence as appendices to focused propositions. Time-space markers, in particular, frequently form the crux of a proposition. For example, when *I caught them kissing this morning* is uttered in response to *When did you catch them kissing?*, then, evidently, we will expect *this morning* to be treated as [+ focus], and *I found them kissing* as [– focus]. Thus, when time-expressions like *this morning* are said to belong to Category II, this should be taken to mean that when *I caught them kissing this morning* is uttered in response to, for instance, *What are you so excited about John and Mary for?*, the expression *this morning* will be typically treated as [– focus], despite the fact that the information provided by the expression may be assumed to be 'new' to the hearer. Note also that it is not impossible for such expressions to be [+ focus] **in addition to** a [+ focus] marking for some other part of the utterance. When this is the case, they require a focus domain to themselves. An example of a focussed time adverbial which appended to another focussed element is given in (42). Here the focus for *this year,* in addition to that for *the eleventh*, serves to bring out the high frequency of dental treatments that the hearer, an office worker, claims to have to undergo.

(42)   A: You had a ∨ DENtal appointment this morning?
         B: \YEAH
         A: The eleventh this /YEAR? [R]

Category II is the category of [–focus] expressions that is discussed by Bing (1979: Ch 2), who calls them Class O expressions, taking the view that they lie outside ('O') the domain to which 'prominence tones' (equatable with nuclear tones) are assigned. This latter domain is filled by Class 1 ('inside') expressions. In addition to challenging Bing's inclusion of certain expressions in the category of Class O expressions and her exclusion of certain others, I will argue that this particular view of 'intonational domain' is incorrect. But first, let us turn to the expressions themselves.

5.1 Time-Space Markers
Time

This is a particularly frequent class. It is noted, for instance, in Brown (1977: 89) that 'time-phrases which modify a predicate are very frequently placed last in the tone group and do not receive the tonic'. These time-markers often denote 'time-when' (including 'relational' words like *yet, (not) any more*), but may also refer to 'duration' and 'frequency' (including *again*). Bing (1979), who has a general category 'sentence adverbials', gives one time-space marker among her examples, the time-frequency adverb *from time to time*. Firbas (1980), however, explicitly refers to 'adverbials of time and place'. The following examples are representative (cf also (18)):

(43) G: I booked his\DAD today
(44) G: \EH/WAIT a minute
(45) O: I always like to tuck her ∨ IN last thing at night
(46) G: Special oc/CASion tonight
(47) G: I haven't got the\BALance anymore
(48) G: I was reading the ∨ PAPer the other day ...
(49) O: You moved a ∨ ROUND a lot [all DBR]

Space

Only the most general place indicators fall in this class. They occur considerably less frequently than time indicators.

(50) O: \LOOK. Do your ∨ COAT up while you're here
            [DBR]
(51) O: Does...a Mr...eh George\ROPer live here
            [FK]
(52)   Trevor did \WELL in life [R]
(53)   Have your Cosmic Reseachers /LED you anywhere? [R]

There are of course examples of focussed locatives in the corpus. In (54), the focus for *your* serves to contrast the liveliness at her mother's house with the depressing tedium of her own.

(54) M: (on the telephone to her mother) It sounds pretty
 \LIVEly| at V YOUR end [SD]

5.2 Cohesion Markers

This class comprises expressions that make explicit the logical relationship between the utterance they are appended to and its context. This relationship may be:

> (parenthetically) ADDITIVE, expressing something like 'Now that you've mentioned it', exemplified by *in fact, as a matter of fact, really, actually*. These often have a downtoning effect, and the latter two in particular may be apologetic in force;

> INFERENTIAL, exemplified by *then* or *so... then, of course;*

> CONCESSIVE, exemplified by *though;*

> REINFORCING, exemplified by *thank you very much, of course, if necessary;*

> CONTRASTIVE, exemplified by *for a change, on the other hand.*

Many others exist (cf. *for example, however, in other words, in that case*), as can be seen in Quirk et al (1972: 821-3), although not all of those listed there would actually be placed in the tail. Many of those that do, moreover, can also be placed in sentence-initial position, in which case they are often given a fall-rise tone, less frequently a fall (cf Allerton and Cruttenden, 1974). The meaning of many items varies according to whether they occur initially or finally. *Really* is strongly reinforcing initially, but 'downtoning' finally (compare *REALLy*| I think you should GO and *I think you should GO really*). Also, the same expression may serve different functions in final position, such as *of course*, which may be inferential or reinforcing, or *then*, which may be inferential or serve as a hearer-appeal marker (see Section 4.3). Note that *then* is not typically used as a time-space marker, a fact that, not surprisingly, is capitalised on for 'comic' effect:

(55) (A and B are talking about how miserable life is and of fear of death)
 A: Well what\DO you think that happens then?
 B: \WHEN?
 A: After\DEATH [R]

The following are representative examples:

(56) G:	Her hooter wasn't ∨ THAT big. Bit like ∨ YOURS really [DBR]
(57) G:	Nothing to ∨ DO with you in fact [DBR]
(58) O:	Still \DOESn't (approve of sex) as a matter of fact [DBR]
(59)	Is sex a\PROBlem then? [R]
(60)	I've just got over Cliff\RICHard's rebelliousness thank you very much [R]
(61) M:	Bit by \BIT if necessary [SC]
(62) G:	Not your own flesh and ∨ BLOOD of course [DBR]
(63) O:	Nice to be on our\OWN for a change [SC]
(64) O:	Must have been a bit of a\SHOCK though [DBR]

Crystal (1975: 25) mentions a few of the above items under the heading 'Final adverbial disjuncts/conjuncts'. In Bing's list, they fall under the general heading of 'sentence adverbials'. As such, they are also mentioned by Schubiger (1958: 91), Bauer et al (1980: 230) and, with refinements, by Firbas (1980).

5.3 Hearer-Appeal Markers

The class comprises items that are used by the speaker to appeal to the hearer. Most of them serve to enhance the solidarity the speaker intends to establish with his hearer, but some are 'challenging' and as such have a distancing effect. Another term for them might therefore be 'solidarity modifiers'. They fall into two groups:

1. A variety of expressions, often conventionalised sentence fragments (*I mean, you know*). They are called 'softeners' or 'softening phrases' by Crystal (Crystal, 1975: 6, Crystal and Davy, 1975: 92). In Bing (1979) they are called 'polite expressions'.

2. Vocatives. They are collectively referred to as 'phatic elements' by Firbas (1980).

Softeners

In the corpus, the following occur: *you know, I mean, then, thanks* and *please*. Examples are:

(65) G:	I was only obeying me ∨ ORDers you know [DBR]
(66) O:	If you'd\HAD one I mean [FK]
(67) O:	I'll say cheeri\O then [DBR]
(68) O:	Not for \ME thanks (declining an offer of sherry) [SC]
(69) G:	I'd like a word with Bill \ALbright please [DBR]

97

Unlike what is suggested in Crystal and Davy (1975: 92-100), these items, when final, are typically included in the tail. It may be true that many of them typically co-occur with a fall-rise in the host sentence, and that they are therefore frequently associated with the rise-element of the fall-rise, but this does not elevate them to the status of a separate tone group. While *you know,* for example, occurs far more frequently with the fall-rise in the host sentence then with the fall, the latter type does occur.

(70) O: It's time you learned to do this for your\SELF
you know Ann [SC]

(71) We have a\BRANCH| in Milton\KEYNES you know [R]

There are no instances in the corpus of *you know* being appended to a host sentence that has a rise, however. The expressions *you see, mind you,* though unattested in the corpus, also belong in this group (Crystal and Davy 1975: 79-9). The item *see,* which occurred once:

(72) O: I mean I'm a shop\STEward| /SEE [FK]

may well be different from *you see, y'see* in typically requiring its own tone group, like *eh* (cf. Section 5.3.1.), but without further data, we cannot be certain that the analysis of (72) is correct. It should in any event be kept distinct from the *see?* meaning 'I told you so' or 'QED', which certainly forms a separate tone group, as in

(73) O: \AH| /SEE? [FK]

Vocatives

Vocatives occur frequently. In DBR alone there are 26 occurrences. They are included in Crystal's list and in Bing's. Examples from the corpus are:

(74) G: Hel∨LO Moby
(75) M: O hel/LO love
(76) M: \ NO George
(77) G: Good _NIGHT Son
(78) O: Mr and Mrs\ ROPer Sir [all DBR]
(79) O: Don't \ FUSS woman [SC]
(80) G: ∨ GLEETings rotus brossom [SC]
(81) O: Ready for∨ COFFee you two? [SC]

As is well-known, vocatives are given a separate tone group when they occur in initial position.

(82) G: ∨ MILdred. Fancy an early ∨ NIGHT [DBR]

In final position, vocatives contrast with similar expressions that have a different function. Lee (1960: 55), Crystal (1975: 25), Bing (1979: 27) and Pierrehumbert (1980: 96), for instance, note that appositives are given a separate tone group.

(83) G: I'm your\GRANdad | grandad\GEORGE   [DBR]

From the corpus, it appears that also the specification of the sender of a quoted message is so separated from the preceding material:

(84) M: \THANK you | for twenty-six glorious
                \YEARS | All my\ LOVE | \George [FK]

Note that in the latter function, the name is normally given a fall, but that when the name is appositive, it tends to agree with the nuclear tone of the element it is appositive to (cf Palmer 1922: 87ff; Halliday 1967: 209). Of course, names also occur as separate tone groups when the speaker inquires after the hearer's name or identity, adresses the hearer selectively, calls his attention, or introduces somebody to the hearer. An example of the first function is (85) and of the last (86).

(85) O: Ex∨CUSE me | Mr / ROPer? [DBR]
(86) M: It's ∨ ME Mother | \ MILdred [SC]

5.3.1. Tags

There are certain tags that behave like the class of 'softeners' discussed above, but certain others that do not. The regular tag is formed by inverting the polarity of the host sentence and repeating the subject and the predicate in proforms (with modal auxiliaries standing in for the whole predicate). The tag always has subject-verb inversion, and the host sentence is always declarative in form. This tag is referred to as Tag I. There is another type of tag which is syntactically distinct from Tag I, in that it agrees in polarity with the host sentence (normally both are positive, but negative-negative sequences are reported, e.g. O'Connor and Arnold, 1973: 61; Quirk et al, 1972: 392), and can also be appended to host sentences that have the form of yes-no questions. As the two types are also phonologically distinct, I will discuss them separately.

Tag I

Tag I forms a separate tone group. While the tag itself either has a fall or a rise (always on the auxillary), there seem to be no restrictions on nuclear tone choice in the host sentence, and, as far as the present corpus is concerned, no restrictions on the tone sequence between host sentence and tag. (O'Connor and Arnold observe that a rise-fall on the tag requires a rise-fall on the host sentence (1973: 81), as in *It's TERRible,* | ISn't it. This, it seems to me, may indicate that we are here dealing with a parameter that is independent of nuclear tone choice proper. That is, the difference between the rise-fall and the fall may be of a different order from that between the fall and the rise, or the fall and the fall-rise). The following examples are illustrative of the various combinations of host sentence tone and tag tone that occur in the corpus:

(87) G:	Something has up\SET you | \ HASn't it
(88) G:	You're not from the H \ P company | /ARE you?
(89) G:	He's a nice /LAD | \ISn't he?
(90) G:	/NICE | /ISn't it?
(91) G:	He was a ∨ NICE looking lad | \WASn't he
(92) G:	I don't think I ∨ KNOW you | /DO I?[7] [all DBR]

There are more tag-like structures in the corpus that require their own tone group. One is *eh,* which would seem to be obligatorily marked with a rise. It also shows a strong preference for combining with a host sentence that has a fall. While it is thus intonationally more restricted than Tag I, it is syntactically less restricted in that it can also combine with host sentences that are WH-questions:

(93) G:	I got a \DAUGHter-in-law | /EH?
(94) G:	Worth a few \MARBles | / EH?
(95) G:	What are you im \ PLYing | /EH? [All DBR]

Tag I and *eh* have different meanings. Tag I either invites the hearer to respond positively or negatively to the proposition conveyed by the host sentence (rise on the tag), or to confirm it (fall on the tag, as stated by e.g. O'Connor and Arnold, 1973: 59-61, Quirk et al, 1972: 391). The meaning of *eh* seems much more general, and in fact is not unlike the meaning of the rise nuclear tone itself, of which it might be said to be the 'dummy' carrier. That is, it is suggested that the more formal counterparts of (93) to (95) consist of the host sentences by themselves with a rise instead of a fall.

Tag II

Tag II agrees in polarity with the host sentence. If the present corpus is anything to go by, it may occur with host sentences that have the form of yes-no questions ((96)), but not with WH-questions ((97)).

(96) G:	Is it one of your ∨ PREsents is it?
	[SC]
(97)	* What are you im ∨PLYing are you?

100

Significantly, however, in practically all instances in the corpus either the operator or the operator and the subject were ellipted in the host sentence:

(98)   Been $\lor$ WORKing have you? [R]
(99) O: You in the /CHAIR are you? [FK]
(100)   Nail varnish dried $\lor$ OUT now has it? [R]

Unlike Tag I, it does not appeal to the hearer either to confirm or to deny the proposition expressed by the host sentence, but rather expresses the fact that the speaker draws a conclusion on the basis of (non-) linguistic information just received (which conclusion may of course be presented to the hearer for comment). As Quirk et al (1972: 390) say, it is frequently used for sarcastic effect. It also often sounds challenging, and Rando (1980), for instance, refers to it as the 'belligerent' tag. Interestingly, Siertsema (1980), who, following Schubiger's analysis of British English intonation and German modal particles (Schubiger, 1965, 1980), investigated the equivalence between English tags and Dutch modal adverbs, lists only examples of Tag II as the equivalent of Dutch *dus* ('so'). In the present corpus, it is always included in the tail of the nuclear tone in the host sentence, a finding that confirms Bing's analysis of the status of Tag II (1979: 37). The host sentence either contains a rise or a fall-rise, which may account for the fact that Quirk et al (1972: 390) state that Tag II (seen by them as a separate tone group) 'always has a rise': the 'rise', then, is either the rise element of the fall-rise, or a continuation of the rise nuclear tone. Examples are:

(101) G: \OH | About the $\lor$ CREDit card is it? [FK]
(102) G: Gonna be la-di-$\lor$ DA are we? [SC]
(103)   Seeing our / NAME| in car park / YELLow are we? [R]
(104)   You specialise in cheering people /UP do you? [R]

It should be observed that a pattern like (102) is 'theory-neutral' in the sense that it could be argued that the pattern might also be analysed as a nuclear fall followed by a nuclear rise. Importantly, however, we did not find instances like (105):

(105)   ? Gonna be la-di- $\lor$ DA | /ARE we?

which would be a counterexample to the generalisation that Tag II is non-nuclear: a non-nucleus interpretation would be impossible, as there is no fall-rise-fall nuclear tone in English. The missing pattern that **is** allowed by the generalisation, viz. one with a fall in the host sentence, is reported by Bald (1980) as occurring in Svartvik and Quirk (1980):

(106)   This is contingent on the central \ HEATing is it
             (S.7.1.a.41)

which pattern is also given by Halliday (1967: 26; 1970: 28).

Because of differences of analysis, we should, again, be cautious when comparing these findings with spontaneous speech data as presented in Svartvik and Quirk (1980). Bald (1980) presents a number of breakdowns of a collection of 439 tag questions taken from this corpus, all based on the tonetic transcription offered in the corpus. His research broadly confirms our analysis in that he concludes that Tag II 'presents a patently different prosodic pattern' from Tag I. Indeed, if we compare Tag I and Tag II on the basis of whether it is classed as a separate 'tone unit', we get a strikingly biased distribution. If we exclude Bald's 'complex' Category VI, containing tags whose syntax is determined by a clause other than the immediately preceding one and for which no tonal specification is given, the figures are for Tag I: 189 separate tone units and 78 tone units shared with the host sentence, while for Tag II the figures are 10 and 69, respectively. Moreover, of the 78 instances in which Tag I was analysed as occurring in the same tone unit as the host sentence, 23 concern the 'theory-neutral' pattern of a fall followed by a rise. In other words, these could also be analysed as sequences of two tone groups. Of the remaining 55, 47 are instances of 'subordination'. Subordination tone groups are, however, intended to constitute **separate** tone units, though of a special type (cf Crystal, 1969: 245; or Bald, 1980, Note 10), and there would therefore seem to be no reason, even remaining within the confines of the transcription conventions adopted in Svartvik and Quirk (1980), to regard these as belonging to the 'shared-tone unit' category.

Of the 10 instances of Tag II as a separate tone unit, 7 appear to consist of \+/ and one of ∧+/, sequences that, again, could be analysed as single tone groups, marked by a (rise-) fall-rise nuclear tone. Thus, Bald's study strongly suggests that the data in Svartvik and Quirk (1980) confirm the analysis offered above. It should also be noted that there are no patterns like (105) in Bald's corpus.

There were two sentences in the corpus of Tag II appended to an imperative host sentence. Although semantically this tag is different from the 'regular' Tag II (e.g. *Get a decent bottle of /SCOTCH will you?* [R]) phonologically it would seem to behave like it in that it is typically non-nuclear. The different distributions of Tag I and Tag II do not support the analysis given in Ladd (1981). In that analysis, Tag II is seen as post-nuclear, as in Bing (1979) and in this article, but Tag I is only regarded as nuclear when it has a fall, not when it has a rise. The examples in the corpus, however, suggest that the freedom of nuclear tone choice in the host sentence is as great when the tag has a fall as when it has a rise.

5.4 Textual Markers

The class of textual markers, also termed 'parentheticals' (e.g. Huckin, 1977: 33) has been supplied from the literature: it is not represented in the corpus. It falls into two groups:

Reporting Sentences

These are mentioned by Crystal ('final direct speech markers', 1975: 25) and Bing (1979), who uses the term 'parenthetical verbs' for this subclass.

(107)   / I don't want to go OUT he said / (Crystal 1975: 25)

Although such reporting sentences would not seem to be infrequent in spoken English, particularly non-standard spoken English, they do not appear to be typically employed in the sort of quasi-spontaneous speech the corpus consists of. There are no occurrences of them, either in tone-group final or in other positions.

Comment Clauses

These are mentioned by Bing (1979: 33), who calls them epistemic verbs. Examples given by Bing are *think, suppose, know, realise, wonder, hope, imagine.* There need be no doubt that such verbs are typically post-nuclear, as in:

(108)   To∨ MORRow I think (Bing 1979: 33)

Curiously, there is only one example of a comment clause in the corpus, and there it was given a separate nucleus:

(109)   .... and found ac\CEPTable | I be\LIEVE [R]

which should perhaps be explained as the actor's attempt at being sarcastic.

5.5 Approximatives

The final class of expressions in Category II is that of the approximatives. It is not mentioned by Crystal, Bing or Firbas. It comprises expressions that indicate the approximative nature of the expressions they are appended to, and it is fairly liberally represented in our corpus. Although the expressions are quite varied from a syntactic point of view, and include adverbials, coordinated expressions and finite clauses, their status as a semantic class is reflected in their being kept outside the focus. Note that clausal approximatives would appear to be restricted to 'empty' comparatives like *the way he did.* Examples are:

(110) O: Oh \ YEAH | I suppose they ∨ ARE in a way
(111) O: Oh it must be eleven \ YEARS or more
(112) G: Just for a /DAY or two
(113) O: ∨ ME | Turning∨ UP like I did [all DBR]
(114)   It's a \RULE | they're always ∨ LOCal or something [R]

(115)   Industrial Tri \ BUNal and all that [R]

(116)   Rotting in the /GROUND? | Burrowing / WORMS and so on [R]

(117)   Do you think we can get on to thinning ∨ HAIR | and
sexual in ∨ ADequacy kind of thing? [R]

	Type	Example
Category I SAAR	1. Subject + {Intransitive verb / (be +) Complement} 2. Object + Verb + Particle 3. WH-movement 4. Subject + Verb + [-focus] Argum 5. [Subject + Passive verb]	I have a feeling the \ KITchen will blast off Keep your \ VOICE down Where does most of our \ COFfee come from Mrs ROPer has been helping me [CLASSes have been cancelled]
Category II Time-space marker	Time Space	Can we sit \ DOWN for a minute? Do your ∨ COAT up while you're in here
Cohesion marker	Addition Inference Concession Reinforcement Contrast	Her hooter wasn't ∨ THAT big/ Bit like \ YOURS really Is sex a \ PROblem then Must have been a bit of a \ SHOCK though Bit by \ BIT if necessary Nice to be on your \ OWN for a change
Hearer-appeal marker	Softner Vocative Tag II	I was only obeying me ∨ ORDers you know Don't \ FUSS woman He/ LO son/ You in the/ CHAIR are you
Textual marker	[Reporting sentence] [Comment clause]	[NO he said] [FIVE I suppose]
Approximative		Industrial Tri \ BUNal and all that

Table 4. Classification of tail-types in Categories I and II. Bracketed elements are not represented in the corpus, and have been supplied from the literature.

104

6.0 Comparison With Other Investigations

It may at this point be useful to summarise our findings in Sections 3 and 4 in tabular form (see Table 4), and to compare them with the results of the investigations reported in Crystal (1975: 25-6), Bing (1979: Ch 2) and Firbas (1980).

From the point of view of the classification of tail-types offered here, Crystal's list presents a rather mixed picture. In addition to such items as were quoted above, Crystal gives a number of miscellaneous ones, including items that concern what we might call 'pragmatically old' information, as in: A: *That was some terrible ACcident* | WASn't it. B: *a TERRible accident.* In others they would seem to concern compound stress rules, as in *That shelf is a do-it-yourSELF job* or *It's a verPLOORG grammar,* or contrastive accentuation of the type *this book costs FIVE dollars* | and this one THREE dollars, or items that are difficult to interpret out of context, such as *he has a YELLow streak,* while in one case a time adverbial is included: *It's the in-THING these days.*

Bing's list resembles our Category II list rather more closely. However, in addition to vocatives, polite expressions (here:.softeners), sentence adverbs, what I called Tag II, parenthetical verbs and epistemic verbs, all of which were covered above, Bing mentions *epithets* and *expletives.* Among other examples, the following are given to illustrate epithets:

(118)   John wouldn't give me his car the stupid bastard (Bing [47])

(119)   My next-door neighbours, the Finks, have been coming
        over every night (Bing [48b])

Bing quotes O'Connor and Arnold's

(120)   Yes, | confound it (Bing [48b], contour corrected)

as an example of an expletive. I believe Bing is mistaken when she classifies expletives and epithets as Class 0 expressions. Contrary to what this implies, they do not form the tail of the preceding nucleus, but are assigned a separate nuclear tone. What may have led her to including them as Class 0 expressions is that this nuclear tone is typically a low rise, and as such phonetically similar to the optional boundary tone, which is her interpretation of the rise element of the fall-rise. Since the presence of the boundary tone is her main criterion for classifying expressions as Class 0 expressions, it is not surprising to find that her list includes expressions that typically have a low rise. Bing's case for this interpretation of epithets rests, among other things, on the contrast between (119) and (121): in (121) *the Finks* is an appositive with a fall-rise:

(121)   My next-door neighbours, the Finks, have been coming
        over every night (Bing [49a])

Since the two tones cannot be interchanged, so she argues, they differ in the way she says they do. I would agree that the patterns do have the meanings given, but of course this could also be used as an argument for saying that the low rise does not mean the same thing as the fall-rise in English. Note that Class 0 expressions, e.g. vocatives, to give Bing's canonical example, have the following characteristics:

- They are not assigned a prominence tone;
- They may be assigned a boundary tone.

Translated into a nuclear tone description, these two characteristics would come out as:

- They may not be assigned a nuclear tone;
- If the sentence they are appended to is assigned a fall-rise they will carry the rise element of that tone.

Below I will retain Bing's terminology. If we compare epithets and vocatives, three differences emerge that Bing's analysis cannot account for:

1. After a completed A-rise contour (a fall-rise), vocatives cannot be given an optional boundary tone, but epithets can:

(122)   They are my next-door|neighbours the Finks

(123)   *They are my next-door|neighbours Pamela

Note that the pattern in (123) would have been well-formed if *Pamela* is added, after a suitable pause, as a means of (literally) calling the hearer's attention (see Section 5.3). It would then not be a vocative in the sense employed here, and be assigned a separate tone group.

2. Vocatives can occur without the optional boundary tone, but - paradoxically - epithets **must** have the optional boundary tone ((126)).

(124)   They're my next-door|neighbours Pamela

(125)   *They're my next-door|neighbours the finks

(126)   They're my next-door|neighbours the finks

3. If a B-contour (a high-rise) is used, a vocative is high in the pitch range (continuing the rise started on the nuclear syllable), but an epithet picks up from the bottom of the pitch range:

(127) Were they your next-door neighbours Pamela?

(128) *Were they your next-door neighbours the finks?

(129) Were they your next-door neighbours the finks?

Observe, incidentally, that (129) may be given a different interpretation. Since appositives are characterised not just by the fact that they are assigned a nuclear tone, but also by the fact that this tone agrees with the tone on the element they are appositive to (see Section 5.2), (129) is ambiguous between an appositive reading and an epithet reading. It may in fact be felt that an appositive reading is the more immediately probable one, possibly because questions like (129) are not easily compatible with declarations of the type expressed by epithets. This should not, of course, allow us to lose sight of the important point, and that is that all three differences noted above are naturally explained by assuming that epithets are separate tone groups, that is, Class I expressions. In (122) it follows a fall-rise, in (126) it follows a fall, and in (129) rise. Similar reasoning would show that expletives, too, are given a low rise nuclear tone. Summarising, vocatives are included in the tail, appositives are given a separate tone group and agree in tone with their 'head', and epithets and expletives are given a separate tone group and are typically assigned a low rise nucleus.

Firbas (1980), finally, attempts to account for the frequent occurrence of predicates in the tail not by postulating a focus-realisation rule (like SAAR), but by appealing to semantic factors. He would thus view our Category I as a subpart of Category II. It is difficult to see how this can be done. Neither is Firbas' account very clear: "[It] is because in the development of discourse the primary function of the verb is an introductory one. It consists in introducing into the discourse notions conveyed by context independent elements. This explains why the verb comparatively rarely comes to carry the highest degree of CD (communicative dynamism) and to function as an IC (intonation centre) bearer."

7.0 Theoretical Implications

It is in the nature of things that tails must be assigned to Category III (pragmatically [–focus] expressions) will not be amenable to the same sort of 'linguistic' generalisations that were made for tails in Categories I and II. At this point we will therefore turn to justification of the interpretation of the falling-rising pitch contours that was adopted in Section 1.3. The first section below argues against certain interpretations proposed in the British literature, the second against a recent proposal by Bing (1979).

7.1 The Status of the Fall-Rise

When placed beside treatments of English intonation like those found in Trager and Smith (1957), Liberman (1975) or Pierrehumbert (1980), descriptions in the 'British tradition' begun by Palmer (1922) are conspicuous in showing considerable agreement with respect to broad questions concerning the segmentation of intonation contours (cf. e.g. Ashby (1979) for a short characterisation). On closer inspection, however, certain differences of opinion emerge, most significantly in the very area we are dealing with here, that of the designation of particular pitch-marked syllables as either nuclear or non-nuclear. Most notably, the disagreement concerns the theoretical status of:

1. rising movements followed by falling movements;
2. falling movements followed by rising movements,

in situations in which the two movements do not occur on the same syllable. If we ignore Bing's treatment for the moment, such sequences have, between them, been described as:

> a sequence of two nuclear tones;
> a compound, bi-nuclear tone, with both pitch-marked
> syllables characterised as nuclear;
> a simple nuclear tone on the first syllable;
> a simple nuclear tone on the second syllable.

Such issues are of theoretical significance, and need not simply be considered out of an Occam's razor-guided desire for descriptive elegance. Their chief importance lies in the implications different solutions will have for a semantic analysis of intonation: different interpretations of pitch movements may affect our decision about what is 'given' (or [−focus]) and what 'new' (or [− focus]), in addition to determining our classification of the pitch movements in terms of the paradigm of nuclear tones, which, after all, are widely held to be strong candidates for meaning-carrying units.

The present analysis of tails can really only claim to have a bearing on the interpretation of the second of the two pitch sequences mentioned above. The first, a rise followed by a fall, is either uncontroversially interpreted as a 'rise-fall', marking a single nucleus, as in (4), or is variably interpreted without affecting the decision about what is 'tail'. Thus, if Crystal (1975: 27) analyses| /ROUND the CORner | and Crystal and Davey (1975: 127)|/PULLing his BAT away| the way they do, i.e. as compound rise-plus-falls, where Deakin (1981) would analyse these utterances as having nuclear falls preceded by rising heads, or if Svartvik and Quirk (1980: 294) analyse| actually you'd go /DOWN to Fulham PALace Road| as a compound rise-plus-fall, where Brazil, Coulthard and Johns (1980: 8) would analyse the same thing as a sequence of a rise and a fall, we end up with the same interpretation of what is 'tail', since the falling movement is seen as nuclear in all three analyses. A different case is presented by the second of the two patterns mentioned earlier, a fall followed by a rise, because here, one of the rival analyses - the one adopted in Section 1.5 -claims that it is only the fall that marks a nuclear syllable, the rise being placed later in the tail(irrespective of its length), and together with the fall forming part of a single nuclear tone, the fall-rise. This may be said to be Kingdom's position (1958: 19) (who, confusingly, does have a 'compound tone' in his analysis, which would seem to be equivalent to a falling head followed by a nuclear rise in other analyses, as in /DO sit DOWN (1958: 127; cf. Schubiger 1961). It is probably also Schubiger's position, who, however, distinguishes between a unitary (distributed) fall-rise and a fall followed by a tail which is 'modified by a rise' (1958: 2 Note), and, less ambiguously, Gimson's (1980: 279), although he adds that both the fall and the rise take place on 'accented syllables'. It is also explicitly the position adopted by Firbas (1980), who, in order to emphasise the distinction between his view and one espousing a bi- or double-nucleus analysis, chooses to replace the term 'tail' with the term 'shade'. Such a 'unitary' analysis, contrasts with an analysis of the two pitch movements as separate nuclei (Brazil, Coulthard and Johns, 1980), as well as with one in which both movements are seen as nuclear, but together make up a single, compound 'fall-plus-rise' nuclear tone (Halliday, 1967; Crystal, 1969; O'Connor and Arnold, 1973). For some analysts, both a unitary nucleus interpretation (with the rise in the tail) and a compound one are available, with (optional) phonetic differences being claimed between them (Halliday's Tone 4 vs Tone 13, 1967: 20, or O'Connor and Arnold's simple vs compound fall-rise, 1973 29). Ignoring this potentiality for alternative analyses by some authors, three interpretations are therefore possible for (2) (repeated here):

(2)   It's true as a matter of fact

(i) | It's ∨ TRUE as a matter of fact |
         (e.g. Bauer et al, 1980: 231)
(ii) | It's \ TRUE as a matter of /FACT |
         (e.g. Halliday, 1967: 15)
(iii) | It's \ TRUE | as a matter of /FACT |
         (cf Brazil, 1978: 59)

Our analysis of tails in this article has assumed the first of the above three interpretations. It follows that all the generalisations arrived at in Sections 4 and 5 will have to be abandoned, if we adopted either the analysis under (ii) or that under (iii). Any arguments for preferring either of the latter two analyses to (i) must therefore be seen as pitched against this, what I would regard as overwhelming evidence to the contrary. Clearly, drawing a distinction between a fall-rise and a fall-plus-rise nuclear tone would considerably complicate the description of the data.[8] This conclusion is in

109

direct conflict with that reached by Crystal (1969: 220), who says: 'The phonetic and linguistic contrast between complex (e.g. a monosyllabic $\lor$) and compound (e.g. a distributed $\backslash$ + $/$) tones thus seems sufficiently great to justify separate phonological discussion.' Crystal's conclusion, however, is misleadingly strengthened by the very misconception it seeks to establish: because he regards both the fall element and the rise element as nuclear, he is able to contrast the compound fall-plus-rise not just with a (phonetically different?) pattern which is described as having the fall-rise in the position of the fall element in the compound version, as in $|\lor$ YOU don't know $|$: well, who does, then! versus $|\backslash$ YOU don't/KNOW $|$: So why are you saying you do!, but also with one in which the fall-rise is placed on the syllable that has the rise element in the compound version, as in $|$ I thought it would $\lor$ RAIN $|$ versus $|$ I $\backslash$ THOUGHT it would $/$ RAIN$|$. Three of the four supporting examplers he gives are of the second type. It should be clear that in the rival, uni-nuclear analysis, comparisons of the latter type concern a difference of nuclear-tone position, not one of nuclear-tone type.

Our analysis also makes it clear that an across-the-board interpretation of such sequences of falls and rises as separate tone groups (i.e. interpretation (iii)) would equally effectively wipe out the generalisations we have made. Observe, however, that although the generalisations may be used as a guiding principle in a large number of cases where a distinction between a one-tone group and a two-tone group solution is at issue, a problem that remains to be solved is how to draw the distinction between a tone group with a non-final fall-rise and a sequence of two tone groups, one with a nuclear fall and one with a nuclear rise, both of which are of course allowed by our analysis. Unlike Schubiger, who plays down the significance of this question to an uncomfortable extent (1958: 89 Note), I believe that the question is - or should be - answerable in an absolute sense, and should not be 'a matter of convention', as Schubiger says. For discussion of this question see Kingdon (1958: 33-7, 78-80), Crystal (1969: 236-9, 248), Gussenhoven (forthcoming, b).

There is, as far as I can see, only one other analysis possible that would leave the generalisations intact. This is an analysis whereby the rise element of the fall-rise is partitioned off from the nuclear-tone paradigm, and accommodated in a separate, two-term paradigm of boundary tones (an analysis which is perhaps implied in Schubiger (1958: 19, 84), at least for part of her data). In such a description, (2) and (130) would be said to have the same nuclear tone (a fall), but to differ in that (2) has a high boundary tone and (130) a low boundary tone, or, alternatively, no boundary tone. If it is possible to define a certain subset of tails, say Category II expressions, then, obviously, the generalisation that can be made is that, that subset is the purview of the boundary tone paradigm.

(130)   It's true as a matter of fact

It is precisely such an analysis that has been proposed by Bing (1979). The next section is devoted to it.

7.2 The Question of a Separate 'Intonational Domain'

Bing's description of Class 0 expressions differs from a description of such expressions in terms of the more traditional 'British' concepts of nucleus and tail, such as the one offered here, in that she sees those expressions as falling outside the domain for the assignment of the 'prominence tones'. In her system, there are four such tones (the second and fourth of which are subsequently argued to be variants of each other). They are given here with their 'British' translations (Bing 1979: 10):

A contour	: fall
A-rise contour	: fall-rise
B contour	: high rise
C contour	: low rise

Class 0 expressions are then given either no tone or a (low rise) boundary tone. That is, the domain formed by Class 0 expressions is **separated** intonationally from the stretch of speech to which these expressions are 'appended' (Liberman (1978) speaks of 'tags', although his position with respect to the question of domain appears to be neutral). Put differently, the host sentences, which contain Class I expressions, are assigned 'prominence tones' and these tones are not allowed to spill over into the Class 0 expressions. Thus, (2) would be said to consist of the A contour followed by the boundary tone, and (130) to have the A contour, but not the boundary tone. Conversely, (131) and (132) would be said to contain different prominence tones (an A-rise contour and an A contour respectively) and also to differ in that (132) has the boundary tone but (131) has not.

(131)   I suppose you can take the car (Bing [60])

(132)   I suppose you can take the car honey [*]

There is, moreover, an important semantic correlate of these two tonal paradigms: prominence tones have meaning, the boundary tone does not. The notion of separate tonal paradigms also occurs in Pierrehumbert, who, in order to generate the Fo contours of American English intonation, postulates three paradigms: pitch accents, phase accents and boundary accents (Pierrehumbert 1980: 16).

I believe that the notion of separate domains and the associated concept of boundary tones lack theoretical justification. Before arguing against these notions, let us see what Bing's arguments for her solution are. If we discount the discussion about the different derivational histories of Class I (coming from Root Sentences) and Class 0 expressions (coming from Non-sentential Expressions) as irrelevant to the point at issue, there being no reason to assume that differences in syntactic status, certainly those of the deeper type she is concerned with, should be precisely paralleled by differences in

111

intonational structure, Bing puts forward only two arguments whose force does not depend on àn a priori analysis of the data in terms of the analysis she proposes. (Bing in fact concedes that part of her argumentation is circular). Both arguments focus on the most important consequence of her boundary-tone analysis: the fact that, in that analysis, the addition of a boundary tone to an utterance does not alter the semantics of that utterance. In an attempt to demonstrate that this prediction is borne out, Bing starts from the well-known pair (133) and (134):

(133)   John doesn't drink because he is un|happy   (A contour, Bing [22])

(134)   John doesn't drink because he is un|happy   (A-rise, Bing [23])

For (133), the most probable interpretation is 'Because of his unhappiness, John doesn't drink', while for (134) it is 'John drinks for reasons other than his unhappiness' (Bing 1979: 27). Now, instead of comparing these variations with (135) and (136)

(135)   John doesn't drink because he is un|happy, Pamela   [*]

(136)   John doesn't drink because he is un|happy, Pamela   (Bing [25])

which would be the respective counterparts of (133) and (134) in a nuclear tone analysis, Bing argues, as indeed she is forced to argue, that (136) is the counterpart of (133), since here a meaningless boundary tone has been added to an A contour (a fall). While leaving (135) undiscussed, she then boldly states about (136) that it gets the same interpretation as (133). Although discussions of this sort should really not take place outside the context of independently obtained judgements (and Bing does not provide any), it is not difficult to choose from 'Why don't you try and cheer him up' and 'He drinks because he is a bloody alchoholic' the most natural sequel to (136). Although, as far as my own intuition is concerned, either sequence would be well-formed, the most immediately probable one is that with the latter sequel, and not that with the former, quite the reverse of what Bing claims. Observe further that by equating (136) with (133), Bing is left with the problem of giving a vocative counterpart to (134). She does this by allowing the rise element of the fall-rise (or the boundary tone, in Bing's terms) to set in a little earlier than in (136), representing it as follows:

(137)   John doesn't drink because he's un|happy Pamela

                (A-rise + boundary tone, Bing [25])

Now at least in standard British descriptions of English intonation, it is not uncustomary to describe the rise element of the fall-rise as picking up from a syllable before the last rather than from the last, either from the first post-nuclear syllable (e.g. Jones, 1975: 303), or from the last secondarily accented (stressed) syllable (e.g. Gimson, 1980: 268), the assumption in this tradition apparently being that any semantic or phonological differences between (136) and (137) are spurious. But even if we assume that the situation in American English is different, Bing is left with an awkward gap in her analysis, provided by (135), as well as with an awkward case of overgeneration: the apparently non-existent pattern consisting of (134) followed by a vocative without the boundary tone.

Bing's second argument likewise tries to capitalise on the fact that her treatment predicts that presence or absence of the boundary tone is semantically neutral. Thus, in (138) and (139), where we are dealing with expletives (which, it will be recalled, are regarded as Class 0 expressions by Bing), the addition of the boundary tone does not alter the meaning of the expletive:

(138)   Screw the shelves! (A contour)

(139)   Screw the shelves! (A contour with boundary tone) (' Bing [138a,b])

Note that the assumption here is that when an expression in Class 0 occurs in isolation, it must receive a prominence tone, which is then optionally followed by a boundary tone. Bing contrasts this pair with the pair in (140) and (141), which are not expletives, and which do differ in meaning:

(140)   Screw the shelves (A contour)

(141)   Screw the shelves (A-rise contour)

                        (i.e. but leave the sides for me to do) (Bing [139a,b])

Bing then notes that this difference is accounted for by the fact that different prominence tones have different meanings ((140) and (141)), and that (138) and (139) after all have the same prominence tone. The argument is faulty, even if we take the view that expletives are post-nuclear (which as we saw they are not). Note first of all that no reason is given why part of the contour in (139) is assigned a prominence tone and part a boundary tone. What, in other words, would the contour look like with an A-rise contour? And how would its meaning differ from (139)? Note, second, that if (138) and (139) are said to have the same meaning, this sameness refers to the fact that they are both *expletives*: at best, a different tone can modify the effect of the expletive, but not 'change its interpretation'. And note, thirdly, that if it did, it would no longer be an expletive, and Bing could dismiss the 'change' as being the result of a shift from Class 0 to Class I! The argument is wholly void.

An observation made by Liberman (1978: 13) might well have provided Bing with another argument for her proposal. Liberman notes that (142), in which the predicate has the nucleus and *my friend* follows in the tail, differs from (143), where *my friend* is a vocative, in that the fall in (142) is allowed to spread on to *my*, but in (143) is completed before *my*, the net effect being that *my* in (143) has lower pitch.

(142)   Sam struck \ OUT my friend
(143)   Sam struck \ OUT, my friend (Liberman 1978: 13)

It would, to my mind, be a mistake to try and account for this difference by postulating different units - tones - or domains - in the intonational system. Neither, to be sure, do we postulate a long /t/ phoneme by the side of a short /t/ phoneme to account for the durational difference in the alveolar closure for /t/ in *out*, which may be another phonetic difference accompanying the syntactic difference. It is suggested that the only 'emic' difference is a syntactic one (cf Liberman, 1978: 10), and that the phonetic differences noted are 'etic' effects of this difference. Of course, low-level phonetic rules, whether segmental or non-segmental, will have to be made sensitive to the difference in syntactic bond between *struck out* and *my friend*, but adding units either to the intonational system or to the phoneme inventory to account for cases represented by (142) and (143) would open the floodgates to whole regiments of phonological units that will soon make a mockery of the concept of a 'phonological system'. In a sense, this is what is proposed in the section on tags in Pierrehumbert (1980: 95-102), in whose description the phonological level and the phonetic level largely coincide. It should be noted that Bing does not bring Liberman's example to bear on her hypothesis.

What are the arguments against Bing's proposal? There are, it would seem, two major problems. One is that the boundary-tone-is-meaningless theory conflicts with the semantic facts, and the other that the boundary tone paradigm leads to the generation of pitch contours that do not occur.

1. One consequence of the fact that the boundary tone is meaningless is that (144) and (145), to take one example, cannot differ in meaning:

(144)   I $\vee$ KNOW, Mildred (A contour + H%) [*]
(145)   I \ KNOW, Mildred (A contour + $\emptyset$) [*]
             (H% is here used for Bing's boundary tone, $\emptyset$ for
             its absence)

Bing's only comment on this type of difference is that (144) would be characteristic of female speakers and (145) more characteristic of male speakers, but, she adds ingenuously, 'both patterns are acceptable to either' (1979: 22). The following frame brings out their different semantic effects rather glaringly:

114

(146) Mildred: And what's ∨ MORE | the police will
                       find out that you haven't returned
                       that \ CREDit card you found

George: (I \KNOW, Mildred)
                                    Shut \ UP about it!
                                            [*]
         (I ∨ KNOW, Mildred)

where the use of the fall on *know* will cause *shut up about it* to sound like an injunction to Mildred to stop talking about it to George, but the use of a fall-rise may well be taken by Mildred to mean that she is not to let on about it to the police, or to other people in general. Tne effects would not, of course, be different from those achieved by *I* \KNOW and *I* ∨ *KNOW*, respectively, which Bing would regard as having different prominence tones. And what to think of the ludicrously pally effect if Julius Caesar were to be portrayed as saying

(147)   Et ∨ TU, Brute (Shakespeare, *Julius Caesar*
             Act III, Sc I)

when receiving the final stab from Brutus (instead of /TU, \TU or —TU)? Surely, this is not caused by the fact that Julius Caesar is a male rather than a female character, as Bing would presumably have it.

Another consequence of her analysis is that (131) and (132) (p.) **do** differ in intonational meaning, since (132) has an A contour on *suppose* and (131) an A-rise contour. It would be difficult to demonstrate that these utterances differ in anything other than a measure of politeness introduced by the addition of the vocative.

2. Bing's postulation of separate Class O domains generates many patterns that do not occur. Among them are the following:[9]

(148)   * No\Mildréd (A-rise + H%)

(149)   * Nǿ Mildred (C contour + Ø)

(150)   * Nó Mildred (B contour + Ø)

In fact, the only patterns that do occur are the ones predicted by the standard view of vocatives being included in the tail of the nuclear tone:

(151) M: It's ri\DICulous George (A contour)

(152) M: Look at it ∨THIS\way George (A-rise contour)

(153) O: I would have /MARRied her George (C contour) [all DBR]

115

In summary, Bing's proposal to look upon Class O expressions as constituting a separate intonational domain must be rejected. All the evidence points to the correctness of the traditional view whereby the tail is included in the domain of the nuclear tone, also when this tail is filled by a Class O expression.

8.0 Category III: Pragmatically [−Focus] Expressions

8.1 Preliminary Remarks

Sentence accents, in the sense of the things that are assigned by rules like SAAR, are either there or are not there. Phonologically speaking, there is no place for 'degrees' of them. As such, they must be distinguished from other phenomena that might conceivably be discussed under the heading 'sentence stress'. These phenomena include at least the following:

1. The existence of suprasegmental durational structure in tails (i.e. durational variation that is explained by the presence of 'word accent', the potential location for 'assigned accents'). Thus, in

(154)   Why \ DID you get rid of Lucy? [R]

rid may be more prominent than *get*, reflecting a potential pronunciation *get RID (of)*.

2. Various suprasegmental means of making a syllable stand out so as to cause the meaning of the word it is part of to be 'significant'. These concern modifications of duration, loudness and voice quality. Examples are:

(155) O: Of course I could wade through yesterday's
                ac\ COUNTS [FK]

where *wade* was lengthened, and pronounced with softer-than-usual, lax voice, and

(156) M: Don't you \ LIE to me! [FK]

with *me* extra loud, and with harsh voice. While such paralinguistic features may be expected to be amenable to systematic description, they are unrelated to the concept of focus and sentence accent.

3. The employment of pauses to create suspense. An illustrating example here is (157)

(157) O: I think it's pretty ∨ OBvious ... dad [DBR]

116

where the pause serves to underline the fact that the speaker continues to regard George as his father, in spite of the latter's remonstrations. The pause, however, does not disturb the mapping of the fall-rise: the rise element goes to the stranded *dad* just as it would have done if no pause had occurred.

4. High-pitched onsets of tone groups in other than sentence-accent positions such as

(158) O: Shall we have a little \ SIDE bet |
               Say a / POUND? [SC]

where *say* has high onset, but is not assigned an accent by SAAR (*say* being a cohesion marker, cf *a POUND say?*)

The sentence accents that we are concerned with, in other words, are those that are assigned by SAAR on the basis of the focus marking of the utterance. Recall that, unlike what is sometimes assumed, 'accent' and 'focus' are not directly relatable in the sense that what is unaccented is therefore [−focus]. In particular, we say in Section 3 that predicates in focussed argument + predicate combinations are unaccented, and that therefore an utterance like *Your FRIEND has called* is ambiguous between a sentence with [+ focus] just for *your friend* and one with full focus marking. In its turn, the intonational option [+ focus], like the syntactic option [±past], is available to speakers to express certain meanings. As is well-known, these meanings are not easy to describe. The most convenient shorthand descriptions of them are probably Halliday's terms 'given' and 'new' (1967: 204).[10] The marking of [+ focus] is invariably reserved for what speakers consider to be the crux of their contribution to the conversation (hence 'new'), while [−focus] goes with what speakers somehow assume - or want to be seen as assuming - to be the starting point of what they are contributing (hence 'given'). (Note that Halliday used 'given' and 'new' to refer to the terms in the focus paradigm themelves, rather than to their meanings.)

It would clearly not be worthwhile to attempt to bring order into the large collection of Category III tails on the basis of formal linguistic criteria of the type 'repetition of words', 'second mention of concept', 'use of proform', etc. For one thing, such a classification would soon prove to be void, inasmuch as there would almost certainly be a [+ focus] example in our corpus for every sub-category that is set up. For another, the basis of a description of pragmatically [− focus] expressions must surely be pragmatic. It is not clear to me, however, to what extent such a description is either possible or desirable.

So, rather than attempt to give a more complete definition of what 'focus' means, I would in a final section like to select from the corpus some examples of focus distribution that are used to create particular effects. This, at least, will make it clear that focus is a semantically powerful linguistic option.

117

8.2 Focus Effects

Special effects of focus distribution as employed in the corpus are of two kinds:

1. ***narrative effects,***
    i.e. such effects as are used to give structure to the narrative;
2. ***'comedy' effects.***

8.2.1 Narrative Effects

A strategy that is not infrequent in the G and M data is to allow [-focus] marking to suggest the occurrence of a preceding conversation. The technique enables the producer of the drama to leave out bits of verbal exchange that would only serve to lead up to 'comedy' situations, and thus results in a higher density of such situations. For example, a scene may begin as follows:

(159) G: Well of \COURSE I remember ve night [DBR]

suggesting a preceding opener *Do you remember v/E night?* Another example of such an opening is

(160) O: And \ THAT'S | my opinion of \ YOU |
                    What do you think of \ THAT?
        G: Well, some people might be of V FENDed by
                    the phrase "arrogant little twerp" [DBR]

A somewhat different technique involving [−focus] occurs in the Roath instalment, where a character speaking on the telephone uses [−focus] to represent the speech of his interlocutor, who, as a character in the series, remains imaginary:

(161)   I do \ NOT see too many spy films | I V DON'T
                    know the facts and fallacies of call tracing ... [R]

While techniques of this kind would also appear to be employed in novels, the spoken medium clearly offers much more scope for them.

8.2.2 'Comedy' Effects

Within this group, two types can perhaps be distinguished: conventional 'comedy' uses of [−focus], and specific ones. In neither case, incidentally, need we be dealing with focus distributions that exclusively occur in 'sitcom' speech. The conventional type, in particular, would seem to be fairly frequent also in real spontaneous speech.

Conventional uses Conventional 'comedy' effects of [— focus] rely on the [—focus] marking of semantic material that could objectively be characterised as unexpected, but that, incongruously, because it is not marked [+focus], acquires a certain measure of self-evidence. That is, the effect is created by the presentation of the unexpected material as material that both the hearer and the speaker had taken for granted all along. In all cases that this technique occurred in the corpus, the preceding nucleus had a fall-rise. For example, in (162), the focus for marking suggests that, contrary to fact, it is somehow common knowledge that Rolls Royces need two parking bays:

(162)   G (temporarily employed as a traffic warden):
               I gave out thirty ∨ TICKets today |
               Thirty-\ ONE | if you count the Rolls ∨ ROYCE
               parked at two meters [DBR]

   Other examples are:

(163) A: (muttering and moaning)
      B: You're quite ∨ HANDsome when you are paranoic [DBR]
(164) (shopkeeper, reluctantly replying to a request to produce an invoice):
                 It'll only take an ∨ HOUR or two to trace it [FK]
(165) (on receiving news that his boss wants to see him):
                 THAT'll be the sack | I had hoped to ∨KEEP
                 this job long enough to buy a toupee [R]

   In a related type, it is unfavourable attendant circumstances that are incongruously not marked [+ focus], the [+ focus] marking being restricted to the conjunction *and*, as in

(166) O: Last year I queued all ∨ NIGHT for Harrod's
                 sale | ∨ AND it was raining [SC]

where the effect depends on the contrast between the suggestion that the two events expressed by the sentential conjuncts naturally go hand in hand and the objective fact that they are unrelated.

   And, stretching the term 'comedy' effect somewhat, we should here perhaps also include conventionalised [- focus] uses as are given by Firbas (1980) and are represented in our corpus by (167) - (169):

(167)   \THAT's for sure! [DBR]
(168)   ∨ THAT'll interest you [DBR]
(169)   ∨ THAT'll be the sack! [R]

119

Specific uses In the group of specific uses of focus distribution for 'comedy' effects we find both instances of the (objectively unjustified) absence of [+ focus] marking, and of its presence. To begin with the latter, tly popular structure here is reflexive verbs, like *to KILL oneself, to TALK to oneself, to asSERT oneself,* which are accented on the verbal element when they are [+ focus] (cf Section 4.0). Observe that for the purposes of SAAR, these verbs are predicates rather than predicate + argument combinations: when they are combined with an argument, SAAR applies regularly (B's reply in (170) being entirely [+ focus]):

(170) A: What's all the \ RUCKus about?
      B: Uncle \ SID's killed himself! [*]

When, however, the [+ focus] marking is restricted to the reflexive pronoun, this will get the nucleus. It is this restricted focus distribution that 'ought' to have been used in O's utterance in (171). Instead, O used full focus for the reflexive verb, which results in a Catgegory I tail for *yourself*:

(171) O: (to George, who keeps intruding on O)
                Mr —ROPer | do you ever / TALK to yourself?
      G: / NO
      O: Now's your \ CHANCE (turns his back on George) [FK]

The same ploy is used in

(172) M: (to George, who is playing scrabble all by himself)
                What are you \ DOing?
      G: I'm \ PLAYing with myself [FK]

Tails resulting from the unwarranted absence of [+ focus] marking are theoretically less interesting. An example is (173), where the 'comedy' effect relies on the occurrence of a homophone, constituting a case of pseudo-repetition:

(173) G: Germany CALLing, Germany CALLing! (cf (40))
      M: (about visitor who just left, bored by George's war stories)
                \ HE won't be calling again! [DBR]

Another example is (174), where [−focus] for the dependent question enhances the sarcastic effect: the utterance was intended as a dismissal of the hearer. Observe that full focus (i.e. with the nucleus on *door*) would have been less effective. The immediacy of the dismissal depends crucially on the (untruthful) suggestion that the hearer must already have been working on the logistics of his retreat, and was about to go anyway.

(174)   \ NOW | DO you V KNOW how the door works? [R]

Finally, observe how in the following exchange the 'comedy' effect relies on George's ignoring the well-formed focus distribution in the first clause of Mildred's utterance, treating it as if not *you* was [+ focus], but *bought a present* (which ought to have given the nucleus on *present*):

(175) M: I bought ∨ YOU a present, George |
            Now what are \ YOU going to do?
      G: I'll say ∨ THANK you, Mildred [FK]

9.0 Summary

As a result of our analysis of tails, a number of important theoretical points about the intonation of English could be established.

1. SAAR expresses an important generalisation. No theoretical consequences could be detected that necessitated a reformulation. Its explanatory power goes well beyond that of statements that NPs are stressed in preference to VPs (Section 4).

2. There is no direct relationship between focus and accent such that what is [+ focus] is necessarily accented. Examples of [+ focus] elements that are unaccented include predicates in focussed argument + predicate combinations, certain compound constituents in focussed arguments, and adverbs of 'proper functioning' and reflexive pronouns in focussed predicates (Sections 4.0, 8.2).

3. A large subclass of [−focus] tails (Category II tails) can be given a semantic characterisation (Section 5).

4. No justification could be found for the postulation of bi-nuclear tones. Indeed, the postulation of a bi-nuclear fall-plus-rise causes important generalisations (cf 1 and 3 above) to be lost (Section 7.1).

5. A theory postulating a separate intonational domain for Category II expressions, served by a paradigm of boundary tones, causes important semantic distinctions to fall outside the scope of its explanatory power. Moreover, such a theory generates controus that do not occur. Neither problem exists in the theory it seeks to replace, that of the theory of nuclear tones (Section 7.2).

6. While we have been unable to give structure to the set of pragmatic conditions under which speakers feel it is justified or imperative to use [−focus], it was demonstrated that focus is a semantically powerful linguistic option, which can readily be exploited to give temporal structure to a narrative, and to produce particular 'comedy' effects (Section 7).

Footnotes:

1. I should like to thank Flor Aarts, Ton Broeders, Gill Brown, Bob Ladd and Elizabeth Couper-Kuhlen for the helpful suggestions they made after reading an earlier version of this article. I thank Pieter de Hann for helping me count the nuclear tones with the help of a computer.

2. I should like to thank Mr James Corsan, Ms Alexa Dably and Mr Bob Louie of Thames Television Studios for their cooperation in making the tapes available to me. The instalments transcribed were **Days of Beer and Rosie** (Series 4, Episode 2), **Finders Keepers?** (Series 5, Episode 1) and **On the Second Day of Christmas** (Series 4, Episode 7). The series was written by Johnnie Mortimer and Brian Cooke and the main characters are played by the late Yootha Joyce and by Brian Murphy. I thank all those involved for permission to reproduce extracts from the instalments here, the copyright to which belongs to Thames Television Limited. The instalment from the Roath material is **Endangered Species**. This series is written by Peter Tilbury, who himself plays the main character in it. The copyright also belongs to Thames Television Limited.

3. Other numerical data for British English are the histograms given in Pellowe and Jones (1978, 1979) and Local (1982), which are based on the figures given in Quirk et al (1964), who give a breakdown over a number of parts of speech. A rough estimate of these percentages, applying the same conversations as for the Davy data, is \ 53, V 14, / 25, –4, V 3. Although they are based on a corpus of spontaneous speech, the figures seem closer to those for reading-style than to those for conversation, as given by Davy (1968). Fries (1964) presents interesting figures on panelists taking part in a radio quiz programme. The panelists, who were speakers of American English, attempted to elicit information from a number of contestants by just asking yes-no questions. Lee (1980) presents similar data for British English, and compares his data with data for yes-no questions in radio programmes in which the questions are not quite so densely packed. Although Lee discusses the difference between his two corpora, the proportions he gives are not in fact significantly different. The overall figures given by Fries are: falls 61.7%, and rises 38.3%, and those by Lee: falls 43% and rises 57%. No attempt has been made to separate out the data in the G and M corpus according to sentence type.

4. The non-assertive role of George as the fall guy can also be related to the differential use by him and Mildred of tag questions (**You're not from the H P company** | / **ARE you?** cf Quirk et al, 1972: 390): out of 16 tag questions in DBR, 14 were spoken by George and none by Mildred, and the other instalments show a similar pattern. (Five of the 14 tags by George were not in fact in the script.) In addition, there were five instances of EH (e.g. **What are you im PLYing** | / **EH**), all of them by George, and unscripted.

5. The terms 'argument' and 'predicate', also used by Schmerling (1976), are chosen so as to underscore the fact that focus marks semantic constituents, rather than syntactic ones.

6. *Observe that this is the solution to the problem offered in the Preface to Postal (1971). Postal notes that topicalised **him** in e.g. **Him Charlie wouldn't put the bag near** (from **Charlie wouldn't put the bag near him**) is no longer ambiguous between a coreferential and a non-coreferential reading, as it is when it is not topicalised. If **him** is to be topicalised, it must be [+ focus]; if it is to be [+ focus], it must be treated as 'new' by the speaker; if it is 'new', it cannot be coreferential with **Charlie**. The fact that **him** and **Charlie** have 'crossed over' (Postal's explanation) is not really relevant.*

7. *Note that in the last example the negative in the host clause is raised to the main clause, and that this does not affect the polarity of the tag, as is pointed out by Quirk et al (1972: 392).*

8. *Note, for instance, Crystal's statement that adverbial disjuncts/conjuncts are 'expounded as a nuclear tail (or as prosodically subordinate, or as the second part of a complex (**sic**; read: compound) tone)' (1975: 25), and his lamentation after his rather mixed collection of tail-types that 'it is unlikely that any greater precision will be introduced into the anlaysis of the semantic conditioning of pre-final tonic placement until more adequate studies of semantic relationships are written' (1975: 26).*

9. *Bing is none too explicit about what the eight patterns that are generated by her description (four prominence tones times two boundary options) look like, and the three patterns given here may not represent her own idea of the realisations of the phonological representations given. Neither, by the way, is any indication given with which, if any, of those eight contours the four contours that are generable for **No mill did** (as an answer to **Which mill used child labour?**) correspond, or why whatever contours are possible on **No, Mildred** but not on **No mill did,** should be so restricted.*

10. *As Brown (1982) observes, it is to be deplored that the 'given/new' distinction has come to be applied to linguistic options of a completely different nature, like pronominalisation, word order, (in)definite articles and second mention of the same referent, which concern syntactic options in their own right and do not necessarily go hand in hand with the way speakers employ focus.*

AN INTEGRATED APPROACH TO STUDYING INTONATION AND ATTITUDE

D Robert Ladd, K R Scherer, Kim Silverman

1. Background: Two Approaches to Intonation and Attitude

The role of intonation in expressing attitude or emotional state, while it is surely relevant in the long run to "discourse", is something that many linguists and phoneticians would rather ignore. By contrast, for many psychologists, emotion and attitude are of central interest, and intonation is often considered a prime carrier of affective information. Not surprisingly, this difference can lead to rather considerable divergences of opinion about research strategies and assumptions, when, as was the case in our project, a linguist and two psychologists come together to study intonational meaning.[1]

One approach to the problem - let us call it the A approach in order to avoid stereotyping linguists and psychologists - would be to produce quantifiable descriptions of both the medium (the non-segmental part of the speech signal) and the message (the various types of affective information conveyed), and attempt to state correlations between the two. More specifically, if we adopted such an approach, we would start with utterances that reliably and unambiguously convey certain affective messages (e.g. anger or surprise) and attempt to identify acoustic features of the signal that are consistently present when those messages are conveyed. (For example, we would hope to be able to make statements like: "Angry utterances are characterised by relatively wide pitch range.") One frequently used method of obtaining utterances that convey specific affective messages is to have speakers pronounce fixed texts with simulated emotions; one frequently used method of determining what affective messages are conveyed by utterances is to have listeners rate the utterances on a variety of judgement scales. The basic goal of a project conceived in this way would be to find correlations between experimentally obtained judgements and measured acoustic cues. (For reviews of the results of this approach see Williams and Stevens, 1972; Scherer, 1979 and 1981.)

The second approach - the B approach - would be to start from observed contrasts of intonational form and interpretation, attempt to generalise from those to the system of formal distinctions of intonation, and at the same time investigate the ways in which intonational distinctions affect the interpretation of utterances. These are essentially descriptive linguistic tasks and as such (it might be argued) not really suitable for experimental study; fieldwork and analysis of corpus material would be much more useful procedures at this stage of the investigation. Furthermore, in developing such descriptions, it would be important to consider the relation between 'grammatical' and 'affective' uses of intonation, and to consider the effects of non-intonational linguistic choices, like modals and particles, on the affective message conveyed. This means that acoustic measurements should not be correlated directly with attitude judgements, but should be taken as evidence about the phonetic correlates of the intonational contrasts posited in the linguistic description. (For a more thorough discussion of this approach see Ladd 1980, Chs. 5 and 6; for a good example see Liberman and Sag, 1974.)

This paper is essentially a report on the several months of theoretical discussion that were necessary for the three of us to get beyond the opposing positions just outlined, and to agree on a reasonable strategy for research. It identifies what we see as the basic theoretical assumptions underlying the two approaches, and it suggests ways in which some of those assumptions can be experimentally tested. In addition, it shows how certain seemingly contradictory views can be incorporated into a more complex theoretical picture that will help us to refine both approaches.

2. Practice and Theory of the Two Approaches

Shortcomings and methodological difficulties in both approaches to 'intonation and attitude' are quite apparent even to enthusiastic proponents of one view or the other. The A approach is forced to make assumptions about the nature of emotion and relies on statistical approaches to validation, which leaves it open to questions like the following: How do you know simulated emotions and real emotions produce the same vocal cues? How do you decide which emotion/attitude descriptors to use in designing a judgement task? How do you evaluate utterances that evoke no clear pattern of judgements? And so on. The B approach, meanwhile, tends to operate with the linguist's assumptions that form and function can be described independently and that one individual case is potentially as revealing about the structure of the system as any other. This provokes questions like: How can results be replicated? What predictions are being made? And why can they not be tested experimentally? And so on.

More generally, the striking thing about both approaches is that neither has ever produced very satisfactory results. Both have so far yielded only fragmentary descriptions in which approximate functions are associated with ill-defined forms. Using the A approach, Uldall (1964) found that "raised weak syllables" make intonation contours more "unpleasant"; using the B approach, Ladd (1980) defined the meaning of fall-rise in English as 'focus within a given set' and derived affective nuances as 'disagreement' or 'polite reply' from that basic meaning by way of informally stated pragmatic inference. In both cases, the explanations of intonational meaning that such descriptions make possible are, "like good astrological readings, not demonstrably inconsistent with the facts, but far too vague to be of much predictive value" (Liberman and Sag, 1974:420).

Despite the fact that both approaches produce similarly unsatisfying results, it is easy for advocates of one approach to point to the obvious shortcomings of the other as justification for continuing their own plan of attack. The reason for this inability to acknowledge fundamental problems appears to lie in the self-confirming nature of theoretical assumptions. That is, the assumptions underlying the two approaches are not readily disproved by the empirical work -experimental and descriptive - that they stimulate. On the contrary, they provide explanations for their own failures and justification for continuing research along the same lines.

Consider the A approach first. The search for correlations between intonational form and conveyed attitude is motivated by the assumption that intonation is (or includes) a system of non-verbal acoustic parameters directly involved in expressing affect. In a sense, it takes the intonational expression of speaker attitude to be similar to other phenomena of non-verbal communication, such as facial movement. The fact that research based on this assumption has failed to find the consistent correlations it is seeking can be seen as showing the need for more precise definition of the variables to be correlated, i.e. more accurate measurement of the acoustic parameters and better understanding of the nature of attitude judgements. That is, the inconclusive results so far can be attributed to insufficiently refined techniques; the underlying theory that intonation directly conveys attitude is unaffected.

Much the same is true of the B approach. In this case the search for formal contrasts in uncontrolled data is motivated by the assumption that intonation is organised much like the rest of language, into an inventory of units of some sort, with specifiable forms and functions. The fact that such analyses do not successfully explain the attitudinal effects of intonation can be explained by further assuming that the intonational expression of speaker attitude is inextricably linked with grammatical and discourse-related intonational function, and that both are part of the more general problem of pragmatic inference and interpretation - the processes by which speaker intentions and presuppositions are understood by the listener. Given that premise, the failure of linguistic analyses to account for attitude judgements simply shows the need for a better understanding of pragmatic interpretation. The underlying assumption about the indirect role of intonation in conveying attitude remains unaffected.

3. One Issue: Direct vs. Indirect

When the assumptions of the two approaches are stated in the form just given, it can be seen right away that one basic issue between the two is the question of *directness* or *context-dependence*. The A approach assumes that the intonational form is directly linked to the affective force of utterances, and implies that affective messages could be superimposed on otherwise neutral texts. By contrast, the intonational meanings often posited in the B approach

127

are more "grammatical" - contradiction, contrast, focus, etc. - and the attitudinal messages that come through are taken to be indirect inferences based on the intonation in its total context.

This issue can be tested experimentally. Two studies, which we are currently carrying out, will provide evidence on the general question of directness and context-dependence.

(1) *The context-switching experiment.*

What happens to attitude judgements when utterances are put into a different linguistic context? In the literature there are many discussions of the context-dependence of intonational interpretation (see in particular Cutler, 1977); our study will construct spliced dialogues by means of digital signal-processing techniques, and thus permit utterances to be judged in different contexts without changing any other variables).

Figure 1 gives an example of the experimental stimuli we will construct. The "original" dialogues will be spoken by pairs of informants with instructions to simulate normal office conversation; the "spliced" dialogues will be constructed by splicing the answer from the first "original" dialogue onto the question for the second, and vice-versa.[2] Since in the first answer the accent on **München** represents so-called normal stress, while in the second it signals a "narrow focus" or "contrastive stress", we expect that the phonetic realisation of the two will be slightly different. We predict that in the spliced dialogues the "contrastive" answer will have too much intonational emphasis for the "normal" context and will be perceived as insistent or annoyed, while the "normal" answer will have too little intonational emphasis for the "contrastive" context and will be perceived as bored or distant. If the expected judgements are obtained, we will have strong evidence that the pragmatic effect of an utterance depends on its immediate context as well as its suprasegmental structure: identical intonation in a different context can signal a rather different attitude.

Dialogue Number	Question	Answer	Expected Judgements of Answerer's Attitude
(i)	Ist Herr Müller da?	Nein, er ist nach München gefahen.	polite, courteous.
(ii)	Herr Müller wollte heute nach Hamburg, oder?	Nein, er ist nach **München** gefahren.	
(iii)	Herr Müller wollfe heute nach Hamburg, oder?	Nein, er ist nach München gefahren.	uninterested, bored.
(iv)	Ist Herr Müller da?	Nein, er ist nach **München** gefahren.	irritated, annoyed.

Figure 1 **Example of the Stimuli to be used with the Context Switching Experiment**

(i) and (ii) give the "original" dialogues.
(iii) and (iv) are constructed by splicing the answer from one of the "originals" onto the question from the other, and vice-versa.

(2) *The stimulus-masking experiment.*

What happens to attitude judgements when parts of the whole speech signal are systematically removed (e.g. by presentation of written text only, by electronic filtering, etc.)? If some part of the whole signal (i.e. the intonation) has a direct context-free connection to attitude, then attitude messages should be lost in some masking conditions and not in others. If, on the other hand, attitude judgements are entirely a question of pragmatic inference from the whole context, then all the masking conditions should weaken the attitude judgements significantly.

4. Results

Preliminary results from the masking experiment clearly contradict the strongest version of the B approach. From a large tape-recorded corpus of practice interviews between welfare agency workers and actors playing clients, we selected 66 simple questions spoken by 11 different welfare workers and had subjects judge the attitudes these questions conveyed.[3] A second group of subjects was asked to make the same attitude judgements on the basis of the written text of the questions; a third group (in a pilot study on only 8 questions) made the same judgements on three different "degraded signal" versions of the questions.[4]

Table 1 shows the intercorrelations across all 66 utterances between the adjectives in the "full audio" and "transcript" conditions. The pattern along the main diagonal suggests that the text alone does not contribute much to the attribution of emotional arousal states (such as ungeduldig and gelassen) or more positive speaker attitudes (freundlich, höflich and verständnisvoll). Tables 2a, 2b, 2c and 2d show the correlations between the different conditions over the 8 utterances selected for the degradation pilot. The "audio" degradations (i.e. all except the "transcript" condition) correlate negatively with the "transcript" and positively with the "full audio" condition, and no single degradation consistently correlates better than the others with the "full audio".

129

	TRHOEF	TRUNGE	TRYORW	TRZWEI	TRFREU	TRUNSI	TRGELA	TRYERS	TRAGGR
FAHOEF	.12 p=.166	-.15 p=.115	-.22 p=.037*	-.03 p=.418	.10 p=.219	.02 p=.444	.04 p=.370	-.10 p=.221	-.22 p=.036*
FAUNGE	.08 p=.259	.14 p=.134	-.01 p=.456	.07 p=.301	.13 p=.157	.02 p=.426	.02 p=.440	.04 p=.390	.26 p=.016●
FAYORW	-.27 p=.015*	.13 p=.149	.64 p=.001***	.43 p=.001***	-.20 p=.051	.12 p=.172	-.32 p=.004*	.09 p=.227	.49 p=.001***
FAZWEI	-.23 p=.035*	-.08 p=.256	.29 p=.009**	.33 p=.003**	-.16 p=.104	.16 p=.097	-.18 p=.075	.11 p=.184	.06 p=.329
FAFREU	-.03 p=.400	.02 p=.448	-.26 p=.018*	-.09 p=.247	.04 p=.388	.11 p=.180	.08 p=.257	-.08 p=.267	-.16 p=.098
FAUNSI	-.09 p=.228	.03 p=.397	-.08 p=.251	-.18 p=.072	-.14 p=.129	-.15 p=.108	-.02 p=.436	.02 p=.440	-.05 p=.360
FAGELA	.02 p=.449	.10 p=.202	-.13 p=.151	-.19 p=.151	-.13 p=.142	-.05 p=.332	-.04 p=.372	-.17 p=.080	-.15 p=.114
FAVERS	-.07 p=.300	-.06 p=.320	.01 p=.473	.14 p=.139	-.05 p=.331	.18 p=.076	-.02 p=.430	.13 p=.154	-.12 p=.166
FAAGGR	-.16 p=.104	.15 p=.116	.19 p=.063	.28 p=.011*	-.07 p=.302	.16 p=.097	.01 p=.463	.07 p=.298	.37 p=.001**

Table 1

130

Table 1 Correlations between Full Audio (FA) and Transcript (TR) Judgements. Correlations are between percentages of judges selelcting each adjective in the FA (16 judges) and TR (23 judges) for each of the 66 utterances. Significance levels are indicated by asterisks: * p <0.05; ** p <0.01; *** p <0.001. Adjectives are: höflich (HOEF); ungeduldig (UNGE); vorwurfsvoll (VORW); zweifelnd (ZWEI); freundlich (FREU); unsicher (UNSI); gelassen (GELA); verständnisvoll (VERS); aggressiv (AGGR).

ungeduldig

	FA	TR	BW	CF	RS1
TR	-0.66				
BW	0.93***	-0.50			
CF	0.77*	-0.31	0.90**		
RS1	0.84**	-0.77*	0.76*	0.52	
RS2	0.85**	-0.59	0.92**	0.77*	0.82*

Table 2a

gelassen

	FA	TR	BW	CF	RS1
TR	-0.37				
BW	0.78*	-0.51			
CF	0.84**	-0.21	0.67		
RS1	0.87**	-0.48	0.57	0.57	
RS2	0.93***	-0.51	0.79*	0.90**	0.71*

Table 2b

131

freundlich

	FA	TR	BW	CF	RS1
TR	-0.43				
BW	0.50	-0.62			
CF	0.81*	-0.31	0.47		
RS1	0.48	-0.69*	0.58	0.64*	
RS2	0.60	-0.66*	0.63*	0.84**	0.81*

Table 2c

zweifelnd

	FA	TR	BW	CF	RS1
TR	0.01				
BW	0.43	0.31			
CF	0.58	-0.27	-0.33		
RS1	0.45	0.17	0.10	0.58	
RS2	0.36	0.00	0.16	0.63*	0.42

Table 2d

Tables 2a, 2b, 2c, 2d Correlations between Different Degradation Conditions.

Correlations as in Table 1, over the 8 uttterances used in the "degraded signal" pilot (18 judges). Only the 4 adjectives shown produced enough variance of the different utterances to yield interpretable coefficients. Significance levels are indicated by asterisks: ● $p < 0.05$; ** $p < 0.01$; *** $p < 0.001$. Stimulus conditions are: full audio (FA); transcript (TR); backwards (BW); content- (i.e. low-pass) filtered (CF); random-spliced (two different random orders: RS1 and RS2).

In short, it appears that much less of the original affective message is conveyed in written text presentation than in any of the three degraded signal conditions. Subjects find the written-text task unreasonable, and their judgements are not often consistent with judgements of the original utter-

132

ances, whereas they have few complaints about the various degraded signal tasks and their judgements of the degraded stimuli are in general rather consistent with the judgements of the originals. From this it seems clear that something in the non-segmental part of the speech signal can directly convey affective information even when other types of contextual information are drastically reduced or entirely absent.

However, this result is not the clear endorsement of the A approach that it might appear. Many adherents of the B approach would readily concede that "voice quality" and other paralinguistic cues directly convey affective information, but that intonation is not to be lumped together with para-linguistic phenomena. This (so the B approach might argue) is all that the masking experiment proves: the intonation contours in this experiment were chopped up, run backwards, and left unchanged in the three degraded signal conditions, yet affective information came through in all three. The experiment also shows the difficulty of trying to extract acoustic parameters of specific attitudes, since the affective information in voice quality is so redundantly encoded that it can be perceived and interpreted even when a great amount of acoustic information is removed.

Furthermore, the question of context-dependence and directness is not really a dichotomous issue anyway. Proponents of the A approach could grant the distinction between voice quality and intonation, and even the existence of interactions with context, without abandoning the more basic assumption that intonation has some fundamental direct link to the expression of attitude. Indeed, such was very nearly the view of Pike (1945) who, in his analysis of intonational contrasts, was nevertheless clearly a believer in the B approach. Another intermediate position is held by Labov and Fanshel (1977:43) who treat intonation together with voice quality, tempo, etc. as "paralinguistic cues", and state that "there is often a one-to-one iconic relationship between the movement of the voice and the emotions being conveyed"; at the same time, they also point out that "the same physical signals can have radically different interpretations in different contexts" (356).

5. The Real Issue: Categorical vs. Parametric

All the foregoing suggests that the issue of directness and context-dependence, while certainly relevant, is not the real source of the disagreement between the A and B approaches. Even if they had agreed to control carefully for context and voice-quality, proponents of the two views could still have exchanges like the following:

A: Well, of course I agree with you that there are interactions with the context and that intonation and voice quality may work separately, but it should still be possible to make objective measurements of overall slope, average Fo, amount of Fo variability, etc., and do statistical analyses of their interactions with the other factors in determining the attitudinal message.

133

B: But if you quantify the acoustic parameters that way, you are not taking into account the linguistic structure of the intonation system. Your procedure simply rules out the hypothesis that intonation is organised into linguistic categories, and that the abstract information conveyed by choices among those categories influences the pragmatic interpretation.

Now the real issue emerges. The disagreement turns not on the directness or indirectness of the link between intonational cues and attitudinal judgements, but on the very nature of the intonational cues themselves. A is talking about acoustic parameters, B about linguistic categories.

In general statistical terms, the question is whether we are dealing with quantity variables or category variables, and whether their role in expressing attitude involves the *interaction of multiple parameters* or the *structured configuration of categories*. The former is characteristic of perceptual processing and is the sort of situation to which ordinary statistical models apply. The latter is in effect what is involved in a grammar. If the variables of intonation are categorical to any significant extent, then we must be cautious in applying ordinary parametric statistical models to intonation data; in particular, we must be careful not to equate intonation - a system of categorical distinctions - with Fo - a parametrically describable acoustic phenomenon. In any case, we have now extracted a further empirically testable question from the clash of assumptions between the two approaches: to what extent, if at all, does intonation involve categorical distinctions?

The most appropriate technique for testing this question appears to be experiments in which subjects attempt to discriminate or categorise utterances with artificial (e.g. digitally resynthesised) Fo contours. On the basis of specific hypotheses about what the categorical distinctions of the intonational system are, we can create sets of stimuli with gradual variations in the contours along dimensions to be tested. For example, supposing we hypothesise that the exact location of the intonational peak with respect to an accented syllable will yield a categorical distinction between "fall" and "rise-fall", we can then create a set of stimuli like the following:

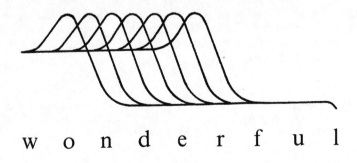

w   o   n   d   e   r   f   u   l

Listeners could then be asked to make various judgements about these stimuli, and the judgements analysed to see whether they fall into two discrete ranges or clusters corresponding to the hypothesised "fall" and "rise-fall" of the linguistic analysis. If they do, then this would constitute strong evidence that the intonational stimuli are being perceived in terms of linguistic categories, even though in strictly acoustic terms there is a stepwise continuum from one stimulus to the next.

Experiments of this general sort have been done by Hadding-Koch and Studdert-Kennedy (1964), Collier (1975), and Bassey and Ashby (Micheal Ashby, personal communication), with results that strongly suggest the existence of categorical distinctions. Part of our project will involve experiments aimed at confirming this finding under a number of specific conditions. While we have no results at this point, it is nevertheless worth noting some of the basic considerations to be taken into account in designing such experiments.

The most serious methodological problem is the absence of a metalanguage in which subjects can express their judgements. In the classic categorical perception study on phoneme boundaries by A. Liberman et al (1957), subjects were asked to classify synthetic syllables as beginning with [b], [d], or [g]. These category names are known to any literate speaker and were thus available for use in the experiment. For intonation, however, there are few such obvious labels. Hadding-Koch and Studdert-Kennedy asked their subjects to label synthetic contours "question" or "statement", which are undoubtedly as familiar to ordinary speakers as [b], [d], and [g], but allow few direct conclusions about intonational cues to attitude. Collier avoided the problem by simply having subjects assign the stimuli to groups; his stimuli were actual endless-loop cassettes that the subjects could pick up and put in piles. Bassey and Ashby avoided the problem in a different way by using trained phoneticians as subjects, they used a set of stimuli quite similar to the ones just illustrated above and asked subjects to decide whether the intonation was "high fall" or "rise fall".

If we want naive subjects to label intonational stimuli, it seems clear that we need a metalanguage that is directly related to the pragmatic effects of the intonation in the specific context of the stimulus - for example, in the illustration of "wonderful" above, something like 'objective' vs. 'emotionally involved'. This runs the risk of being, on the one hand, too crude to express distinctions even if subjects can hear them, and, on the other hand, too closely tailored to the stimuli to prove anything more general: once again we encounter the problem of which attitude descriptors to use in our judgement experiments. In some sense, the absence of an obvious metalanguage is a reflection of the very problem we are trying to investigate.

In addition to a metalanguage, of course, categorical perception experiments must be based on a set of hypotheses about what the categorical distinctions of intonation are - that is, a linguistic analysis of intonation. This analysis must be phonetically explicit enough to serve as the basis for resynthesising stimuli. A framework for such a description has been developed within our project by Ladd (in press). It treats the linguistic structure of intonation as involving choices at structurally significant points in the utterance, such as boundaries and accented syllables; these choices are represented as features of intonational segments. (For example, in many languages a feature may specify the delay of an accent peak with respect to the accented syllable, as in the "wonderful" illustration.) We plan to do resynthesis experiments which we hope will show that the categories of this description are relevant for attitude judgements. Such results could then be taken as evidence for the validity of the lingistic description.

Note that in general it is neither customary nor useful to validate descriptive linguistic statements by experiment (e.g. one does not need to do an experiment to confirm that the plural of *child* is *children*). Once a descriptive framework for intonation is well established, this will presumably be true for intonational analyses as well. However, at this point it is clearly appropriate to muster experimental evidence, precisely because the very existence of categorical linguistic distinctions is in question. That is, by these experiments we are not really validating the description, but testing the entire approach that assumes such a description is needed.

6. Integrating the A and B approaches

If experiments of the sort just described are able to confirm the existence of categorical distinctions in intonation, this will represent substantial experimental evidence for the assumption that intonation involves a linguistic system of formal contrasts. This in turn will provide some justification for adopting elements of the B approach. In particular, it will show the empirical relevance of work on pragmatic inference to the study of intonation and attitude, and justify treating acoustic measurements as correlates of intonational categories rather than as correlates of specific attitudes.

At the same time, by establishing the validity of the B approach in this way, we can provide a firmer basis for A approach experiments that investigate the direct expression of attitude and emotion through paralinguistic cues. That is, if we wish to investigate paralinguistic acoustic parameters while at the same time respecting the non-parametric nature of intonational distinctions, then in effect we must 'control for intonation'. A solid B-approach analysis of intonational categories will make this possible.

To take a speculative but by no means entirely hypothetical example: suppose we are able to distinguish categorically between a "baseline low" and a "raised low" following high peaks. (Impressionistically this is the difference between "terminal fall" and "non-terminal fall".) Suppose further that one of the vocal parameters involved in signalling tension or emotional arousal is "raised baseline". In order to be able to detect such a variable, we need to know **what to measure**. That is, if we can identify those parts of the contour that are most directly affected by parametric modifications - in this case, baseline low - we will be in the best position to find the acoustic variables that directly convey affect. Conversely, if we are able to identify those parts of the contour where parametric effects might be masked by categorical distinctions - in this example perhaps "raised low" - then we can account for the failure of parametric studies that average whole contours, and we may be able to avoid confounding our parametric measurements with irrelevant variation.

It is conceivable, of course - to continue the same illustration - that the raising of "baseline low" would have measurable effects throughout the contour, and that these would be manifested in measures as gross as average overall Fo. In fact, however, some parametric studies find higher average Fo as a correlate of arousal and some do not (cf. Höfer, Wallbott and Scherer, in preparation). Our investigations of vocal attitude cues will be much more precisely focussed and much less likely to yield disappointingly approximate results, once we are able to compare parametric variables in linguistic environments that are actually comparable.

The overall goal of our project might best be described as laying the groundwork for the integrated approach to intonation and attitude just outlined. Specifically, as we said, our masking and context-switch studies are intended to provide evidence about the directness of intonational attitude cues, while our experiments with resynthesised intonation contours will investigate the extent to which intonation involves categorical distinctions. Insofar as we find evidence both for categorical distinctions in intonation and for the direct expression of attitude, we feel that an approach that carefully distinguishes intonation from paralinguistic cues and designs its studies with that distinction in mind will be the most productive way to investigate the role of intonation in expressing attitude. In addition, it may provide a way to bridge the mutual misunderstandings between scholars from diffferent disciplines who bring such different assumptions to the investigation of intonational function.

Footnotes:

1. *The research reported here is funded by the Deutsche Forschungsgemeinschaft. An earlier and much shorter version od this paper was read at the 24th Tagung Experimentell Arbeitender Psychologen in Trier in April 1982, and the experimental results reported in Tables 1 and 2 were presented in a poster session at the 33rd Kongress der deutschen Gesellschaft für Psychologie in Mainz in September 1982.*

2. *A pilot study has already shown such splicing to be technically possible (i.e. such spliced dialogues are not detectably "artificial" or "unnatural".)*

3. *Subjects were asked to judge the utterances using any combination of the following adjectives: höflich (polite); ungeduldig (impatient); vorwurfsvoll (reproachful, critical); zweifelnd (doubtful); freundlich (friendly); unsicher (uncertain): gelassen (relaxed, composed); verständnisvoll (understanding); aggressiv (aggressive). Instead of, or in addition to, these they could write a description of the attitude using their own words. Most simply selected one or two adjectives. For a fuller description of the larger corpus from which the test utterances were taken, see Scherer and Scherer (1979).*

4. *The utterances were masked in the following ways: by low-pass filtering, which preserves the Fo contour and some amplitude information but little else; by random splicing (Scherer, 1971 and 1982), which preserves information about voice quality, amplitude, and pitch range but destroys any temporal organisation; and by simply playing the recording backwards, which preserves pitch range and apparently voice quality, and in effect creates a new Fo and amplitude contour. In all three conditions, intelligibility is destroyed, though on rare occasions individual words are recognisable in random splicing.*

ON THE ANALYSIS OF PROSODIC TURN-TAKING CUES

Anne Cutler and Mark Pearson

1. Introduction

Would you mind just letting me finish?

Why can I never get a word in edgeways?

What's up? Cat got your tongue?

When a conversation breaks down, the problem can often be traced to a failure in the turn-taking procedure, i.e. the smooth interchange of speaking turns between conversational partners. For a conversation to function successfully, each speaker's turn should not go on too long, and should be accomplished without interruption; and at the end of one speaker's turn another speaker should take over without too long an intervening pause. Of course, at what point a turn of an inter-turn pause becomes "too long" may depend upon the particular conversational circumstances - e.g. on such factors as how well the participants know one another, their relative age or social status, and the difficulty of the subject matter under discussion. For any given conversation, however, it is usually obvious whether or not it is proceeding smoothly.

To take over the turn at the appropriate moment, without undue hesitation, it is obviously useful to be able to decide as early as possible that the previous speaker has finished or is about to fininsh. Clearly, syntax, semantics and reference to the discourse context play the largest role here. A completed utterance usually forms a syntactically complete unit. Questions usually signal that a response is required. Anecdotes have ends (if not always punch lines). And there are many more text-internal cues to whether or not a speaker has finished.

External to the text, however, there exists a considerable range of cues which speakers may employ - consciously or not - to inform hearers where the current turn will end. Some of these cues are paralinguistic in nature - i.e. not part of the speech signal at all. For example, speakers often look away from the interlocutors while speaking, but look towards them again as they finish talking (Kendon, 1967), especially if speaker and interlocutor do not know each other well (Rutter et al, 1978) and especially if the topic under discussion is difficult (Beattie, 1979). Termination of a hand gesture has also been claimed to be associated with turn-final utterances (Duncan, 1972). But there are also text-external cues which are part of the spoken utterance, and it is with these cues - specifically, those borne by the utterance prosody - that the present paper is concerned.

2. Prosodic Structure and Turn-Taking

The prosodic structure of speech comprises variation in three dimensions - fundamental frequency, duration and amplitude. All three dimensions exhibit specific effects which are dependent upon utterance position. Thus in the unmarked case fundamental frequency declines across the utterance (Maeda, 1976), as does amplitude (Lieberman, 1967); violations of these effects are marked as carrying information - for example, the terminal rise associated with certain question forms. Timing relations vary similarly; a given word will be uttered with longer duration in phrase-final than in non-phrase-final position (Oller, 1973), although there seems to be no evidence that utterance-final lengthening is greater still (Oller, 1973; Lehiste, 1980). Thus at the end of any utterance, whether or not it completes the speaker's turn, we would expect to find a fall in baseline pitch, a decrease in amplitude and some segmental lengthening. Prosodic turn-yielding cues, if any, would have to be overlaid upon this characteristic utterance-final prosodic pattern. Very closely related to this prosodic configuration, in addition, are certain voice quality features - e.g. creaky voice - which may also function as turn signals.

Duncan (e.g. 1972) has claimed that prosodic turn-ceding cues indeed exist. In a series of papers (Duncan, 1972, 1973, 1974, 1975) he has reported a major study in which two 20-minute two-person conversational interactions were transcribed in detail from videotape. In this study Duncan identified six "turn signals", three of which were prosodic, namely:

(1) "The use of any pitch level/terminal juncture combination other than 22/ at the end of a phonemic clause" (22/ here refers to a sustained "mid" pitch level in the Trager and Smith (1951) system).
(2) "Drawl on the final syllable or on the stressed syllable of a phonemic clause".
(3) "A drop in paralinguistic pitch and/or loudness in conjunction with [one of several stereotyped expressions such as "but uh", "or something" or "you know"]". (All quotations from Duncan, 1973, p.37).

With hand gesture termination, the stereotyped expressions referred to under (3) above, and completion of a syntactic clause (!), these cues are said to comprise the repertoire of potential turn signals. By labelling them in this way, however, Duncan is clearly begging the question; the term "signal" implies a communicative function between speaker and receiver which is in no sense justified by Duncan's analysis. Take, for example, the "signal" of syntactic clause completion. Clauses are completed frequently in speech, but only a small proportion of them also complete conversational turns. If clause completion were indeed an effective "turn signal" we would presumably find our interlocutors wanting to resume speaking every time we finished any clause. As this does not generally happen - at least in the authors' experience - we can assume that the effectiveness of clause completion alone as a turn-yielding signal is in fact very slight.

140

It is not clear from Duncan's publications how he arrived at his particular set of signals, although it is implied that they were simply collated after inspection of the transcriptions of those utterances which ended speakers' conversational turns. A more proper term for the phenomena he listed would therefore be "correlates of end of speaking turn". Duncan used his compilation of "turn signals" to generate and test predictions about the relationship between number of "signals" produced at once and interlocutors' attempts to resume speaking at that point. This procedure is logically circular, and in this particular instance the results were also statistically very shaky (see the criticisms advanced by Beattie, 1981).

Moreover, Duncan's prosodic descriptions are extremely ill-defined. Signal (1) is described in terms of a particular Trager-Smith pitch level; but this kind of pitch notation is notoriously subject to influence from the syntax and semantics of the utterance (Lieberman, 1965). Furthermore, (1) is not even expressed as turn-yielding signal at all, but rather as what is *not* a turn-yielding signal - what it says in effect is that a sustained middle pitch (that is, presumably, neither a rise nor a fall) is a signal that the speaker wishes to *hold* the turn. Signal (2) is "drawl", which is not defined - although the term presumably refers to a phrase-final lengthening which is greater than would be expected in the default case, no metric is given for determining the relation between expected and observed phrase-final lengthening for any particular utterance. (This is a somewhat complicated procedure, but it is clear how it should be done; Lehiste (1980) gives an excellent and instructive example. She computed the average duration of every segment of a particular type - e.g. voiced stops, diphthongs etc. - in a stretch of speech, and then compared the actual length of words in phrase-final, paragraph-final and non-final positions in comparison with their expected lengths as computed by summing the average durations of their constituent sounds.) Finally, signal (3) - a drop in pitch and/or loudness - is, as we saw above, the default case for utterance-final phrases whether stereotyped or not. One suspects that here Duncan is actually talking about vocal quality features - creaky or whispery voice. But as with the other "turn signals" one retains the impression that Duncan merely recorded a subjective impression of what he heard. As all the speech in his study was apparently transcribed with full reference to the discourse context, there would have been considerable scope for the record of the prosodic features of any utterance to be affected by the syntax and content of the utterance as well as by its known position in the discourse.

We may conclude, therefore, that neither the perceptual effectiveness of prosodic end-of-turn cues nor even their existence has been unequivocally established by Duncan's work. We found only two further studies addressing the issue of prosody and turn-taking, both of which preceded Duncan's. The first was a study by Yngve (1970), in which the turn structure of an experimentally elicited two-person conversation was analysed in depth. Although impressionistic, the findings of this study succeeded in ruling out one plausible hypothesis by establishing that pausing is *not* a turn signal. In other words, it is not the case that speakers simply take over the turn after a sufficient period of silence has elapsed since the last speech from anyone else; rather, they take over when they have received active cues from the previous speaker. The second study, by Meltzer, Morris and Hayes (1971), dealt with only one prosodic dimension: amplitude. Meltzer et al recorded the amplitude fluctuations of individual speakers' voices during sixty two-person problem-solving discussions lasting forty minutes each. Perhaps unsurprisingly, they found that raising one's voice from the normal amplitude baseline correlates well with success at taking over the turn, or keeping it in the face of attempted takeover, and that the absolute difference in amplitude between the two speakers' output efficiently predicts the outcome of an attempted interruption, particularly if simultaneous speech continues beyond a word or two.

3. Methodological Issues in the Study of Turn Signals

These latter two studies raise an interesting question, namely the extent to which one can study conversational structure using non-natural material. Although all the speech Meltzer et al recorded was produced spontaneously, the situation in which it was elicited was experimentally contrived, and designed specifically for collection of the amplitude data they sought. Similarly, Yngve's study used an artificial paradigm in which speakers matched for their conversational ability participated in a conversation designed to be co-operative. Other studies of prosodic factors in conversational interaction, however, have analysed natural speech. Duncan's material was drawn from real-life interviews. French and Local (1982, and this volume) conducted an extensive analysis of natural conversation which produced, inter alia, similar conclusions about the role of amplitude in interruptions to those reached by Meltzer et al. Beattie (1982) and Beattie, Cutler and Pearson (1982) analysed the turn-taking structure of television interviews with politicians; Beattie, Cutler and Pearson analysed prosodic cues in particular. They transcribed a subset of sentence-final phrases "blind", i.e. without reference to the discourse context, and then identified a number of prosodic and vocal quality features which appeared on turn-final and turn-medial utterances respectively. Turn-disputed utterances (i.e. points at which the speaker had been interrupted) could then be analysed in terms of these features, and it could be determined whether they more closely resembled the turn-final or the turn-medial norm.

All such naturalistic studies have one, potentially very serious, drawback: they are based on data from a very limited number of speakers. Duncan's material was produced by three speakers only; Beattie and his colleagues analysed interviews with only two politicians. In contrast, Meltzer et al's experimental study employed 120 speakers; one can be reasonably certain of the generalisability of their amplitude findings. Generalisability cannot, however, be predicated of the naturalistic studies: there is no guarantee that

142

(a) features characteristic of one speaker's turn-final utterances are also used by other speakers, even other speakers of the same dialect; (b) features which are perceived as effective turn-yielding cues by one listener are effective for others; (c) features which listeners perceive as turn-yielding cues in one speaker's productions are equally effective cues when spoken by others.

The present study forms a first attempt to assess the possibility of using experimental techniques to establish whether perceptually effective prosodic turn signals do indeed exist. Of necessity, the experimental situation was far more constrained than that used by, say, Meltzer et al. In their experiment, only baseline amplitude and excursions from it were at issue; such gross measurements are relatively independent of speech content, so that it was not necessary to constrain the content in any way. Other prosodic characteristics, however - e.g. pitch and timing variation - are more heavily dependent on the speech material in conjunction with which they occur. It is not possible to compare final tone group durations, for instance, when they are realised over different numbers of words. A pitch rise realised on a yes-no question is not necessarily directly comparable with a similar rise realised on a string of words which does not form a question. Thus investigation of such prosodic cues demands careful control of the speech underlying them.

The ideal situation, in fact, would obtain if we had syntactically and semantically identical utterances, produced by the same speaker, which differed only in that one occurred at the end of a conversational turn while the other did not. In the absence of realistically occurring material of this nature, it was therefore decided to approximate it as closely as possible by the simple device of having speakers read aloud short dialogues; the dialogues were written such that the same utterances occurred in either turn-medial or turn-final position in different versions of the texts.

We do not pretend that this experimental design simulates natural conversation. It is, primarily, a device for eliciting the same utterance from the same speaker twice, once in a context in which the speaker is invited to provide turn-final signals and once in a context to which turn-medial signals would be appropriate. By presenting the resulting utterances to listeners, we can determine whether or not listeners fasten upon any particular prosodic features to guide their judgements as to whether a particular utterance is turn-final or turn-medial. In addition, of course, we can determine whether or not speakers do systematically distinguish their turn-final from their turn-medial utterances by prosodic means. Note, however, that this latter issue - the production question - is much less well addressed by the experimental design than is the former - the perception question. The situation in which speakers produce the experimental utterances is far removed from normal spontaneous conversation. The speech is not in the least spontaneous - the task of reading aloud contains at least as large a perceptual as a productive component, and, because the message is given, reading aloud short-circuits the message-formulation stages of the normal production process. Although professional actors may possibly be able to produce a full range of natural prosodic turn signals when reading a written text aloud, our speakers were untrained in such arts. Even were we to find consistent prosodic differentiation between turn-final and turn-medial utterances in this experiment, therefore, there is no guarantee that such differentiation would reflect the state of affairs in the speakers' normal conversation.

The listeners, on the other hand, at least have a task which approximates the normal case. Though for them too the experimental situation is perhaps somewhat artificial, all they are required to do is to judge utterances as to whether or not they are turn-final. The very premise of this study, as of all other studies of turn signalling, is that such judgements must regularly be made in the course of normal everyday conversation.

4. Description of the Experiment

4.1 Materials

Five dialogues were constructed, each in two versions. An example dialogue is:

Speaker 1:	Foster was pretty upset that you rejected his design - any particular reason?
Speaker 2:	It's simply not good enough, and that's all I have to say on the subject! I don't see why I have to justify my decisions.
Speaker 1:	OK - sorry I asked!

The second version of this dialogue was identical except that Speaker 2's turn read:

| Speaker 2: | I don't see why I have to justify my decisions. It's simply not good enough, and that's all I have to say on the subject! |

Thus each pair of dialogues provided two sentences which were word-for-word the same, but each was turn-final in one version of the dialogue, turn-medial in the other. The complete set of dialogues is listed in Appendix 1.

4.2 Production Task

Both versions of each of the five dialogues were read onto tape by ten native speakers of British English (six males, four females). For each dialogue, five speakers read one version first while the other five read the other version first. The speakers were instructed to read the dialogues in a natural manner.

Each of the two crucial sentences from each of the ten recordings of each of the two versions of each of the five dialogues was then spliced out of its original context, digitised, and recorded on disc in a computer. The extracts from the example dialogue above, for instance, were "I don't see why I have to justify my decisions" and "that's all I have to say on the subject", each read twice (once turn-finally and once turn-medially) by each of the 10 speakers. There were 200 utterances in all.

4.3 Text Perception Task

Although each dialogue used in the experiment was constructed in such a way that both orderings of the two crucial sentences sounded quite natural, it was nevertheless possible that some individual sentences, out of context, sounded more or less intrinsically turn-final than others. Since in the audio perception tasks the sentences were to be presented out of context, gross differences between the utterances in the "finality" of their texts alone could bias the listeners' judgements. Accordingly we collected "finality" judgements on the sentence texts alone.

The ten crucial sentences were presented in written form to twenty-three native English speakers, none of whom had participated in the production task. They were asked to rate each sentence on a scale from 1 to 5, where 1 represented "definitely still has more to say", 2 "probably still has more to say", 3 "could be going on or could be finished", 4 "probably finished" and 5 "definitely finished". Since the sentences had been chosen to fit equally naturally into turn-final or turn-medial position in context, the ideal result would be a mean rating of 3 for each sentence. In fact, there is one confounding factor which renders this unlikely: although any sentence in the language can be uttered in turn-medial position, i.e. can be followed by some other utterance, not all sentences are suitable for turn-final position. Thus any **randomly** selected sample of sentences might show a slight bias towards medial ratings; but because all our sentences were chosen so that they **could** (in our judgement) occur naturally in turn-final position, their ratings might be slightly biased towards the final end of the scale. Thus we predict that the mean finality ratings for all sentence texts will lie between 2 and 4, with the overall mean perhaps slightly above 3.

4.4 Audio Perception Task 1: Isolated Presentation

The 200 utterances were presented singly in random order to twenty subjects, all native British English speakers, who judged for each one whether it sounded turn-medial or turn-final. Ten of the twenty subjects were the speakers who had taken part in the production task. None of the twenty had participated in the text perception task. The subjects were tested individually and heard the utterances over headphones in a soundproof cubicle; they signified their decision by pressing one of two response keys.

This task provides the purest test of whether any general cues to turn-finality (or turn-mediality) are available for listeners to use. Moreover, the fact that speakers in the production task also participate in this task, judging their own as well as others' utterances, provides an extended test of the production question; it may be the case that there are cues which are not easily perceptible to others but which will at least be recognised by the speakers themselves.

4.5 Audio Perception Task 2: Paired Presentation

Twenty-seven subjects, all British English native speakers, none of whom had participated in the production, text perception or first audio perception tasks, heard a tape containing all 200 utterances, paired such that both versions of any one sentence by any one speaker occurred together. In half the pairs the turn-final production occurred first, in the other half the turn-medial. The subjects were tested as a group and heard the tape over loudspeakers in a classroom. They were given a response sheet on which the text of each utterance pair was provided, and recorded their judgements by ticking against each sentence in one of two columns labelled "first" and "second" respectively, to signify which member of the pair they considered to have been the turn-final version.

This test should give more scope than the first audio task for speaker-particular turn signals to become obvious to listeners. Although a given utterance may sound ambiguous in isolation, when it is paired with the alternative version of the same text by the same speaker crucial differences between the two might suffice to enable listeners to make a reliable judgement.

5. Results

5.1 Text Judgements

The results of the text perception task are given in Table 1. The overall mean was, as predicted, a little above 3 at 3.43. However, it was not the case that all sentences received mean ratings in the middle range; two were obviously biased towards sounding final. These were "that's all I have to say on the subject", with a mean of 4.83, and "we haven't heard a word from him since", with a mean of 4.30. (When these are removed from the calculation the overall mean lies at 3.15, and the range runs from 2.30 to 3.57.)

146

That's all I have to say on the subject	4.83
We haven't heard a word from him since	4.30
I really should find out what happened to him	3.57
I don't see why I have to justify my decisions	3.52
- the nicest present I've ever had in all my life	3.48
But she's still there	3.39
I told him to get out and never come back	3.39
You have to take it with a pinch of salt	3.04
He stole all our ideas for the new series	2.48
It was a surprise party	2.30

Table 1   Text perception task: mean finality ratings (1 = most medial, 5 = most final)

The mean number of end judgements elicited by a given sentence in the isolated audio presentation experiment, averaged across speakers and versions, correlated significantly with these text ratings: r(9) = .824, p <.01. However, when the two high-rated sentences were removed, the correlation was no longer significant: r(7) = .58, p <.10. Thus there were grounds to believe that subjects' perceptions of these two sentences might have been biased towards turn-final judgements. With the remaining eight sentences, however, we may be confident that no intrinsic bias was confounding the effects of the auditory cues.

5.2 Audio Judgements

As pointed out above, the audio judgement results address two separate questions, which we termed the production question and the perception question. The production question - do speakers consistently produce cues to distinguish turn-final from turn-medial utterances? - can be answered by simple calculation of the correctness scores across speakers and utterances. If listeners are able to categorise utterances correctly with respect to turn position, then we have reason to believe that speakers indeed differentiate between turn-final and turn-medial productions of the same sentences in a consistent way. However, this answer is itself dependent on the perception question - do listeners make consistent use of auditory cues to distinguish turn-final from turn-medial utterances? If they do not, the production question cannot be answered by correctness scores, but must be answered by auditory analysis of the utterances themselves.

The perception question, similarly, must receive a positive answer if correctness scores are high. If not, then two distributions of the results are possible: either all utterances receive about 50% turn-final judgements (i.e. listeners cannot decide about any of them), or some utterances consistently receive more and some fewer turn-final judgements (but these are' not

147

necessarily correct judgements). In the first case, the answer to the perception queston is no, and we must attempt to answer the production question by exhaustive auditory analysis of each utterance. In the second case, we can resort to auditory analysis to answer the perception question; and again, two possible approaches present themselves. On the one hand, if one has a hypothesis about which auditory features will be used as turn signals, one can analyse each utterance for the presence of such features and test the prediction that their presence will be associated with particular categorisations. On the other hand, if one has no a priori expectations of particular auditory features, one can select those utterances with a high proportion of, say, turn-final categorisations, and determine whether they have in common any features which are not shared by utterances without high turn-final ratings.

To begin our anlysis of the audio judgements, we computed the overall correctness scores; these are shown in Table 2. As can be seen, in neither experiment were they very different from chance performance (50%). Removal from the analysis of the two sentences which were intrinsically biased towards "end" judgements did not significantly alter the mean proportion of correct judgements.

	All sentences	Unbiased sentences only
Isolated presentation	51.40	51.44
Paired presentation	53.44	52.60

Table 2 Audio perception tasks: mean percent correct

Interestingly, the ten speakers were no better at judging their own utterances than others were at judging the same utterance, or than they were at judging the others' utterances. No speaker's mean correctness score for his own utterances exceeded 65%, and the mean own-utterance score across the ten speakers was exactly 50%.

There was also no difference between male and female speakers with respect to proportion of correct judgements elicited by their utterances.

Thus the correctness scores force us to resort to auditory analysis to assess the implications of our results. First, however, we must decide whether our auditory analysis should primarily attack the production question (by comparing turn-final with turn-medial productions) or the perception question (by comparing utterances judged as turn-final with those judged to be turn-medial). As we pointed out above, there is reason to believe that the production question might be the less profitable one to investigate, since the nature of the experimental situation did not encourage speakers to indulge in natural speech behaviour. Moreover, the perception judgements lead us to

148

suspect that listeners' responses were by no means random. We mentioned above that approximately 50% end judgements for all utterances would necessitate an emphatic no to the perception question; but this was definitely not the case. In the isolated presentation experiment the range of end judgements per utterance varied from 0% to 100%. In addition, the mean scores for each utterance pair show a significant, albeit small, positive correlation across the two audio experiments: $r(99) = .221$, p $<.03$. This suggests that the two sets of listeners were making similar decisions about each utterance pair. Finally, the speakers' poor performance at categorising their own utterances also weighs against choosing the production question, since one might expect that if the speakers had in the production task been distinguishing systematically between turn-final and turn-medial product-ions, they ought to be able in the perception task to detect whatever distinctions they had made. For these reasons we decided to address our further analyses to the perception question.

Since the literature we reviewed above had not provided us with clear hypotheses as to the specific prosodic phenomena involved in turn signalling, we chose not to analyse all utterances and test the correlation between particular prosodic features and particular patterns of listener judgements. Instead, we concentrated upon certain utterances which listeners had clearly perceived to be turn-final or turn-medial. In the isolated audio presentation experiment, 26 of the 200 utterances had been judged turn-medial by 75% or more of the listeners, and 39 had received 75% or more turn-final judgements. Among the latter group, however, we were not surprised to find a total of 24 productions of those two sentences which had proved in the text perception task to be intrinsically biased towards turn-final judgements. In view of the likelihood that categorisations of these utterances were influenced as much by their content as by their prosodic characteristics, we decided to exclude them from this analysis. Thus we had 41 utterances which our listeners had felt to be clearly turn-final or clearly turn-medial.

Before any of the perception experiments had been run, a prosodic transcription of all 200 utterances had been prepared by one of the authors, without knowledge of the context from which each utterance had been taken. The transcriptions of the 41 perceptually unambiguous utterances were now selected and inspected. It was immediately obvious that the utterances which had attracted turn-final judgements had quite different pitch contours from the utterances which had been judged turn-medial. Briefly, turn-final judgements were associated with downstepped contours on the final tone group of the utterance, while turn-medial judgements were associated with final tone groups having upstepped contours. By downstep we mean a tonic syllable starting significantly lower than the previous syllable -Crystal's "drop" and "low drop" (1969, 144-5). Upstep refers to a tonic syllable which starts on a higher pitch than the previous syllable - Crystal's range of "boosters" (1969, 145). Table 3 shows the distribution of upstepped and downstepped contours across the entire corpus of utterances (excluding those which were textually biased). The distribution is significantly different from chance ($\chi^2 = 38.3$, p $<.001$).

	75% or more turn-final	Ambiguous utterances	75% or more turn-medial
Upstep	0	38	99
Downstep	100	19	1
	(N=15)	(N=119)	(N=26)

Table 3 Percentage of utterances with stepped contours

Figure 1 shows pitch contours and amplitude traces of both versions of the utterance "It was a surprise party" by speaker PC. The top version, with the upstepped contour, received mostly "middle" judgements, while the bottom version, with the downstepped contour, received mostly "end" judgements.

As Table 1 shows, some of the ambiguous utterances also had stepped contours. Inspection of the perception data for these showed that even in this middle range there was a tendency for utterances with downstep to receive more turn-final judgements than utterances without, and for utterances with upstep to receive more turn-medial judgements than those without. We are in no doubt that this feature was used by our listeners as a basis for categorising utterances as turn-final or turn-medial.

No other clear differences between the set of utterances judged turn-final and the set judged turn-medial could be observed in the transcriptions. We also made a range of acoustic measurements on this subset of our data, but on none of them did the two sets of utterances differ significantly, nor did any of the measures correlate with the perception judgements. There was a slight tendency for utterances eliciting a high proportion of turn-final judgements to have a greater overall duration (mean: 2.25 sec) than their pairs which were not considered particularly turn-final (mean: 2.07 sec), but this difference also failed to reach our criterion of statistical significance (F = 4.66, p $<.07$).

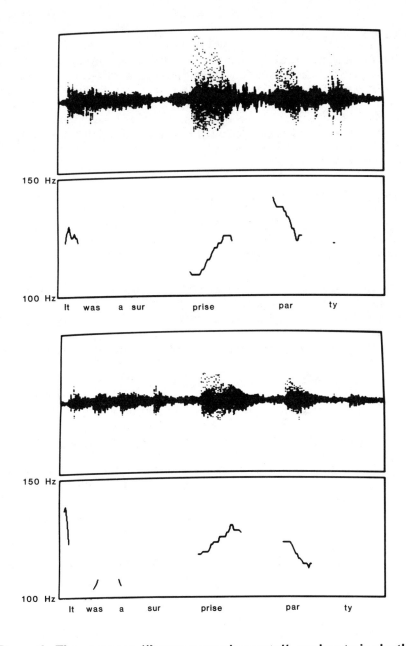

Figure 1 The sentence "It was a surprise party", spoken twice by the same speaker. The top version received mostly "middle" judgements, the bottom version mostly "end" judgements.

151

6. Conclusion

Our attempt to extend the methodology available for the analysis of turn-taking signals into the laboratory, by using precisely controlled speech output, has met with only qualified success. Our speakers did not differentiate consistently between turn-medial and turn-final utterances, so that we have not been able to give a positive answer to what we termed the production question. However, as we pointed out above, the responsibility for this lies in the shortcomings of our experimental technique, not necessarily in limitations on speakers' use of prosody.

We have, on the other hand, provided clear evidence that the answer to the perception question must be yes. This in itself implies that a positive answer to the production question should be attainable with appropriate methods - if listeners have learned to use cues to turn structure, they surely must have learned by being exposed to cues produced by speakers.

One major cue, we have found, is carried by the fundamental frequency contour of an utterance. The process is more complicated, though, than is suggested by Duncan's (1972) statements that any terminal contour other than a sustained mid-level pitch functions as a turn-yielding signal; our listeners found a downstep in pitch a good turn-yielding cue but a pitch upstep a good turn-holding cue.

This is clearly not the whole story, because many of the utterances which our listeners found ambiguous also had upstepped or downstepped pitch. Other prosodic or vocal quality features which occurred on these utterances may also function as effective turn-holding or turn-yielding cues, and may have cancelled out the stepping contour effects. In natural speech, therefore, there may be quite a range of further turn signals available to speakers and listeners; description of the entire repertoire is a task for future analyses.

However, we are not surprised to have established a clear effect of pitch contour on the perception of turn signals, since there is a body of independent evidence which points to the importance of fundamental frequency contours in discourse structure. Brown, Currie and Kenworthy (1980), for example, found that speakers changing the topic of a conversation signalled this by raising the pitch of their utterance in comparison with their previous pitch level. Exactly the same finding emerged from a study by Menn and Boyce (1982) of parents' conversations with their children. Menn and Boyce also found that a pitch rise (expressed in relation to a speaker's baseline) in comparison with the previous speaker's utterance accompanied any disruption of discourse structure; for example, verification questions, requiring the conversation to back up temporarily, produced as much pitch raising as did a topic change.

Of course, fundamental frequency is not the only prosodic dimension in which turn signals may manifest themselves. Future studies could well also find turn-taking cues in the amplitude contour of an utterance, since as Meltzer et al (1971) and French and Local (1982) found, amplitude variation plays a large role in determining the outcome of interruption attempts; and Goldberg (1979) also found that speakers changing the topic of discussion tended to do this with an utterance of higher amplitude than their previous utterance. Durational effects specific to the ends of larger discourse units have yet to be established; although the slight tendency in our results for longer utterances to be judged turn-final suggests that here too more sensitive experimentation may be able to establish a perceptual effect.

Methodologically, our experimental paradigm did not prove itself as a useful alternative to natural conversation for studying the production question. However, we did demonstrate that the perception question can be attacked by the rather artificial means of having listeners judge utterances heard in isolation. Accordingly, we recommend the following combination of methodologies for a definitive investigation of prosodic cues to turn-taking: (a) analysis of natural conversation to answer the production question by establishing a repertoire of features characteristic of turn-final and turn-medial utterances respectively; (b) use of speech resynthesis techniques to impose each of these sets of features on otherwise identical utterances, thus creating a range of carefully controlled stimuli which would allow one to ask not only whether a given feature was an effective cue, but which cues were relatively more and which relatively less important. By such means the perception question could be answered in far greater detail than was possible in the present study.

Footnote

This research was supported by the Science and Engineering Research Council and the Social Science Research Council. We are grateful to Stephen Isard and Donia Scott for helpful discussions, and to Peter Clifton for stepping in at the right time.

153

Appendix 1

Dialogues used in the experiment:

1. *In an advertising agency: an executive and his cantankerous boss*

A: Foster was pretty upset that you rejected his design!
    Any particular reason?
B: It's simply not good enough, and that's all I have to say
    on the subject! I don't see why I have to justify
    my decisions.

OR

    I don't see why I have to justify my decisions. It's
    simply not good enough, and that's all I have to say
    on the subject!
A: OK, OK, sorry I asked!

2. *A shop assistant and one of her regular customers*

A: Hello, you're looking particularly happy today!
B: Well, I am happy! It was my birthday yesterday, and I
    got the nicest present I've ever had in all my life.
    I got home, and there were about thirty of my friends,
    all waiting for me - it was a surprise party!

OR

    Well, I am happy! It was my birthday yesterday, and
    when I got home, there were about thirty of my friends,
    all waiting for me - it was a surprise party! I think
    it was the nicest present I've ever had in all my life.
A: Isn't that nice! No wonder you look pleased!

3. *Two neighbours on campus*

A: I haven't seen that friend of yours lately - Roger,
    was that his name? He used to be round here all the time.
B: You know, that's a funny thing. I was thinking myself,
    only the other day, I really should find out what happened
    to him. You see, he went off to Africa - it was supposed
    to be just for a holiday - and we haven't heard a word
    from him since.

OR

You know, that's a funny thing. He went off to Africa - it was supposed to be just for a holiday - and we haven't heard a word from him since. I was thinking myself, only the other day, I really should find out what happened to him.

A: That's weird. I hope he's all right.

4.   *Two colleagues in a TV studio*

A: I hear you and Joe had a bit of a row.
B: You're damn right we did! Do you know what the bastard did? He stole all our ideas for the new series! I told him to get out and never come back!

OR

You're damn right we did! I told him to get out and never come back! Do you know what the bastard did? He stole all our ideas for the new series!

A: Hey, you know this isn't the first time that's happened with him. Why do you think he lost his job in London?

5.   *Conversation between two friends*

A: Hey, I saw Carol at the weekend.
B: Oh yeah?
A: She was really pissed off with living in that flat.
      She reckons she's moving out, and if Chris wants to stay there, that's up to him.
B: Well, so she says, but I think you have to take it with a pinch of salt. I don't know how many times she's sworn she was moving out - but she's still there.

OR

Well, so she says. I don't know how many times she's sworn she was moving out - but she's still there. I think you have to take it with a pinch of salt.

A: Well, she seemed pretty determined to me.

155

PROSODIC FEATURES AND THE MANAGEMENT OF INTERRUPTIONS[1]

Peter French and John Local

1. Aims

The aim of this paper is to explain some aspects of the operation of conversational interruptions.[2] In pursuing this aim, it is shown that conversational participants make use of certain phonetic features of speech with a high degree of systematicity both in producing interruptive utterances and in identifying the specific interactional function that the interruptive speech of others is performing. These features, (for example pitch height and tempo variations) having to do with the non-segmental characteristics of speech, have been termed 'prosodic' (Crystal, 1969).

2. Methodology

A more precise indication of this paper's focus is provided in the next section. Before proceeding to this we shall attempt briefly to explain something of the methodological principles the analysis adopts. This may be helpful in view of the fact that many readers of the volume who have backgrounds and interests in the fields of linguistics or social psychology will be unacquainted with the Conversation Analytic approach to interactional data.[3]

The central concern of Conversational Analysis (henceforth C.A.) is to explicate the competencies social participants draw upon in producing, understanding and co-ordinating interactional behaviour. Quite obviously, there is more to social interaction than just language, but in that language occupies such an important position among the constituent 'channels' of information exchange (gaze, gesture, posture, facial expression), it has quite naturally come to provide a major focus for studies within the C.A. tradition. The skills at language production and comprehension which C.A. investigates are, in the main, generalised ones. Unlike most other approaches to socially-situated language - for example sociolinguistics or the ethnography of speaking - C.A. is not directly concerned with either the ways in which individuals effect adjustments in their modes of speaking from one social setting to another or with the ways that certain linguistic forms or speech activities may be indexed to particular social roles or identities (Jefferson, 1981; Wootton, 1981a). Thus, even though the recordings upon which the present study is based reflect a range of types of social encounter - academic seminar, unscripted radio panel-discussion, family consultation with a general practitioner - the analysis we produce makes no reference to social setting or participant identity. Rather than, say, attempting to plot differences in the incidence of interruptions across the various settings, or examining the possibility that certain types of interruption may be more in evidence in the speech of men as opposed to that of women, in the doctor's speech rather than the patients' etc., we set aside these issues in order to address the more basic question of **how** interruptions are produced and responded to - irrespective of who is involved in the encounter or the purpose for which the participants have convened. Language variation is an issue which does interest us (see Local's chapter in this volume) but, as we have argued elsewhere (French, 1983), an over-concentration on speaker and situation differences may lead one away from the basic skills at talk production and comprehension which unite interactants of vastly disparate social identities as members of the same communicative community.

As work within the C.A. tradition advances, it is becoming clear that these generalised skills are extremely complex and may involve participants utilising knowledge of lexico-syntax (Wootton, 1981b), as well as broader cultural knowledge (Button, 1977) in signalling to one another the interactional functions of their utterances.[4] The intention of the present study is to develop understanding of these competencies by extending analytic consideration to the ways that participants make use of prosodic features in the design of their interruptive speech.

In characterising the role of prosody in interruptions, we have attempted to ground each analytic claim in features of transcribed excerpts of conversation. This strategy is informed by a central methodological canon of C.A. The principle guiding the inclusion of detailed transcriptions of data alongside analytic points is that in their absence claims come to stand 'insulated from any kind of rigorous public inspection'. Given access to the data, however, readers can follow through the logic of any interpretations of it as well as proposals about how they were produced' (Atkinson and Drew, 1979: 26).

As long ago as 1935, the linguist J.R. Firth called for a form of enquiry that treated speech forms as contextualised productions. However, in the course of that appeal he also issued a warning against developing 'a loose linguistic sociology without formal accuracy'. The C.A. strategy of research presentation could be seen as one way of answering this type of warning. Juxtaposition of data and analysis raises the relationship between the two elements of the research report to a point of high visibility. The accuracy of the analysis thereby becomes open for assessment, assent or challenge.

When attempting to warrant analytic claims in the observable features of data we frequently use the term 'participant orientations'. The analysis we put forward of how interruptions operate is intended to be commensurate with a participant's analysis. Thus, where we make claims that, for example, a particular prosodic feature is an important element in the structuring of a certain type of interruption, we attempt to provide evidence that participants themselves treat it, or 'orient to' it, as important. This type of evidence could take a variety of forms. We might find, for instance, the feature being routinely incorporated in the speech of interrupters. Or we might find that those who are interrupted show signs that they are monitoring the interruptive talk for the feature. Or we might find that participants act as though something is 'amiss' should the feature be absent from an interruption of that type. As the analysis proceeds it will become apparent that the search for evidence of participant orientations may involve the analyst in protracted examination of small fragments of data. The claim that one's analysis is more than a purely analytic construct but reproduces and explicates the bases of participants' understandings is a strong one. In view of this, the painstaking, 'inch-by-inch' approach to interactional data that C.A. recommends becomes understandable not as a matter of quirk or indulgence, but as one of necessity.

3. Types of Interruption: Turn-competitive and non-competitive

As we hinted above, the analysis is based upon recordings of multi-party conversations. Simultaneous or overlapping speech is a recurrent feature of these settings. It is clear that such speech may occur for reasons other than a speaker having misjudged the completion point of another's turn or the timing of his own beginning. Researchers have identified a variety of conversational activities that speakers can perform by timing their speech to begin interruptively (Jefferson and Schegloff, 1975). In analysing interruptions, reference has been made to the syntactic and segmental characteristics of the interruptive speech (Jefferson and Schegloff, 1975), to the place at which it enters a turn in progress (Schegloff, 1973; Zimmerman and West, 1975; Edelsky, 1981) and to the thematic relation of such speech to a turn in progress (Bennett, 1980). In short, researchers have shown that participants gauge very precisely both when and how to begin their talk relative to an ongoing turn (Jefferson, 1973; Sacks, Schegloff and Jefferson, 1974).

The focus of the present study is rather more restricted than previous treatments of this topic in that it is concerned with only one particular type of overlapping interruptive speech[5]: that in which one speaker comes in clearly prior to the completion of another's turn and can be heard as directly competing with the other for possession of the turn. We use the term '*directly competing*' to circumscribe those occasions on which we get a sense that the interrupter has something to say and that he is treating the in-overlap position as an undesirable or unsuitable place to say it. We hear him as wanting the floor to himself not when the current speaker has finished but **now**, at this point in the conversation. In order to give some preliminary indication of our focus consider the following excerpts:

(Transcription conventions can be found at the end of the paper.)

(1)   CTB, Z: NKB

K: ...I was- I was gonna ask about those (0.5 cos (.) in terms of your
       stuff about hints in the first thing because it seems to me that
       something like .hhhhh Fionna's not letting me have her scissors .hhhh
       is as much a threat to Fionna (0.7) as it is a hah hint h to-is a-
       is a hint to her father
                        (1.6)|

F: x::

N:→   oh yeah I mean it ⌜'s some sort of-/
                          ⌜   <dim> →|
                          ⌜   <accel> →|
                          ⌜   /
K:→   └y' know I mean and/this is your thing ab ⌜out the/two
                          ⌜h⟩ ────────►⟨h⟩   ⌜
                          ⌜f⟩ ────────►⟨f⟩   ⌜
                                                                    ⌜
N: └nyeah/

K: edged (0.4) way that these things work=

N: =nyeah (0.4) nyeah

(2)   UVY, 2: WBB

A: ...and at the- the outset these things go relatively smoothly and- and .hhh it's
       only in fact er:: .hh the problems in fact only arise when you get a clear(er)
   →   idea of what you want (and) when you set up some ⌜thing as a basic standard/
                                                        ⌜f⟩ ─────────►⟨f⟩|
                                                        ⌜<decel>────────►
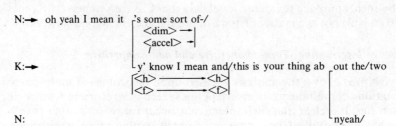
W:→   └ but it's- it's always some- (some)/way t
                                                        ⌜h⟩ ─────►⟨h⟩|
                                                        ⌜f⟩ ─────►⟨f⟩|

       go before .hhh one ever reaches what one's (0.2) looking for so- so .h it's
       almost bound to be easier at the beginning of (the) term of employment
                        (0.3)

A: yes and that I think gives us every reason...

(3)   TTM, Z: NKA

F: ...the police house isn't very suitable for- (0.6) for all living together (0.2) ⌈it's/erm (0.3)

D: ⌊m:/

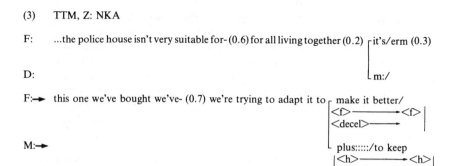

F:→   this one we've bought we've- (0.7) we're trying to adapt it to ⌈ make it better/
                                                                      │<f>————————•<f>|
                                                                      │<decel>————————•|

M:→   ⌊ plus:::::/to keep
                                                                      |<h>————————•<h>|
                                                                      |<f>————————•<f>|

        er (.) er y' know: er (.) now that she's coming (up) nine at school (.) she - she didn't
        seem too bad at Keswick actually (.) er er did she as regards friends

We note first that in fragments (1) to (3), a turn in progress is overlapped by
a co-participant's interruptive speech. Moreover, in each case, the interruptive
speech begins at a place which does not suggest itself as proximal to a likely
completion point for the extant turn (cf Sacks et al, 1974). In (1) its beginning
is directly subsequent to a pronoun occupying the intial subject position of a
clause ("... it↑'s some sort of"). In (2) it begins during the production of the
word 'some↑thing' which in this case carries very little stress thus indicating
the likelihood of more to follow ("... when you set up some↑thing as a basic
standard"). In fragment (3) its beginning is subsequent to the word "to"
which, by virtue of its rhythmical and segmental characteristics (unstressed
with a short central vowel) is constituted as a grammatical item which projects
further talk from the current speaker ("... we're trying to adapt it to make it
better"). However, the point at which interruptive speech begins relative to a
turn in progress does not seem to bear a direct relationship to the directly
turn-competitive character of the interruption.

Consider the following in this respect:

(4)   CTB, Z: NKA

K:→   it would be interesting you know (0.3) to know what kind of categories
        you're gonna play around with if you're gonna (0.4) =achieve both ⌈ instances at the same/ time
N:→   x::=   ⌊ well exactly yeah/
                                                                            |<l>————————•<l>|

E: .h in fact there's possible evidence in the data that- that`Fionna's the next
        Speaker (.)(.) not - not 'n' at all ...
D: m::

This fragment again contains an instance of speech coming in during an
ongoing turn. As in (1) to (3), its entry is at a point where further talk from
current speaker is strongly projected.

161

The word after which the interruption begins, "both", does not carry the degree of stress or pitch movement which one would associate with an utterance-final or turn-final occurrence and so presents itself syntactically as the (pre)determiner of a noun phrase of which the remaining constituents are yet to follow. In this case, however, unlike (1) to (3), the interruptive speech does **not** suggest itself as turn-competitive. That is, we hear N's utterances as being produced in the course of K's turn but as unequipped for and unaddressed to the task of securing the turn from K. Our first observation then is:

> the *positioning* of interrupter's speech at a non-completion point in current turn does not alone make for a hearing of that speech as directly competitive for the turn.

One aspect of the interruptive speech in (4) which distinguishes it from that in (1) to (3) is its lexical constitution. At first sight this looks as if it might provide for the absence of a directly turn-competitive character. Through the affirmative tokens ("well exactly yeah"), N's utterance displays support for, or agreement with, current speaker in a much clearer way than does the interruptive speech in any of fragments (1), (2) or (3). This support, however, is related specifically to the thematic matter contained **within** K's turn. And consideration of fragments (5) and (6) reveals that thematic concord or dissent need not bear a simple relation to any sense we may have of the interrupter's wish for the securing or continuation of a turn in progress.

(5)   UVY, 2: AVA

B: ...the way in which these things are written of course places
      them (way and) beyond the - the comprehension of the average well-informed
      person and - .hhh and occa:sionally I think (.) (be-) beyond the
      lawyers themselves who draw them up in the first place
V: yes (0.2) I'm sure though that they - (0.2) that everyone involved in
      the transaction knows full well what's going on we go out and we
      find someone who will for a large sum of h money hah .hh phrase the agreement
      in the most difficult terms possible in the belief that when we speak
  →   in these (.) terms we really are ta ⌐ ken   seriously ´⌐
                                                          <f>⟶<f>⌐
                                            ⌊<decel>──────────⌋

A:→   ⌊ yes   ye: s: ⁄ I- I'd agree with
                                              <h>⟶<h>⌐
                                              <f>⟶<f>⌐

      that because the way people look upon words is .hh as - as though
      they can (.) somehow transform er ::: once they're written down er .hh can
      transform ....
B: (* *)

(6)   TUX, 1: PSA

S: I think the — I think the great thinker Spiro Agnew .hhhhh I'll - I'll quote
      him before Norman does (0.2) got it right when he said an inthhellectual
      was a man who didn't know how to park a <u>bike</u> (0.9) 'n what I (.)
      want to say is that I claim it was a - it's a relic of the
      thirties left over from then because .hh the <u>wor:d</u> was applied
      to someone who was wearing a hairy green suit a pastel
      yellow tie .h check shirt .hh an' who (.) no chin (.) glasses an'
➤   looked as thoug he wasn't goo ⌈d for / much el ⌈se than writing novels that / nobody

P:➤   ⌊ but-/   ⌊ but this is shit you're talking/
                                                 |<hh>| |<hh>————————►<hh>|
                                                 |<pp>| |<pp>————————►<pp>|

S: read (0.2) now   if/ (.) er (.) what I - (.) I just labour it (.) just very

N: (* *)/
      |<h> |
      |<pp>|

S: slightly then <u>Spiro</u> says...

      In (5) the entry of the interruptive speech is at a noncompletion point in the
current turn (i.e. medial to the production of a projective verbal element
("taken")). As in fragment (4), we again have agreement with the content of
the current turn explicitly signalled ("... yes ye:s: I-I'd agree with that ...").
Here in (5), however, the interruptive utterance does clearly suggest itself to us
as directly competitive for the turn. Conversely, in fragment (6) P's interruptive talk which enters the current turn at a non-competition point signals
dissent in no uncertain terms ("but this is shit you're talking"), but does **not**
suggest itself to us as directly turn-competitive. We do not hear P as projecting
that there is anything further to be said or as competing for the turn. Our
second observation then is:

      the *thematic relation* of interrupter's speech to the content of the current
      turn (agreement or disagreement) does not in itself constitute the character
      of that speech as either directly competitive or non-competitive for the
      turn.

      So far we have suggested that the interruptive speech in fragments (1), (2),
(3) and (5) is hearable as directly competitive for the turn, whereas that in (4)
and (6) is not. We have also indicated that neither the positioning of the
interruption nor its thematic relation to the speech in progress can provide a
systematic basis for these directly turn-competitive or non-competitive
hearings. In order to provide such a basis we turn to a consideration of some of
the prosodic features of the interruptive utterances.

In each of the fragments (1), (2), (3) and (5) we have subscripted some portion of the incomer's speech with the symbols <h> and <f>[6]. These indicate that the portion is markedly raised in pitch and loudness respectively. By 'raised' we intend the following:

1) That the subscripted portion is both higher and louder than that speaker's norm for beginning turns at points where another speaker has completed his turn;
2) That it is both higher and louder than any portion of interrupter's speech not so marked;
3) That it is loud, but not necessarily high in absolute terms, relative to the speech contained in current turn.

Neither the interruptive speech in fragment (4) nor that in (6) displays this combination of features. In (4) the interrupter's speech is unremarkable in terms of its pitch height; moreover it is quieter than both the speaker's norm and the talk contained in the current turn (indicated by subscript <p>). In fragment (6), although the interruptive speech is extremely high in pitch (<hh>), it is, like that in (4), quieter than that speaker's norm and quieter than the ongoing talk.

From an analytic point of view, then, one thing which systematically collects those instances of interruptive speech which are hearable as directly turn-competitive and discriminates them from those which are not is the presence of the combination of prosodic features high pitch and increased loudness (henceforth <h+f>).

4. Pitch height and loudness in the management of interruptions

It seems clear from our transcribed recordings that the occurrence of <h+f> is not of merely analytic import. Our transcripts provide four kinds of evidence that conversational participants methodically produce and monitor for ('orient to') <h+f> as a non-incidental, constitutive, property of directly turn-competitive interruptions.

The first kind of evidence for this concerns the extent of interrupter's speech over which the prosodic combination <h+f> is present. The most prevalent pattern in this respect is represented in fragments such as (1), (3) and (5) where

it begins with speech onset and is sustained exactly to the point of turn occupant's termination. This suggests firstly, that interrupters are closely monitoring for the ending of current turn. Secondly, it suggests that <h+f> is being deployed to signal the fact of turn competition, for once termination has occurred and the turn has been secured by the interrupter then any competition is over and <h+f> is dropped.

Only occasionally do we find these features being sustained beyond the point of current speaker's termination. In each such case the post-overlap portion of the interruption for which <h+f> is held contains not more than one stressed syllable. In phonological terms, the combination <h+f> is not sustained beyond completion of the already begun rhythmical unit - the 'foot' in progress (Abercrombie, 1964).

(7)   TUX, 1: SPA

P: ...if you're a - a woman you learn very quickly to suss out an er i-
interesting or boring man .hhh but if he's interesting (.) .hhhh erm in the
course of a train or a plane jour ⌐ney I can come to no harm/

U: ⌐can spot if he may be an intellectual within fifty heh
                                 yhehards
    heh heh/
P: and I can have a fascinating conversation I mean
→   it's a bonus I'm re ⌐garded as (* *)/
                      ⌐<dim>⎯⎯⎯|

S:→   └I wonder- I wonder/how they start these things up
                  |<h> ⎯⎯⎯⎯⎯⎯⎯→ <h>|
                  |<f> ⎯⎯⎯⎯⎯⎯⎯→ <f>|
(because) I- I- I'm reminded of er reminded of dear Stephen Potter
(who we) referred to earlier (0.2) hhh his technique in railway
carriages he said was to bound in and if the lady was
reading the Times as I imagine you would be ...

(8)   TUX, 3: GUA

U: ...by using the word quarrel you're suggesting it's really rather
pointless I mean at least following the - that - you know the
definition we were talking about before it's not really about
anything (.) whereas I mean this was about something .hhh this
was about a point .hhh this was about the chalk coming up
in - on a particular ser:ve in which it was quite clear from the
replay that McEnroe was absolutely right .hhhh
→   now are w ⌐e suggesting-
                 ⌐<dim>→

G:→   └I don't thi- I do/n't think you can defend his behaviour
                 |<h>⎯⎯⎯⎯⎯⎯→ <h>|
                 |<f>⎯⎯⎯⎯⎯⎯→ <f>|
I think you either liked it appreciated it (er) or enjoyed it or
you didn't .hhh erm I think it's probably fair to say
objectively that it's a bit of a cheap shot .hh that he
did take all the conventions of Wimbledon and try and smash
them .hh but of course there's a certain perverse pleasure in
that for the audience ...

(9)   UVY, 2: NVA

V: ...in spite of all one might- might say about
      tacit understandings (* *) and- and such
      like .hhh the fact (0.2) still remains that at some
→   point an ag reement's got to be reached/
                 |<f>————————————→<f>|
                 |<decel>————————→<decel>|

N:→   that- that's not- that's not the- that/'s not
      |<h>——————→<h>|
      |<f>——————→<f>|
      the one (.) we're worried about though .hh
      it's when a- (.) a formal (or) explicit
      understanding .h (one) which has been er:
      (0.3) consciously entered into by two or more
      parties is then treated by one of those...

In other words, except when an interrupter has already begun a rhythmical unit which straddles a turn-occupant's completion point, <h+f> is present only for so long as turn-competition may be an issue.

The second kind of evidence that conversationalists orient to <h+f> as constitutive of directly turn-competitive interruptions concerns the in-overlap speech of current turn-occupants.

Notice first of all that in fragments (4) and (6) which contain instances of interruptive speech not marked with <h+f> we have not notationally subscripted the portion of turn occupant's speech which is overlapped by that of interrupter. In these cases we hear no alteration in the prosodic features of the ongoing speech either upon or subsequent to interrupter's point of commencement. That is, turn-occupants appear to carry on speaking in overlap with interrupter at much the same loudness, pitch and tempo as they were prior to his beginning. In distinction to these cases, the fragments in which interrupter's speech is marked with <h+f> and is hearable as directly turn-competitive all involve prosodic changes in the speech of the turn-occupant. These modifications, which principally concern the features of loudness and tempo, take one of two forms. In each of (2), (3), (5) and (9) turn occupants increase the loudness of their speech and decrease its pace either directly upon, or at the latest one syllable subsequent to, the onset of the interruption.

The decrease in pace and increase in loudness directly following interruption can be seen in (2) 'something as basic standard'; (3) 'to make it better'; (5) 'are taken seriously'; and (9) 'an agreement's got to be reached'. These two features, decreasing pace (<decel>) and increasing loudness (<cresc>/<f>) combine to produce the sort of speech effect one might refer to as 'emphatic'.

Taken together with the fact that in each of these cases turn-occupants do not directly yield the floor to interrupters but continue to produce turns which are recognisably complete, such emphasis might be seen as constituting a return of competition.[7]

The second form of prosodic modification turn-occupants effect may be termed 'fade-out' (<dim>). This can be seen in (1) 'I mean it↑'s some sort of'; (7) 'it's a bonus I'm re↑garded as'; (8) 'now are w↑e suggesting'; (10) 'just been describing bu↑t at least that'.

(1)   CTB, Z: NKB

K: ...I was- I was gonna ask about those (0.5 cos (.) in terms of your
        stuff about hints in the first thing because it seems to me that
        something like .hhhhh Fionna's not letting me have her scissors .hhhh
        is as much a threat to Fionna (0.7) as it is a hah hint h to-is a-
        is a hint to her father
                                    (1.6)│

F: x::

N:→   oh yeah I mean it ┌'s some sort of-/
                          │   <dim> →│
                          │   <accel>→│

K:→   └y' know I mean and/this is your thing ab ┌out the/two
                          ┌<h>──────────→<h>│   │
                          │<f>──────────→<f>│   │

N: └nyeah/

K: edged (0.4) way that these things work=

N: =nyeah (0.4) nyeah

(7)   TUX, 1: SPA

P: ...if you're a - a woman you learn very quickly to suss out an er i-
        interesting or boring man .hhh but if he's interesting (.) .hhhh erm in the
        course of a train or a plane jour ┌ney I can come to no harm/
                                           │

U: └can spot if he may be an intellectual within fifty heh
                                             yhehards
        heh heh/
P: and I can have a fascinating conversation I mean
  →   it's a bonus I'm re ┌garded as (* *)/
                            │ <dim>──────│

             S: └I wonder- I wonder/how they start these things up
  →   │<h> ───────────→<h>│
                            │<f> ───────────→<f>│
        (because) I- I- I'm reminded of er reminded of dear Stephen Potter
        (who we) referred to earlier (0.2) hhh his technique in railway
        carriages he said was to bound in and if the lady was
        reading the Times as I imagine you would be ...

167

(8)   TUX, 3: GUA

U: ...by using the word quarrel you're suggesting it's really rather
      pointless I mean at least following the - that - you know the
      definition we were talking about before it's not really about
      anything (.) whereas I mean this was about <u>some</u>thing .hhh this
      was about a point .hhh this was about the chalk coming up
      in - on a particular ser:ve in which it was quite clear from the
      replay that McEnroe was absolutely right .hhhh

→   now are w ⌐e suggesting-
                 │   <dim>→

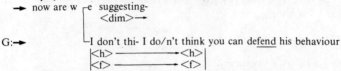

G:→   └I don't thi- I do/n't think you can de<u>fend</u> his behaviour

      I think you either liked it appreciated it (er) or enjoyed it or
      you didn't .hhh erm I think it's probably fair to say
      objectively that it's a bit of a cheap shot .hh that he
      did take all the conventions of Wimbledon and try and smash
      them .hh but of course there's a certain perverse pleasure in
      that for the audience ...

(10)   TUX, 1: SUB

U: ...the way in which they manage to .hhh convince
      themselves there is no such person is by
      inventing these radio fun caricatures you've just
→   been describing bu ⌐t (at least) that-/
                          │   <dim>→

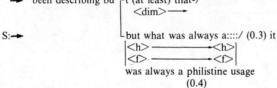

S:→   └but what was always a::::/ (0.3) it

      was always a philistine usage
                    (0.4)

U: but you keep copping out of answering the
      question .hh that...

   Again prosodic changes take effect approximately from interrupter's point
of onset. In these cases, however, the principal change is one of a decreasing of
volume (<dim>). Because, in addition to this, in (1), (8) and (10) turn-
occupants do not continue to a possible turn-completion point (in (7) the issue
cannot be determined as the volume of speech decreases to a point of
unintelligibility) one might look upon the in-overlap as a 'fade-out' or yield to
interrupter's competition.

   It appears, then, that where <h+f> is a feature of the interruption, turn-
occupants begin to modify their speech prosodically in such ways as to render
it hearable as either a return of competition or a relinquishment. When
<h+f> is absent from the interruption, as in (4) and (6), no such
modifications are made.

We have, in addition to those so far discussed, a set of fragments where the interruptions are in fact substantially lower in volume and in some cases lower in pitch than both the interrupter's norm and the speech contained in the ongoing turn. We shall now consider these as our third type of evidence of speakers orienting to <h+f> as constitutive of direct turn competition:

In fragments (11), (12), (13) and (14) the turn occupant yields almost immediately to the interrupter.

(11)   TUX, 1: SNA

```
N:       ...so élite and élitist intellectual's about the worst thing
         you can say: of anybody these days .hh and er: i- it reminds
         me of the erm of the man who: erm (0.7) the African
  →      who er ┌ re -                        (0.2) who refused to perform (.) some

S:→             └ fasten your seatbelts
                 |<I> ─────────→ <I>|
                 |<p> ─────────→<p>|
```

```
U:       heh heh heh heh
N:       humdrum duty that he was given by Albert Schweitzer .hhh and erm
         Schweitzer said why- why- why won't do this rather humdrum
         (* *) he says I can't do that it's beneath me I'm an
         intellectual .hhh and Schweitzer replied .hh h well I too had thoughts once
         of being an intellectual .h (0.3)but I found it was too difficult
```

(12)   TUX, 1: USB

[S is taking an extended turn]

```
S:       now ┌ if/ (.) er (.) what I- (.) I just labour it (.) just very

N:           └ (* *)
             |<h> |
             |<pp>|
```

```
S:→      slightly then Spiro says th ┌ at/
                                     │         (0.2) Spiro says that about not

U:→                                  └ slightly more
                                       |<I> ─────────→ <I>|
                                       |<p> ─────────→<p>|
```

```
S:       being able to park a bike .hhh and all I'm saying is (0.3) that it's
         obviously a caricature of someone who never existed .hh that kind of ...
```

169

(13) TUX, 1: SNB

S: ...I'm wearing glasses at the <u>mo</u>ment but I don't read - wr - wr - write
        unreadable novels and by George if you saw my bike outside
        Broadcating House .h its <u>beautifully</u> pa ⌐rked/
U: └i-/ isn't he defensive you're right

        he (doe ⌐s agree *)/
                │ │<dim> │
                │ │<accel>│

Ni:→   └ I'm - I'm on / your   ⌐s-   (.) I'm on your side Stu because I
        |<h> ————→<h>|
        |<f> ————→<f>|

S:→   └on the run

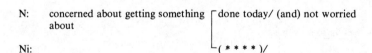

Ni: think (0.4) Unwin defines a man that I don't recognise (0.2) and
       Norman talks
       about where do we put ourselves in this league (.) now what is the league
       it
       seems to me you're either .hhhh on the top (.) of division one or you're
       elsewhere ...

(14) TUX, 1: UNA

N: ...but now the intellectual as far as I can see .hh is someone who- (.) who
        <u>pon</u>ders who <u>won</u>ders who ex<u>am</u>ines .h these are people .h who go
        out be<u>yond</u> and deeper .h than people like yourself
   →   who are ⌐:   (0.2) (y' know) are basically)
U:→   └ sock it to him Norm (.) sock it to him
                  <I> ————————————→<I>

N: concerned about getting something ⌐done today/ (and) not worried
        about   │
Ni: └(* * * *)/

N: tomorrow at all

yield is almost immediate. In (11) and (12) only one syllable is produced in
overlap by turn-occupant, and in (13) and (14) only a single sound segment.

   Notice here that in each case turn-occupant yields to interrupter without
completing his turn. However, unlike the turn-yields in (1), (7), (8) and (10)
where turn-occupant carries on in overlap to produce several syllables or
words on decreased loudness before yielding prematurely, in these cases the

Moreover, in (11), (12), (13) and (14) the original turn-occupants do not recommence speaking immediately upon interrupters' completions but fractionally delay their restarts. One plausible interpretation of this delayed restart is that original turn-occupants are giving interrupters 'time to complete' thus exhibiting that they are treating the interruptive speech as non-competitive. When we compare the conversational activities which interrupters are performing in these cases with those they perform with speech which is raised in pitch and loudness we find some clear differences. These interruptions are markedly shorter in duration and are characterisable as, say, 'interjections', 'asides', 'quips', etc., rather than as serious attempts to take an extended turn.

This characterisation is, of course, essentially a retrospective one. It depends on having available for scrutiny interrupters' completed turns. It would seem that there is no way of specifying the length or type of conversational activity interrupters will perform at the point of onset of their speech as no lexico-syntactic clues are available (given that turn-occupant yields almost immediately). However, insofar as turn-occupants do drop out directly upon the production of interrupters' onset syllables or speech segments, it would seem that such prospective analyses of activity-type can indeed be performed by participants. In the absence of any substantial lexico-syntactic clues with which turn-occupants could be working, it appears that their material for analysis is prosodic. Specifically we would suggest that it is the downgrading of interrupters' onset syllables away from <h>, and in some cases <f>, that serves as the basis for such prospective analyses[8].

The fourth kind of evidence in our transcripts which suggests that conversationists orient to <h+f> as constitutive of turn-competition concerns the way in which turn-occupants continue their turns subsequent to a hesitation where another speaker attempts to take the floor.

(15)   TTM, 1: D-FA

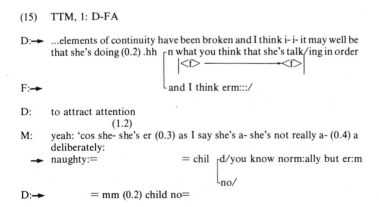

D: to attract attention
                   (1.2)
M: yeah: 'cos she- she's er (0.3) as I say she's a- she's not really a- (0.4) a
      deliberately:
   → naughty:=   = chil ⌐d/you know norm:ally but er:m
                                               └no/

D:→   = mm (0.2) child no=

171

(16)   TTM, 1: F-MA

D: ...is this why you're- you- you're (.) thinking of buying a house
        in (* *) er: (1.1) Missus Dobson in order to er (.) stablise
        the situation

F:→   (0.3) well the erm::─┌the idea was/ to some extent h (.)
                                                     │
                                                     │<f>─→<f>│
M:→   (0.9) ye └s: really/

F: you know because we had erm: (0.5) Gran was living at Keswick (0.6)
        and the nearest after eight years I managed to get to Keswick
        from Carlisle was Windermere well at that progress...

(17)   TTM, 1: D-FB

F: ...there is one particular teacher who: (1.5) she seems to clash with as it were=

D: =which (was) that
                        (0.3)
F: erm
M: (0.8)
D: who's the tea ┌cher you cla-/

            M: └Missus/
                        (0.6)
C: Missus Handley
                        (0.2)
D:→ M ┌issus Han/dley is it .hhhh ┌erm: I (won't be a mo/ment just let me go and see
       │   │<f>─→<f>   │
       │   │
F:→   └Missus Ha-/   └erm yeah I-/

       ┌(if there's /been
       │
       └okay/

D: a little (1.2) child

                        [D leaves surgery]

   In fragments (15), (16) and (17) turn-occupant hesitates at a non-
completion place in his turn at which point another participant comes in. In
each case the original turn-occupant either immediately or almost immediately recommences speaking and does so in a way that renders his speech more
audible than that of the other speaker. Crucially, this greater audibility is not
achieved by the production of the speech with **both** increased pitch height **and**
increased loudness but by an increase in loudness **alone** until the turn is
regained. Now, if it is the case, as we have suggested, that participants orient to
increased pitch and loudness as constitutive of directly turn-competitive

172

interruptions, then there might be some premium for speakers in these situations in **not** combining these features in their recommencements. For, if they were to do so they would thereby present themselves not as simply producing a continuation of a turn which was legitimately theirs but as competitive interrupters - hence signalling acknowledgement that the turn had changed hands.

5. Further characteristics of interruptive speech

So far we have discussed only the prosodic characteristics of speech in which direct turn competition seems to be an issue. There are, however, further, non-prosodic features of talk which recur - more variably and sporadically - in the in-overlap portions of interruptions. In particular, it appears that interrupters utilise resources of sound sustention and repetitious incomplete syntax in displaying their turn-requirements from within overlap. In (3) for example:

... we're trying to adapt it to ⎡make it better/
　　　　　　　　　　　　　　　⎣ plus :::::/to keep her ...

interrupter sustains the final sound segment of the initial, in-overlap component until turn-occupant completes. In doing so, he displays simultaneously that he has something to say on the matter being addressed by turn-occupant and that the saying of it is attendant upon turn-occupant's completion or termination. Similarly, by producing either simple or expanded repeats of incomplete syntactic units, interrupters can signal both that there is more to follow and that it is being withheld until they have gained sole occupation of the floor:

(7)　　TUX, 1: SPA

P:　　...if you're a - a woman you learn very quickly to suss out an er i-
　　　interesting or boring man .hhh but if he's interesting (.) .hhhh erm in the
　　　course of a train or a plane jour ⎡ney I can come to no harm/

U:　　　　　　　　　　　　　　　　　　　⎣can spot if he may be an intellectual within fifty heh
　　　　　　　　　　　　　　　　　　　　　yhehards
　　　heh heh/
P:　　and I can have a fascinating conversation I mean
　→　it's a bonus I'm re ⎡garded as (* *)/
　　　　　　　　　　　　 ⎢⎡<dim>————⟍
　　　　　　　　　　　　 ⎢⎣　　　　　　⎮
S:→　　　　　　　　　　 ⎣ I wonder- I wonder/how they start these things up
　　　　　　　　　　　　 ⎮<h> ————————<h>⎮
　　　　　　　　　　　　 ⎮<f> ————————→ <f>⎮
　　　(because) I- I- I'm reminded of er reminded of dear Stephen Potter
　　　(who we) referred to earlier (0.2) hhh his technique in railway
　　　carriages he said was to bound in and if the lady was
　　　reading the Times as I imagine you would be ...

(9)   UVY, 2: NVA

V: ...in spite of all one might- might say about
       tacit understandings (* *) and- and such
       like .hhh the fact (0.2) still remains that at some
  →   point an ag   reement's got to be reached/
       <f> —————→<f>
       <decel>—→<decel>

N:→   that- that's not- that's not the- that/'s not
       <h> —————→<h>
       <f> —————→<f>
       the one (.) we're worried about though .hh
       it's when a (.) a formal (or) explicit
       understanding .h (one) which has been er:
       (0.3) consciously entered into by two or more
       parties is then treated by one of those...

It seems from the corpus of data transcribed, however, that these features
are not constitutive of direct turn-competition in the way that the prosodic
combination <h+f> is. The evidence for this is as follows:

(a) Interrupters may produce repetitions of incomplete syntax without turn-
occupants effecting prosodic modifications to their speech of the type
associated with either returns of competition of yields.

(6)   TUX, 1: PSA

S: I think the — I think the great thinker Spiro Agnew .hhhhh I'll - I'll quote
       him before Norman does (0.2) got it right when he said an inthhellectual
       was a man who didn't know how to park a <u>bike</u> (0.9) 'n what I (.)
       want to say is that I claim it was a - it's a relic of the
       thirties left over from then because .hh the <u>wor:d</u> was applied
       to someone who was wearing a hairy green suit a pastel
       yellow tie .h check shirt .hh an' who (.) no chin (.) glasses an'
       looked as thoug he wasn't goo ⌐d for / much el ⌐se than writing novels that / nobody could

  →
P:→   ∟ but-/   ∟ but this is shit you're talking/
P: |<hh>| |<hh> —————————→ <hh>|
                                     |<pp>| |<pp> —————————→ <pp>|

S: read (0.2) now   if/ (.) er (.) what I - (.) I just labour it (.) just very

N: (* *)/
       <h>
       <pp>

S: slightly then <u>Spiro</u> says...

(18)   TUY, 1: USC

S: ...Spiro says that about not being able to park a bike .hhh and all
       I'm saying is (0.3) that it's obviously a caricature of someone who never
       existed .hh that kind of image of an intellectual .hhhh was the one (0.4) er: sort

→   of er <u>nour</u>ished by peop ⌐le who/wrote to the Daily Telegraph in

U:→   └but all you're/
                                      |<h>─▸<h>|

S: about nineteen   thirty eight/

U: but all you're/doing (.) is describing I think as
                           |<f>─────────<f>|

       Norman has- 'as- 'as- 'as- 'as- 'as so succinctly put it I mean what
       you're doing .hhhhhh is des<u>crib</u>ing the attitude o:f people in this
       country towards intellectuals...

(19)   TUX, 1: SNC

S: ...all three words intellectual(.)cogniscenti and er intelligentsia.hhh are <u>mo</u>dels (.)
→   very very vague models .hh of something that's never ac ⌐tually existed/
                                                                 |
                                                                 |
N:→   └no no no no/ no you're
                                                               |downsteps |
                                                               |from <h> to <⊳|

       quite wrong int- intelligentsia was a term.hh which had a particular
       political connotation particularly in Europe .hhh where: the Russian
       revolution was .h sparked off 'n- an' supported by the intelligenesia
       the intelligentsia were a group of people who were <u>edu</u>cated...

In (6) neither P's initial interruption, which is marked by <hh> and <pp>,
nor its subsequent expanded repeat on <hh> and <p>, occasions any
prosodic modification in the speech of turn-occupant. Similarly, in (18) U's
interruption (on <h> alone) and the repeat (on <f> alone) do not result in
prosodic changes in S's ongoing speech. In (19) turn-occupant's speech post
interrupter's entry retains the prosodic characteristics established prior to the
onset point. The sense we get of these fragments is that the interrupter is
simply, without urgency, talking along with the extant turn until its
completion whereupon he may unproblematically take the floor with minimal
competition from the other speakers present.

(b) Instances of interruptive speech which are hearable as directly turn-
competitive and which contain reptition or sound sustention involve turn-
occupants effecting prosodic modifications to their speech at points clearly
prior to the onset of the repeated or sustained portion:

(7) TUX, 1: SPA

P: ...if you're a - a woman you learn very quickly to suss out an er i-
interesting or boring man .hhh but if he's interesting (.) .hhhh erm in the
course of a train or a plane jour ⌐ney I can come to no harm/

U: ⌊can spot if he may be an intellectual within fifty heh
yhehards
heh heh/

P: and I can have a fascinating conversation I mean
→ it's a bonus I'm re ⌐garded as (* *)/
  ⌊<dim>⎯⎯⎯⎯|

S:→ ⌊I wonder- I wonder/how they start these things up
  |<h> ⎯⎯⎯⎯⎯⎯●<h>|
  |<f> ⎯⎯⎯⎯⎯⎯●<f>|
(because) I- I- I'm reminded of er reminded of dear Stephen Potter
(who we) referred to earlier (0.2) hhh his technique in railway
carriages he said was to bound in and if the lady was
reading the Times as I imagine you would be ...

(8) TUX, 3: GUA

U: ...by using the word quarrel you're suggesting it's really rather
pointless I mean at least following the - that - you know the
definition we were talking about before it's not really about
anything (.) whereas I mean this was about something .hhh this
was about a point .hhh this was about the chalk coming up
in - on a particular ser:ve in which it was quite clear from the
replay that McEnroe was absolutely right .hhhh
→ now are w ⌐e suggesting-
  ⌊<dim>→

G:→ ⌊I don't thi- I do/n't think you can defend his behaviour
  |<h> ⎯⎯⎯⎯⎯●<h>|
  |<f> ⎯⎯⎯⎯⎯●<f>|
I think you either liked it appreciated it (er) or enjoyed it or
you didn't .hhh erm I think it's probably fair to say
objectively that it's a bit of a cheap shot .hh that he
did take all the conventions of Wimbledon and try and smash
them .hh but of course there's a certain perverse pleasure in
that for the audience ...

(10) TUX, 1: SUB

U: ...the way in which they manage to .hhh convince
themselves there is no such person is by
inventing these radio fun caricatures you've just
been describing bu t (at least) that-/
<dim>

S: but what was always a::::/ (0.3) it
  |<h>   <h>|
  |<f>   <f>|
was always a philistine usage
  (0.4)

176

U: but you keep copping out of answering the
question .hh that...

(c) Instances of interruptions marked by <h+f> which turn-occupants respond to as directly turn-competitive may exhibit no repetition or sound sustention:

(1)   CTB, Z: NKB

K: ...I was- I was gonna ask about those (0,5 'cos (.) in terms of your
stuff about hints in the first thing because it seems to me that
something like .hhhhh Fionna's not letting me have her scissors .hhhh
is as much a threat to Fionna (0.7) as it is a hah hint h to-is a-
is a hint to her father
                     (1.6)|

F: x::

N:→ oh yeah I mean it ⌜'s some sort of-/
                       |<dim> →|
                       |<accel>→|

K:→   ⌊y' know I mean and⁄this is your thing ab ⌜out the/two
                     ⌈<h>————→<h>|
                     |<f>————→<f>|

N: ⌊nyeah/

K: edged (0.4) way that these things work=

N: =nyeah (0.4) nyeah

Unlike <h+f>, then, we have been unable to find evidence that participants systematically orient to either repetitious incomplete syntax or sound sustension in the management of directly turn-competitive interruptions.

6. Concluding remarks: the independence of prosodic features and illocutions

Directly turn-competitive interruptions constitute an analytically manageable subset of overlapping speech. Accepting the methodological precept that analytic claims should be formulated by attention to the orientations of participants, we have attempted to explicate systematic features of their management. In examining the ways in which participants manage directly turn-competitive interruptive speech we have made no reference to the types of conversational acts the interruptions perform. Those contained in our fragments in fact span a variety of such acts. In (2), (8), (9) and (10), for example, interrupter may be heard as producing some form of qualification, correction or disagreement vis-à-vis the point being formulated by turn-occupant. Conversely, in (5) interrupter's activity might be characterised as an elaborated agreement. It appears, then, that direct turn-competition is not consistently associated with any particular type of conversational· act.

177

Further, some of the activities contained in the directly turn-competitive interruptions are performed non-competitively within overlap elsewhere (cf (4) for an in-overlap non-competitive agreement and (6) for a disagreement).

Insofar as interrupters can perform a range of conversational activities either turn-competitively or non-competitively, they might be seen to have an interest in the availability of a device which can both signal the competitive status of an activity and operate independently of any particular activity type. Because any utterance or sequence of utterances can, irrespective of its lexico-syntactic constitution, be produced on high pitch and high volume, <h+f> provides a powerful resource for the achievement of such an interest. Furthermore, as we noted at the outset, in the interruptions we hear as directly turn-competitive one gets a sense that the interrupter urgently requires the floor to himself. In that <h+f> is a prosodic combination, it is not constrained by sequential construction or unfolding. Because of this, it provides a device which interrupters may recognisably deploy right from speech onset thereby making the fact of turn requirement immediately available to co-participants.

Footnotes

1. *A slightly different version of this analysis entitled 'Turn-competitive incomings' appeared in the Journal of Pragmatics VII,i. We are grateful to the Journal for permission to reproduce the analysis here. We would also like to thank Peter Auer, David Crystal, Jane French, Gail Jefferson, Graham McGregor, Bill Wells, Susanne Uhmann, Tony Wootton and members of the Ethnomethodology Study Group at Manchester University for their comments on an earlier version of this analysis.*

2. *The paper is a preliminary report of one part of a continuing research project on the achievement of interactional goals in conversation.*

3. *Conversation Analysis does not comprise a homogeneous set of topical interests or methods of working. General statements about C.A. made here are not intended to be exhaustive or definitive. In particular they should not be seen as speaking on behalf of the tradition as a whole. More extended statements about C.A. interests and methodologies can be found in Button (1977), Chapter One of Atkinson and Drew (1979) and in Wootton (1981a). Heritage (1978) and Leiter (1980) provide accounts of the ethnomethodological tradition of social enquiry from which C.A. emerged.*

4. *An indication of the range of empirical issues C.A. studies have addressed is provided by contributions to Sociology 12, 1, Schenkein (Ed.) (1978) and Psathas (Ed.) (1979). Accounts of the centrality of the work of the late Harvey Sacks in initiating and inspiring interest in the variety of empirical interactional matters can be found in the Introduction and Dedication section of Psathas (Ed.) (1979) and the Preface to Jefferson (1981).*

5. *We deliberately use the terms 'overlapping, interruptive speech' to indicate that the sorts of non-overlapping, thematically contradictory speech that Bennett (1980) considers as interruptive stand outside our immediate interest.*

6. *In order to characterise more fully the speech of the participants we found it necessary to include in our transcription the full range of prosodic features discussed in Crystal (1969). For the purposes of this paper, however, we represent only the subset of the originally transcribed features which is relevant to our discussion (polysyllabicity, pitch height, tempo, loudness and pause variations). The features are marked only at points of speech overlap under consideration.*

7. *It is not always clear whether the speech contained in the in-overlap portions marked <decel> continuously decelerated to termination or whether the deceleration was local to overlap beginning. On occasion we felt that some such portions began slowing down and then continued at slower, but not slowing, pace. However, the tempo variations in these stretches were not so dramatic as to warrant transcription as <decel>... <lento>. The same point applies to portions marked <accel>.*

8. *In addition to <l> and <p>, we have sporadically noted the occurrence in these interruptions of increased vocal tract tension. At present, however, the part played by this feature is unclear.*

Transcription Conventions

The meanings of subscript symbols enclosed in angle brackets which relate to prosodic features of speech are explained in the text. These features are marked only at points relevant to the analysis. In order to give some indication of prosodic/paralinguistic characteristics of speech that occur in portions of the excerpts which do not directly figure in the analysis, we have used the following notations. These derive from the transcription system developed by Dr Gail Jefferson.

The linear array of the transcription owes some debt to the system suggested by Dr Sue Foster (1981). The data were independently transcribed by Peter French and John Local prior to analysis. Any problematic portions or indeterminacies were resolved during careful re-listing by Peter French and John Local jointly.

The transcriptions generally follow the conventions established in the Conversation Analysis literature. Syllabic pitch features are indicated, where necessary for discussion, beneath the orthographic transcription in an impressionistic fashion. The following features of the transcription should be noted.

=   indicates one utterance follows on immediately from another.

(.)   indicates a pause of less than a tenth of a second, other pauses are given in figures; thus (1.2) indicates a pause of one point two seconds.

:   placed after a letter indicates a noticeable lengthening of the sound.

.h   indicates outbreath; the more symbols the longer the inbreath.

h   indicates outbreath; the more symbols the longer the outbreath.

[indicates the point at which overlapping talk begins. The point at which such talk ends is indicated by a slash placed on the ongoing speech.

<f>   placed below a given stretch of talk indicates that it is produced louder (forte) than the speaker's norm.

<p>   placed below a given stretch of talk indicates that it is produced quieter (piano) than that speaker's norm.

<cr>   placed below a given stretch of talk indicates that it is produced with increasing loudness (crescendo).

<l>   placed below a given stretch of talk indicates that it is pronounced more slowly (lento) than the speaker's norm.

...   indicates that preceding talk by that speaker has been omitted.

***   indicates obscure utterance. Each asterisk represents one syllable.

PATTERNS AND PROBLEMS IN A STUDY OF TYNESIDE INTONATION

John K Local

1. Introduction

Recent attempts to describe the organisation of intonation in discourse have exposed many shortcomings in traditional accounts of the work done by 'non-segmental' aspects of speech. On the whole, however, these recent attempts have also been less than satisfactory. There seem to be three main reasons for this. First, researchers have tended to make rather simplistic, monosystemic statements about the relationship of functional (phonological/ discourse) categories to phonetic exponents (e.g. Halliday, 1967). Second, they have failed to build descriptions **inductively** from data (this can be seen for instance in the reluctance of many researchers to warrant, from the behaviour of conversationalists, the functional categories they propose (e.g. Brazil, 1975; Brazil, Coulthard and Johns, 1980; Brown et al, 1980.[1] Third, researchers have often been tempted into making far-reaching generalisations on the basis of rather limited data. This last tendency has led some to formulate implicitly pan-English claims which are simply inaccurate when we examine the structure and functioning of prosodic features in localised varieties of English. The last of these shortcomings will be the focus of this paper. To do this I will begin by outlining in general terms some of the pitch characteristics of localised Tyneside English intonation. I will then consider in some detail the prosodic organisation of 'understanding checks' in localised Tyneside speech.

2. Characteristics of Tyneside Intonation

Varieties of English may differ from each other not only in terms of their segmental phonetics and phonology, lexis and syntax but also in respect of their prosodic characteristics.

There is a growing body of evidence which shows that non-segmental systems exhibit regional and social variation (henceforth *lectal* variation) which parallels that documented for other levels of analysis (e.g. Jarman and Cruttenden (1976); Knowles (1974), and also this volume). The intonational characteristics of different varieties of English may differ in a number of ways. Three central kinds of difference may be found in (a) the pitch inventory and its distributional characteristics, (b) the 'rules' for the realisation of particular intonational units and (c) the ways in which phonological/discourse categories and intonational exponents are related (i.e. the different relationships contracted between the 'same' pitch pattern - say utterance final rises - in different varieties).

The first of these differences has been treated in detail elsewhere (Local, 1982; Pellowe and Jones, 1978) and will not be discussed here. I shall examine here the other two kinds of difference illustrated with material deriving from the Tyneside Linguistic Survey (Pellowe et al, 1972; Strang, 1968). I begin by considering differences which may exist between varieties of English which have to do with the phonetics of particular pitch configurations.

If one attends closely to the phonetics of different varieties of English it soon becomes clear that there are often striking differences in their realisations of such intonational categories as falling tone, rising tone and so on. (See Knowles, 1974; Local and Pearson, 1980). As an illustration of this we can take the category 'rising tone' in localised Tyneside speech. I have selected 'rising tone' for consideration here for two main reasons. First, as I will show below, 'rising tone' occupies a functional place in the tonal system of localised Tyneside speech which is rather different from that occupied by 'rising tones' in other varieties of English. Second, I wish to emphasise the fact that the work of doing a phonology of pitch for English (insofar as that is possible without taking account of other phonetic parameters) involves the analyst in having to identify what, under what conditions, 'counts as *the same thing*" (here the category 'rising tone'). That is, there are not any ready-made, simply identifiable 'tones', they are the result (not the starting-point) of phonological analysis (see Brown et al, 1980, for further discussion of this point).

For simplicity I will not describe in detail the realisation of 'rising tone' in other varieties. Details can be found in Crystal, 1969; Halliday, 1967; and Knowles, 1974. The following fragment exemplifies some of the characteristics of rises in localised Tyneside speech:

(1)   TLS:Gsh

Int: ... well (.) e:: (0.2) to start at the beginning

        (.) e: (0.3) could you tell us (.) where

        you were born please

1   Sh: .hh aha (.) I was born in: em: (.) I

2   was: born in Burn Street

                  (0.5)

Int: yeah (0.2) yes (0.4) and e: (0.5) where

        abouts else have you lived since then you

        know how long did you stay there

                 (0.3)

3   Sh: well (.) till the war (.) and then we

4		were evacuated .hh ⌐h you kn ⌐ow
	Int:	⌊ ⌊mm

	Int:	(1.3) and then where
5	Sh:	and then e:m: (.) wel whench (.) when we
6		were evacuated I had tuberculosis

(0.5)

	Int:	aye

(.)

7	Sh:	I had it off and on for y ⌐ears
	Int:	⌊ mm

8	Sh:	(0.3) you know .hh ⌐h (.) and then I came
	Int:	⌊aye

9	Sh:	home (0.4) started work in the factory (.) you
10		know .h (1.3) and then I had e::: (0.7) I
11		went in: couple of factories (0.3) .hh (.) and
12		then I had tuberculosis again for three year
13		and I was away (0.5) you kno ⌐w
	Int:	⌊mm ⌊mm (2.0) and

	Int:	e:

(.)

14	Sh:	and (.) and then (1.1) came home (.) got
15		married (.) an: had a family

(.)

	Int:	e e: .h how long have you been
		down here

(.)

16	Sh:	.hh we've lived here fourteen year

183

Fragment 1   Rises co-occur with the stretches *Burn Street* (line 2), *war* (line 3), *evacuated* (line 4), *tuberculosis* (line 5), *home* (line 9), *away* (line 13), *home, married, family* (line 14, 15), *year* (line 16).

A first characteristic to note is that unlike rises in some other varieties of English (e.g. those described by Crystal, 1969; Halliday, 1967 etc.) not all of these localised Tyneside 'rises' show continuous rise through the nuclear syllable and, if there is one, through the tail. It is clear that in localised Tyneside the phonological category 'rise' is differently realised according to its placement in the tone unit and the vowel which occurs in the nuclear syllable. Where the tonic syllable is final in the tone unit (e.g. war, home, away, year) the rise is realised as a steady sustained rise in pitch over the syllable. If however the tonic syllable is non-final in the tone unit and is followed by one or more syllables (stressed or unstressed) the characteristics of the rising tone are different. In such cases the nuclear syllable is realised as a sustained level pitch (with crescendo loudness) which then steps up to the next syllable which is produced with level pitch (e.g. *married, family).* The post nuclear level pitch is particularly obvious if the syllable is stressed (e.g. *Burn Street).* If there are a number of post-tonic syllables these are produced on the same pitch level as the syllable after the tonic syllable (e.g. *evacuated).* If the tonic syllable is non-final and contains a **long** vowel the rise is realised as a sustained rise in pitch over the syllable. In such cases post-tonic syllables are realised as described above. Realisational differences such as these and the relative proportions of particular 'tones' (outlined above) give localised Tyneside intonation a very distinctive character which, in the course of the TLS research, was often the subject of lay-comment (Local, 1975; Pellowe, 1980).

The third kind of difference which may exist between varieties of English at the intonational level is to be found when we consider phonological and/or discourse categories and their intonational exponents. Remarkably little work has been pursued on the phonology of intonation in English. Much of what passes for phonology in this domain is little more than taxonomic statement of 'types of pitch' informally associated with intuitively-derived semantic categories (e.g. Crystal, 1969; O'Connor and Arnold, 1961). (But see Wells, this volume; and Local, Wells and Sebba, in preparation.) Lack of space does not permit extended discussion here, nonetheless a brief consideration of rather different roles played by 'nuclear rises' and 'nuclear levels' in localised Tyneside and non-localised varieties will serve to emphasise the need for caution in making phonological statements.

3.1 Intonational Exponents of Phonological Categories

Nuclear rises and levels in localised Tyneside varieties do not expound the same range of phonological/discourse categories as in the non-localised varieties described by, for instance, Crystal and Halliday. One of the functions of rising and level tones in non-localised varieties is to mark that the utterance

184

is 'non-final' (Quirk et al, 1972: 1044) as opposed to falls which mark utterance completeness/finality. Quirk et al comment that rises are used:

> '... when we wish to indicate that our utterance is non-final or that we are leaving it open and inconclusive. This may be because we are counting or listing and have not come to the last item; or because another clause is going to follow'

(Quirk et al (1972: 1044-45)).

Of level tone, Quirk et al note that it 'seems to be a variant of the rise ... and it is used to suggest (often somewhat pompously) the exact predictability of what is to follow ...' (1972: 1045). Fragment 1 (above) and Fragment 2 illustrate some of the rather different phonological/discourse functions which nuclear rises and levels can play in localised Tyneside.

<pre>
(2)   TLS:JH

Int: ... e (.) .h could you tell us first of all where

        you were born please e

                (0.5)

1   H: Gateshead

                (0.2)

Int: e (.) where abouts

                (0.5)

2   H: e::m (0.2) Forster Street (0.7) side

3   Saint Joseph's Church there

Int: .h oh aye (.) its not there now

                (.)

4   H: no (.) n o

Int: (***** *)

5   H: doesn't want to be either

    H: (.) ha ha ha

    Int: ha ha

    Int: ... an e: (0.4) .hh where abouts else have

        you lived since then you know (0.3) em

                (.)
</pre>

6   H: just e: (.) Cumberland Street (0.4) same

7   area

              (.)

   Int: yeah

              (.)

8   H: e: then (0.6) up onto this estate

             (0.6)

   Int: oh I see (.) yeh (.) he: you must of only

          moved up here a couple of years ago (.) did you

          cos t ⌐o (***)

9   H: Lwell five year ago we lived on the:: .h (.) other side

10   of the estate (.) .hh

             (.)

   Int: yeah

11   H: in a:: maisonette

             (0.9)

   Int: I see y ⌐eah

12   H: Land e: f:amily came along (0.7)

13   H: we shifted over here (like)

   Int: oh I see yeah (.) cos

   Int: its its not long since this was completed really

   Int: is this part of it (.) mm (1.5) . hh cos I know

14   H: e:

   Int: I was working on it (.) one (.) two three

          years ago or something

15   H: five year

             (0.5)

   Int: aye

              (.)

```
16    H:    must have been up five year
            ·    ·    ·    ·    ·    ─

      Int:  e: its (.) its certain been that (.) I know
```

Fragment 2   Fragment 1 offers ample evidence that in localised Tyneside speech, unlike the non-localised variety described by Quirk et al, rising tone can and does mark 'utterance completeness'. The first occurrence of rising tone in this fragment (co-occurrent with the words *Burn Street*) exemplifies this. The words *Burn Street* form part of Sh's declarative response to the interviewer's indirect WH-question about her place of birth. That this declarative utterance, with tonic rise, is prosodically complete (i.e. a 'possible completion point' in the sense of Sacks, Schegloff and Jefferson (1977) for localised Tynesiders) can be seen from the fact that both interactants treat it as such. That is, after the rise, the interviewer takes the next turn to ask a further question designed to elicit more talk from Sh.(The interviewer's talk 'yeah (0.2) yes (0.4) and e:' can be heard as acknowledging the information contained in Sh's response to his first question before he proceeds to formulate his next question.) Moreover, Sh herself gives no indication that her turn was incomplete. She does not attempt to produce any more talk after *Burn Street* until the completion of the direct question from the interviewer. She thus does not display (as she could have done by interrupting or talking during the interviewer's turn) that she **had** more to say which had been prematurely curtailed by the interviewer having begun to talk.

The rises which are co-occurrent with *evacuated* (line 4), *away* (line 13) and *year* (line 16) are likewise functioning to indicate (in part) utterance completeness. (Sh's 'you know' post *evacuated* and *away* are clearly post-final tags.) The behaviour of both interactants here too shows orientation to this delimitative function of rising tone in localised Tyneside speech. (Notice too that the stepped-up level co-occurring with *years* (line 7) could, on phonetic and functional grounds, be treated phonologically as a rise.)

Fragment 2 reveals that level tones, as well as rises, can in localised Tyneside act as exponents of utterance finality/completeness. Examples can be found by considering the level tones co-occurring with the words *Gateshead* (line 1), *no* (line 4), *estate* (line 8), *maisonette* (line 11), *here* (line 13), *year* (line 16). As in Fragment 1, the prosodic completeness of these utterances is seen in both the responses of the interviewer and the lack of indication from H that these are anything other than complete. In addition to this Fragment 2 shows that *levels* can also expound some of the functions they expound in non-localised varieties. They may, for instance, be exponents of non-completeness of utterance. Consider the words *em* (line 2), *then* (line 8), *the* (line 9), all of which are realised with level tone and all of which are doing some kind of turn holding non-completeness. (Notice that for this speaker at least these 'non-complete' levels may be formally distinguishable from those which mark possible completion points.) All the 'non-complete' levels in this fragment, where they are preceded by talk from the same speaker, are realised on the same pitch as the preceding syllable. Those level tones which delimit 'complete' utterances are stepped up or down. The matter is not clear, however, and more work is required before this observation can have more than a tentative status.

4. Prosodic Realisation of Understanding Checks

From the foregoing brief survey, it should be clear that the phonetics of localised Tyneside intonation and relationship of exponents to phonological categories differ somewhat from many other varieties of English. I now want to examine in some detail a small part of the working out of such differences by looking at the way 'understanding checks' are done by localised Tynesiders. In doing this I will show (a) that such 'checks' are realised by localised Tyneside speakers with different prosodic features from those reported in the literature for non-localised speakers, and (b) that given such differences of realisation any attempt to discuss the prosodic exponents of discourse or conversational categories must be argued from particular texts and based on the observable orientations of participants. The following fragments illustrate the kind of phenomena I shall be concerned with.

(3)   TLS:DW

McN: ..... e (0.2) varnigh

(3.5)

W: varnigh

(0.4)

McN: aye (1.5) you know for nearly

(1.5)

W: I've never heard it but I've heard me mother use it

(4)   TLS:GSh

McN: ..... e (0.5) cree

(1.2)

Sh: cree

(0.5)

McN: mhm (.) m: um (0.3) pigeon cree or a

(0.5)

Sh: cree o ⌜h yes (.) pigeon cree duc/ket (0.3) he he ho he he

McN: ⌞ aye yes mhm mhm/

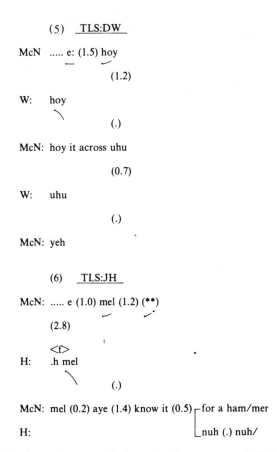

(5)   TLS:DW

McN   ..... e: (1.5) hoy

                    (1.2)

W: hoy

                    (.)

McN: hoy it across uhu

                    (0.7)

W: uhu

                    (.)

McN: yeh

(6)   TLS:JH

McN: ..... e (1.0) mel (1.2) (**)

        (2.8)

        <f>
H: .h mel

                    (.)

McN: mel (0.2) aye (1.4) know it (0.5) ⌐for a ham/mer
H: ⌊nuh (.) nuh/

In part of the interviews carried out in the course of TLS research the interviewer was required to asked the interviewee whether or not they knew, used or had heard used certain putative localised words. These words were presented orally to the interviewee. Frequently, this part of the interview proceeded without problem. However, as Fragments 3-6 indicate, on occasion problems arose in the successful management of this task. In Fragments 3-6 we see that following a 'test word' produced by the interviewer there is a noticeable pause before the interviewee responds. Rather than producing a simple token (say 'yes' or 'no') which would indicate whether or not they recognise the word, the form of interviewee's response is what looks like a repetition of the 'test word'. This is followed in the interviewer's next turn by various formats common to all of which is the presence of some kind of acknowledging or confirmatory token and (in 3,5,8,6) some form of exemplification or clarification of the meaning of the 'test word'. In these interchanges, then, it looks as if the interviewee's turn is 'heard' as doing some kind of work to check that they have heard or understood correctly what the interviewer has said. And in each of these fragments the interviewer offers confirmation that they have.

In the linguistics literature, such repeated utterances as those produced by interviewees in Fragments 3-6 are frequently referred to as 'echo questions', Quirk et al (1972: 408 and following), though this label tells us remarkably little. For the present purposes I use 'understanding checks' as a more appropriate term for the phenomenon (whether the problem lies in the recipient having difficulties determining the phonetics or meaning of what has been said will not be of direct concern here). One reason for adopting this term rather than 'echo question' becomes clear if we consider Fragments 7-10.

(7)   TLS:DW

McN: ... e: (0.2) bairn

         (2.0)

            <f>
W: bed

                    (0.5)

McN: bairn (0.3) little bairn

                 (.)

W: oh bai::rn I thought you sai h.hh (0.5) bairn (.) uhu =

McN: = yeh

(8)   TLS:JH

McN: ..... e (2.5) fettle

         (1.0)

H: chettle

         (0.4)

McN: fet no fettle (0.6) to fettle somebody you know

         (0.2)

H: oh aye (.) yes aye

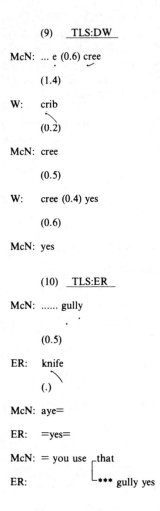

(9)   TLS:DW

McN: ... e (0.6) cree

       (1.4)

W: crib

       (0.2)

McN: cree

       (0.5)

W: cree (0.4) yes

       (0.6)

McN: yes

(10) TLS:ER

McN: ...... gully

       (0.5)

ER: knife

       (.)

McN: aye=

ER: =yes=

McN: = you use ⌈that

ER: ⌊*** gully yes

Here again the interviewee's turn seems to be doing work which elicits from the interviewer a clarification of what word has been said. In these fragments, however, we do not have repetition; in 7-9 the interviewee's utterance can be seen as a malproduction of the test word, while in 10 at this place we find a lexical item which is similar in meaning but not in sound to the test item. Nonetheless the responses of the interviewer in the next turn show similarities to those in this place in Fragments 3-6. That is, he responds in a way appropriate to the interviewee having done an understanding check, which treats his prior utterance as problematic and requires him to clarify what he has said. That the interviewee's turns in all these fragments represent similar objects can also be seen by considering the interviewee's talk subsequent to the understanding check. In all these fragments, the check is done with a single word and the interviewee produces no further talk until after the interviewer's next turn. In each case, the interviewer responds quickly (never longer than 0.5 secs) to confirm/disconfirm the interviewee's version of the test word, always repeating the word where there has been a malproduction. It is only after the interviewer has done this that the interviewee offers any sign of recognition or otherwise of the test item.

A further reason for using the 'understanding checks' term emerges if we consider Fragments 11-15.

(11)   TLS:BC

```
McN:   bray (0.7) for to hi ⌐ t
                              └ <cr>
C:.                           └ bray (0.4) .hhh a ha ha ha ha

C:          .hhhh (0.3) not really I'm very familiar with I

C:        ⌐ have used it

McN:      └ yes    (0.2) but you wouldn't use it now (.) no
```


(12)   TLS:GSh

```
McN:   ... bonny

                      (1.3)

Sh:    bonny aha (0 ⌐.6) I use bonny

McN:               └ aye
```


(13)   TLS:JH

```
McN:   ... e (1.0) clammin (1.0) clammin

                      (0.7)
              <f>
H:     clammin (0.3) a ⌐ ye (0.2) ⌐ definitely (0.2) ⌐ a haye

McN:                   └ mhm       └ yes             └ mhm
```


(14)   TLS:ER

```
McN:   ..... e:m: (0.6) cree

                      (2.6)
              <p>
ER:    cree (1.9) I've heard it

                      (0.2)
```


192

```
McN:   yeh

ER:    mhm (.) cree


(15)   TLS:DW

McN:   ..... e: (.) bait
              ‾  ‾
                    (1.2)

W:     bait (.) mhm hm
       ‾      ‾  .
                 (2.0)

McN:   yeh
```

In all of these, the interviewee repeats the test word but it is clear from the interviewee's subsequent talk and from the placing of the interviewer's talk relative to it that these repetitions are not understanding checks. Notice that even where the interviewee leaves a considerable pause after the repeated test item (as in Fragment 14) the interviewer makes no attempt to come in but waits for further speech from him which will demonstrate recognition. Clearly the interviewee's turns, in Fragments 11-15, are set apart from the kind of work being done by the repetitions and partial repetitions observed in Fragments 3-10. These are, as we might expect, realisational differences between the understanding checks in Fragments 3-10 and those interviewee turns in 11-15. The most interesting of these for my present purposes is to be located in the co-occurrent pitch features of the utterances. (A full discussion of the role of other features in these understanding checks (e.g. pause and loudness phenomena) can be found in Local and French in preparation.)

Pitch features have, of course, been remarked on in discussions of echo questions and clarification requests. For example, Quirk et al remark that 'interrogative echoes bear some of the marks of question classification, in that they can be divided into yes-no and wh-types, the former invariably having **rising** question intonation' (1975: 408, my emphasis). Corsaro too, while discussing three forms of clarification request, notes whole or part utterance repeats with rising intonation. (Compare also the transcripts and comments in Garvey, 1978; Jefferson, 1972; Sacks et al, 1974 and the descriptions in Lindström, 1976). Consideration of the pitch features of the understanding checks produced by these Tynesiders, however, reveals that a *falling* not a *rising* contour is used. To be more precise the contour is a falling one which begins high in the speakers' pitch range and falls to low. Fragments 3-10 share this high to low falling contour. In Fragments 11-15 we find different pitch features realised: 11 has a wide low rise, 12 a rise from mid, 13 a low narrow fall, 14 a low fall and 15 a mid level pitch. (At this stage in analysis it is not clear whether these various pitch movements are in free variation. For further discussion see Local and French in preparation.) An important feature of the

193

pitch characteristics of these understanding checks for Tynesiders is that not only should the fall start high but also that it should end low. We can see this by considering Fragments 16-18 which reveal a somewhat different kind of understanding check.

(16)   TLS:LP

McN: ... bait
             .
                    (2.5)

P: bait h (.) you mean putting lunch e ⌐lunch up and
       ˅   .   .   . .   ˅ |
McN: └mhm
                                              .

P: tha (0.9) well (1.5) wl I don't use i   t I I've/really

McN: you wouldn't use it/

P: got ⌐no:: reason to ⌐use it but me mother used to use it I know that
McN: └(no)   └nm   └yeah   └yeah

(17)   TLS:JH

McN: ..... e (2.4) cree
             .   ─
                    (1.7)

H: cree (.) for hut
               ˅ ─ . ˅
                    (0.2)

McN: aye
                    (0.6)

H: I say hut

(18)   TLS:BC

McN: ..... em: (1.0) gully
             ─   . .
                    (0.6)

C: gully (.) sthat a knife
               ˅ . . ˅
                    (.)

McN: mhm (0.2) ye   ah

C: a gully (.) might do

194

In these fragments the interviewees repeat the 'test word' but here we find a pitch contour which falls to mid or just below mid. After this there is a micropause and then more talk from the interviewee in which they propose a gloss for the test item. In Fragments 16 and 18 the final word in the gloss is realised with the high to low falling pitch movement described earlier. In Fragment 17 this same pitch movement is located on the word *lunch*. In each of these cases the interviewer witholds talking until after this high to low falling pitch movement has begun. He does not attempt to come in with confirmation/disconfirmation or clarification directly after the repeated 'test word' with the high to mid fall. From a functional point of view it appears that the understanding checks in these fragments are different from those in 3-6 for here there is indication in the interviewee's subsequent talk that they have *heard* what was said (i.e. there is not a 'hearing' problem) but are uncertain as to the meaning, and it is specifically the meaning problem which is being presented for resolution. Thus the pitch movement co-occurrent with the repeated 'test word' is not hearable as a 'check', rather as a preface to a check. Certainly this behaviour of the interviewer could be taken to support such an analysis. Such behaviour on the part of the interviewer indicates the interactional salience of the pitch of the end-point of the fall. From this it looks as if end-point of fall has relevance for a system of delimitation wherein falls to low indicate finality (cf Fragments 3-10, where falls from high to low are co-extensive with end-point of the interviewee's turn) while falls to non-low are implicative of non-finality.

The foregoing data show that in particular circumstances 'repeats' or 'echoes' of words can, for localised Tynesiders, be functionally distinct (i.e. can be 'checks' or 'non-checks'). In itself this is neither surprising nor interesting. What is of interest is the **exponents** of such a functional distinction. In contrast with many varieties of English, localised Tynesiders do 'checks' with a falling pitch contour and non-checks with a wide range of pitch types. As with most things of linguistic interest, however, it is not the case that all functionally similar entities have the same exponents. Thus for the same Tyneside speakers where an understanding check is done containing a WH-word for the item being checked the pitch contour used is (as in non-localised English) a rising one. Consider Fragments 19-21.

(19)   TLS:JH

McN: ... I'm gann to stay with the son for the holidays

          (1.0)

H: uh you ganin where

          (0.2)

McN: I'm gann to stay with the son for the holidays

195

(20)   TLS:JH

McN: .... Jack didn't think much to the race

(1.1)

H: Jack (0.3) didn't think much to the what

(0.4)

McN: to the race

(0.4)

H: to the rain

(0.5)

McN: the race

(0.4)

H: .h oh no (.) no

(21)   TLS:BC

McN: ... never mind I'll manage but =

C: = never mind I'll manage what

(.)

McN: I'll manage but

(0.4)

C: but (.) yes that's fine

These fragments derive from part of the TLS research which required interviewees to say whether or not they found certain syntactic constructions 'acceptable'. In each case after a presentation of the original utterance the interviewee partially repeats the utterance but explicitly questions (by using 'what', 'where') a further part of the original. In all of these fragments, the interviewer's next turn is formulated as a whole or repeat of his initial turn.

This apparent overlap with non-localised intonation exponents at this point is interesting ('apparent' because in these fragments the rise is stepped up from the preceding syllable - I do not know whether this is also the case for non-localised varieties). It is of interest because it points to the need for caution in stating the exponents of phonological/discourse functions (i.e. high to low falls for checks other than those containing a focussed WH-word). Such caution occasioned the approach that I have employed in the latter part

196

of this paper. The approach, generally that called conversation analysis, may appear tortuous and nit-picking. However, if we are to understand clearly the relationship of intonational exponents to categories/functions then clearly close attention to detail (both phonetic and interactive) is required. It is not possible to specify functional properties of intonational features in a given variety until we have information concerning the distribution and status of those features within varieties. Such facts can only be gleaned from very detailed analysis of detailed phonetic transcription (see Wells this volume for further discussion of this issue). An examination of localised varieties (such as I have presented here) which have variant intonation features is crucially important if we are to make sense of the structure and functioning of intonation in English.

Footnotes:

1. *Brazil provides no evidence to show, for instance, that his proposed 3-way 'key' choice (9ff) has relevance for conversational participants. Nor does he make clear whether his formalisation of the notion of 'key' (why a 3-way choice anyway?) is intuited or derives analytically from the observable behaviour of interactants. Indeed he eschews such a procedure, for when writing in general about his approach he says:*

    'I shall use invented examples by way of illustration ... The task of demonstrating each point convincingly from data would be a protracted and tortuous business, and the attempt would probably obscure the lines of a pattern I am immediately concerned to illuminate.'

    A similar observation can be made about Brown et al when, for example, they invoke functional notions such as 'delimitative marking' (157-161) and 'conducive question' (30, 177-180) in their description. These notions are asserted as being relevant rather than argued for inductively on the basis of specific instances in the data. Moreover it is not clear what status such 'evidence' as they do produce is intended to have. Nor is it clear whether the functional notions they employ are apriori categories or derive analytically from data based observations.

2. *The reader is referred to Gussenhoven's paper, in this volume, for a full discussion of tone types.*

3. *The transcriptions generally follow the conventions established in the Conversation Analysis literature. Syllabic pitch features are indicated, where necessary for discussion, beneath the orthographic transcription in an impressionistic fashion. See below for transcription conventions.*

4. *Thanks to Peter French, John Kelly and Bill Wells for comments and criticisms.*

The transcriptions generally follow the conventions established in the Conversation Analysis literature. Syllabic pitch features are indicated, where necessary for discussion, beneath the orthographic transcription in an impressionistic fashion. The following features of the transcription should be noted.

=   indicates one utterance follows on immediately from another.

(.)   indicates a pause of less than a tenth of a second, other pauses are given in figures; thus (1.2) indicates a pause of one point two seconds.

:   placed after a letter indicates a noticeable lengthening of the sound.

.h   indicates outbreath; the more symbols the longer the inbreath.

h   indicates outbreath; the more symbols the longer the outbreath.

[indicates the point at which overlapping talk begins. The point at which such talk ends is indicated by a slash placed on the ongoing speech.

<f>   placed below a given stretch of talk indicates that it is produced louder (forte) than the speaker's norm.

<p>   placed below a given stretch of talk indicates that it is produced quieter (piano) than that speaker's norm.

<cr>   placed below a given stretch of talk indicates that it is produced with increasing loudness (crescendo).

<l>   placed below a given stretch of talk indicates that it is pronounced more slowly (lento) than the speaker's norm.

...   indicates that preceding talk by that speaker has been omitted.

***   indicates obscure utterance. Each asterisk represents one syllable.

PROSODIC DIFFERENTIATION OF DISCOURSE MODES

Catherine M Johns-Lewis

1.0 Introduction

Some prosodic characteristics of **spontaneous speech** have received considerable attention. Those that have been investigated include: the relationship between **slips of the tongue and prosody** (Boomer and Laver, 1968; Fromkin, 1973, 1980; Cutler, 1982, 1983); **pauses** (Boomer and Dittman, 1962; Maclay and Osgood, 1959; Goldman-Eisler, 1968; Clemmer, O'Connel and Loui, 1979; Beattie and Butterworth, 1979; Butterworth, 1980a; Duez, 1982); **acoustic bases for speaker recognition** based on long-term spectral properties (Atal, 1972; Larivière, 1975; Hollien and Majewski, 1977; Horii, 1975, 1979; Laver, 1980; Nolan, 1983; Millar and Wagner, 1983); **pitch as an indicator of discourse structure** (Lehiste, 1975, 1978, 1979; Ladd, 1980; Coulthard and Brazil, 1981; Menn and Boyce, 1982); **social and physical determinants of pitch** (Laver and Trudgill, 1979; Lass et al, 1980; Loveday, 1981; Graddol and Swann, 1983; Graddol, this volume); and **kinesics in relation to linguistic systems and pausing** (Gosling, 1981; Ragsdale and Silvia, 1982).

Relatively less attention has been paid to the prosodic differences between **contrasting** discourse modes. (The term discourse mode is used as an amalgam of the sense in which Hymes (1972: 65) uses the term *'genre'* (prayer, lecture, poem, etc.), and of Crystal and Davy's (1969: 74-76) term *modality* (radio, news report, live commentary, interview).) While the **segmental phonetic** differences between casual and careful styles of speech are relatively well understood, as far as English is concerned (see Brown, 1977; and see also comments on Labov, 1972, and others, in Section 1.2), it is true to say that **prosodic** differences between different discourse modes are less well understood.

1.1 Prosodic characteristics of discourse modes: background

Eight studies in the literature on prosodic characteristics of discourse modes will be commented on: Crystal and Davy (1969); Goldman-Eisler (1968); Grosjean and Deschamps (1973); Fonagy (1978); Barik (1979); Duez (1982); Levin, Schaffer and Snow (1982); and Graddol (this volume).

The most comprehensive, in terms of identifying prosodic dimensions along which speaking styles vary, is Crystal and Quirk (1964), which is elaborated and applied to the prosodic and stylistic analysis of spoken texts in Crystal and Davy (1969).

Crystal and Davy identify a number of prosodic dimensions along which speaking styles vary: intonation (involving nuclear placement, boundary location and tone choice); pitch range; loudness; tempo; rhythmicality; tension; and voice quality (the latter Crystal and Quirk, 1964, term *paralinguistic effects*). They note (p 106-109) that **conversation** has certain recurrent prosodic features:

- relatively standardised, narrow pitch contours for many of the monosyllabic response utterances
- high proportion of falling tones
- 'stepping down' heads within tone units (gradually descending syllables from onset to nucleus)
- tendency for short tone units (one to five words)
- tendency for many tone units to be incomplete, and to tail off (diminuendo effect)
- use of silence for contrast, as opposed to breath-intake
- frequent use of voiced hesitation (um, er, etc.)
- uneven tempo within and between utterances

There are a number of comments scattered throughout the book which indicate an awareness of what is prosodically distinctive for a particular mode. For instance, they mention (p 109) the shortness of tone units in **unscripted commentary** (cricket and state funeral commentaries, pp 126-130); the frequency of level tones in the **state funeral commentary**; the absence of voiced hesitation; lengthy, coherent intonational sequences which terminate with a marked (extra low or extra wide falling) contour indicating finality; comparatively slow speed of utterance; use of a relatively narrow pitch range for individual tone units, but within a long pitch sequence with a high start and an extremely low end point (p 131); and use of highly varied pitch patterns - much more varied than conversation.

They note that **the cricket commentary** has long tone units containing up to 10 words, whereas the state funeral commentary has 1 to 6 words per tone unit and is thus (my emphasis) **reminiscent of English that is being read aloud from a written version** (p 133).

Crystal and Davy draw attention to a feature shared by both types of commentary: the phonological differentiation between "the language used to describe important parts of the action, and that used for filling in the background". They suggest that the transition from "action" to "background" is marked prosodically, but the degree and nature of the marking will vary between sports such as horse-racing, which may produce a lengthy buildup to one major climax; soccer, in which the activity is continuous but interspersed with many local climaxes and tennis or cricket, where the structure of the game ensures that bursts of activity will alternate with quiet spells (p 134-135).

Prosodic marking out of "action" is achieved, they suggest, through use of rate (accelerando), loudness (crescendo), stress (staccato), pitch range (wide), which combine to produce dramatic effect.

The discussion on religious language differentiates between **unison liturgical prayer**, where tone and rhythmicality are noted as the defining prosodic characteristics, and **speaking a prayer aloud**, with one person performing, which involves 'narrowness of pitch range, high frequency of level tones, gradual descent of pitch at the end, a tendency to keep units short and rhythm isochronous, together with an absence of marked prosodic or paralinguistic features common in other varieties'.

The section on public speaking in Ch 9 presents extracts from a **sermon**, a **lecture**, a **formal radio discussion** and a **formal speech**. The exercises imply that there are answers to the questions:
- How could one tell clearly that this was written English read aloud (cf. pause and speed systems in particular)?
- Examine in detail the way in which the pitch range system is used....
The implications of the questions are not discussed, however.

In a similar way, Section 7 (Ch 9) on **broadcast talks and news** (i.e. reading aloud) presents questions on prosodic features which have implications for a full taxonomy of discourse modes, including:

> "What evidence of informality is there? (Consider the pause system of Text I in particular. Also, what aspects of the prosodic system would *not* be indicated in the punctuated script?) ...... (Consider the way in which each topic is given its own speech 'paragraph' ... primarily through the use of prosodic features.)

> Crystal and Davy (1969:247)

Crystal and Davy do not compare each of the selected texts on each prosodic dimension (intonation, pitch range, loudness, tempo, rhythmicality, tension and voice quality); at least, they do not do so in a systematic way. Nevertheless, their detailed observations of speaking styles serve as a useful point of departure for comparative work.

Goldman-Eisler's (1968) study[1] examines pause and speech rate in two styles: **spontaneous speech** (discussion, description of cartoons, and interviews) and **reading aloud**. She found that breaths are located at grammatical junctures in 100 per cent of cases in reading aloud, but only in 69 per cent of cases in spontaneous speech. She also found that pausing is sensitive to the requirements of different verbal tasks, **increases** with semantic complexity, and **decreases** with learning or rehearsal of matter spoken. At the sixth repetition, of a description, subjects made about half as many pauses as at the first repetition.

Grosjean and Deschamps (1973), comparing pauses in interviews and in descriptions of visually presented material reached conclusions similar to those of Goldman-Eisler: in descriptions of visual material, pauses are more frequent than in interviews. It would seem that subjects require more time to decode an image and encode it linguistically, than they do to construct linguistic output in interviews.

The study by Fonagy (1978) falls into two parts. The first part reports on a laryngographic study of fundamental frequency in ten texts, each exemplifying one of ten emotions: 1) tenderness 2) anger 3) repressed anger 4) joy 5) fear 6) sadness 7) coquetry 8) disdain 9) longing 10) reproach. The passages were **read aloud** by an actress three times, and three judges selected the rendering that best represented the emotion.

Fonagy then examined fundamental frequency in the 10 samples. He found that

"... joy was characterised by a high pitch-level and large melodic intervals; a low average pitch-level and narrow intervals correlated with sorrow; fear was reflected in mid-high pitch level and reduced intervals."

Fonagy (1978:35)

In the second part of his study, he presented the laryngographic recordings of the ten texts to 58 students. The subjects were able to detect the intended emotion with significant accuracy. However, although he demonstrates that the speaker in question was judged to be marking the intended emotions in the 10 texts, it does not follow that the prosodic features quoted above do in fact generally signify these emotions. If a larger sample of speakers all exhibited the features in question, there would be some justification for concluding that 'those features are the prosodic features of the emotion in question'.

Fonagy went on to report a perception experiment involving laryngographic recordings of a) a lyrical poem (Verlaine) b) a tragedy (Corneille) c) a fairy- tale (Perrault) and d) a conversation, all spoken by the same actress who recorded the 10 emotionally contrasting texts. The recordings were presented to 42 students, who were able to identify the genres of communication significantly more often than chance. Although it is clear from his results that prosodic information is sufficient for accurate categorisation, it is not possible to identify the role of different parameters (intonation, pitch range, pause, rate, voice quality, etc.) in identifying genres. Fonagy suggests that speech synthesis might separate out these parameters.

The study by Barik (1979) reports a comparison of prosodic features in four contrasting speech styles:

- **spontaneous speech** (story-telling based on a picture; discussion of a film)
- **semi-prepared material** (lecture, prepared but not read aloud)
- **prepared material** (live translation into French of a non-technical speech in English)
- **reading aloud** (formal, non-technical article).

He compared male speakers operating in these modes in English and in French. It is assumed that the speakers were native speakers of French, and native speakers of English, although this is not stated, but the inclusion of translation raises some doubt as to whether the English material was also produced by the same (native) speakers of French who produced the French texts. For the **English material**, the same speaker recorded the **story** and the **written text read aloud**, *the other types being produced by a different speaker.* For the **French material**, all the texts **except the lecture** were rendered by the same individual.

The use of different speakers as source for the contrasted modes is somewhat incautious, in view of reported differences between speakers as regards the duration and distribution of pauses (Goldman-Eisler, 1968: 15). The question of the familiarity of the speaking task, which also has a marked effect on the duration and location of pauses (Goldman-Eisler, op. cit.), is not taken into account.

The use of different speakers for different discourse modes raises some doubts about the reliability of the cross-mode comparisons. The results for French are probably less open to doubt than the results for English, in that only the lecture mode figures[2] were not derived from the same speaker. There is certainly a clear indication that for the single speaker who provided three of the modes (ignoring the lecture material), speech to pause duration, mean pause duration, speech rate and proportion of pauses at grammatical junctures are likely to be diagnostic of discourse mode.

	Story	Film	Lecture	Speech	Written Text
Speech duration %	43.5	56.9	81.6	67.4	71.6
Pause duration %	56.5	43.1	18.4	32.6	28.4
Mean Pause duraton (sec)	2.06	1.48	0.96	1.22	1.24
Speech rate (syll/min)	131.8	174.0	209.1	183.3	204.8
Pauses at grammatical juncture %	88.6	53.6	60.0	93.4	85.4

Extract from Barik (1979: 110) Table 1

Further investigation of the contrasting modes, using a larger population as data base, and ensuring that the same speaker provides the modes contrasted, is obviously desirable.

Duez (1982) analysed the frequency, duration and distribution of pauses in three discourse modes in French: **political speeches, political interviews** and **casual interviews**. She found that non-silent pauses are significantly longer in casual interviews than in political interviews. She suggests that this may be because in casual interviews, the lack of constraints on the speaker allows him to spend more time in false starts, hesitations, etc. She also found that articulation rate differed in the three modes, the fastest being political speeches, casual interviews being slowest, with political interviews intervening. This represents a hierarchy of degrees of practice. The fluency effect in political speeches is also reflected in the near total absence of non-silent pauses in political speeches.

Her results cannot be directly compared to Barik's (1979), because different modes were studied under different conditions. Taken together, however, the work of Duez and Barik indicate that the speech to silence ratio is likely to be higher (of the order of 80:20%) in public oratory and interview than it is in speech involving reflective interpretation (44:56%).

Duez's study unfortunately has the same weakness as Barik's: the data for cross-mode comparison derives from different sets of individuals, so that, although the inter-speaker differences are clear, there is less certainty about the cross-mode differences.

The study by Levin, Schaffer and Snow (1982) contrasted the prosodic characteristics of **reading aloud** as opposed to **telling a story**. Four teachers were recorded reading aloud a story to pre-school children, and then telling the same story. The reading and telling recordings were treated with a low pass filter removing frequencies above 312Hz, and filtered and unfiltered extracts then provided the material for a perception experiment.

They found that listeners could tell with great accuracy whether a speaker was reading aloud or telling a story, even when segmental (and therefore lexical, and syntactic) information had been removed.

They examined some of the cues for identification of mode. **Speech rate** was slower in telling than in reading aloud, for all four teachers, by an average of 11.1%.[3] In Barik's data, on the other hand, for the French speaker who provided the story and read aloud text, the speaking rate in the story mode is some 36% slower than in the reading aloud task. The smaller difference between the two modes for the teachers studied by Levin et al may be the result of the practice effect noted by Goldman-Eisler, the teachers having no doubt told the same children's story on other occasions.

Another possible cue for the recognition of mode is **pause**. They report that they had insufficient pause data to do statistical analysis of the differences between modes. However, they suggest that story telling seemed to contain more long pauses than reading; and more of these pauses tended to occur within rather than at grammatical boundaries. They also note that story telling seemed to contain more fillers, false starts, repetitions, concatenatives and non-literary words. These comments are in general agreement with Goldman-Eisler's (1968) data on reading aloud as opposed to spontaneous speech, where she notes that pauses tend to occur at grammatical junctures more often in reading aloud than in spontaneous speech.

The study by Graddol (this volume) explores the contrasting **pitch characteristics** of males and females operating in two discourse modes. His subjects **read aloud** two kinds of text: **neutral technical prose**, and **dramatic dialogue.** Graddol demonstrates that the pitch characteristics of the perform-ance of the technical prose are significantly different from those of dramatic dialogue, as measured in terms of mean, standard deviation, range, skew and kurtosis of fundamental frequency. He also shows that females use a greater proportion of their potential pitch range than males, and suggests that there are important social conditioning forces which constrain males to operate within a narrower band of their pitch potential.

1.2 Sociolinguistic Studies of Speech Style

Sociolinguistic evidence for the effect of context on speech style is overwhelming. Variation in speech style is well documented at the segmental level (Labov, 1972; Trudgill, 1974; Trudgill, 1978; Milroy, 1980); and at the syntactic level (Labov, 1972; Cheshire, 1982; Platt, 1977). (Variation at the syntactic level is also likely - for instance in relativisation and sentence conjunction - but it is questionable whether discourse level variation can be treated in the same way as phonological variation.) Variationist studies on languages as far apart as Farsi, Jamaican Creole and Welsh have brought to public attention the variable nature of speech performance.

Studies of intonational variability are relatively rare (see Pellowe and Jones, 1978; Knowles, 1978; Brown et al, 1980 ; and Local, this volume). None operate within the variationist paradigm: i.e. none assume a stable variable with determinable linguistic meaning, and with hierarchically ranked variants (ranked, that is, for prestige). Rather, they follow the procedure of describing general prosodic characteristics of the speech of pre-defined socio-economic groups. Laver (1980:6), for instance, comments on Norwich working class speakers who use articulatory settings distinct from those of middle class speakers:

... creaky phonation, a high pitch range, a loud loudness range, a fronted and lowered tongue position, a particular type of nasality and a high degree of muscular tension throughout the vocal apparatus.

(Trudgill, 1974: 186-7; Laver and Trudgill, 1979)

Thus, although sociolinguistic studies of prosodic phenomena exist, they do not rely on the variable as a tool for quantitative statements. They do share with segmental studies, however, certain characteristics which set them apart from **prosodic studies of discourse mode** such as those summarised in Section 1.1. A comparison of **sociolinguistic studies of speech style** with **prosodic studies of discourse mode** shows two major differences:

1. Sociolinguistic investigations normally control for non-linguistic variables (e.g. age, network strength score, socio-economic class, etc.) in speakers selected. Studies of prosodic differences between discourse modes, such as those described in Section 1.1, have tended to select "speakers of the prestige norm" and often fail to give information about subjects which could be significant. Barik (1979), for instance, makes no mention of the occupation of the speakers who acted as source of different discourse modes. But a speaker's familiarity, or non-familiarity with the task of telling a story, or giving a lecture, or reading a dense prose text aloud could have a significant effect on speaking rate, pause length and distribution, and general fluency, as Goldman-Eisler (1968) points out. Only Duez (1982), and Levin, Schaffer and Snow (1982) seek out a well defined social group (politicians and teachers respectively) for whom the speaking tasks in question represent a well-rehearsed, familiar activity.

2. Sociolinguistic studies are normally based on fairly large groups (at least 20 subjects, in most cases), whereas work on the prosodic differentiation of discourse modes has tended to involve quite small populations: one for each discourse mode in Crystal and Davy (1969); one for each discourse mode (or nearly one for all discourse modes) in Barik (1979); six speakers for political speeches, five for political interviews, and four for casual interviews in Duez (1982); and four speakers (all teachers) in Levin, Schaffer and Snow's (1982) study. Only Graddol (this volume) has a large population (30 speakers) as a data base for his study of pitch in discourse mode differentiation.

There is clearly a problem, in that instrumental measurement of large numbers of speakers is expensive and time consuming. But without larger population bases, prosodic comparisons of discourse mode to date have lacked generalisability across even one socially well-defined group.

Comparison of work on prosodic differentiation of discourse modes with sociolinguistic studies of distinguishable speech styles suggests that we ought to give consideration to the following criteria in research design:-

1. **Selection**: Control of non-linguistic variables (e.g. occupation)

2. **Authenticity**: Familiarity of speaking task for individuals (i.e. previous experience of discourse mode)

3. **Generalisability**: representativeness of selected individuals of socially defined groups.

These three criteria were regarded as relevant in setting up samples of contrasting discourse modes to form a basis for prosodic comparison, which is described in Section 3.0.

Before presenting the results of the experimental study, however, some discussion of a framework of reference for discourse modes is necessary.

2.0 Discourse Modes: The Place of Taxonomy

It might be an advantage if experimentation on the production and perception of discourse modes could take place in the context of a well worked out taxonomy of spoken discourse.

What existing schemes are there for classifying discourse? Three types of taxonomy will be commented on: Ethnography, Speech Act Theory and Rhetoric.

Ethnography, while rich in detailed observation, has not progressed beyond sporadic and incomplete listing of kinds of speech event (e.g. *verbal duelling, riddles, jokes, ritual insults, stories by children, prayers, orations, lectures*). As Hymes (1972) himself says, these are **instances of genres**, and listing them is not equivalent to presenting a comprehensive taxonomy of types of speech activity in our own society.

Speech Act theory, as developed by Searle (1969, 1975) has been criticised for, among other things, its confusion of linguistic expressions and acts performed by speakers; for its lack of a consistent basis for classification; for its assumptions about speaker intention (Ballmer and Brennenstuhl, 1981); for its lack of principled evaluation of competing classifications (Levinson, 1983); and for the lack of match between levels based on linguistic expressions and actual purposes in human interaction (Stubbs, 1983). In spite of attempts to make Speech Act theory more exhaustive in classification coverage, and more accountable to users' perceptions (see Kreckel, 1981), it is clear that it cannot provide a basis for classification of discourse modes. It represents analysis at a lower level of generality than the notion of modes or styles. Discourse modes cannot be differentiated by reference to their Speech Act composition, since the same speech act (e.g. *belittling, insulting*) can occur in several discourse modes (e.g. *riddles, stories, lectures*).

207

Rhetoric provides classification schemes which are all, essentially, based on written texts. They typically present schemes based on author's purpose (or perceived purpose), and typically present categories such as *definition, classification, comparison, narration, description, process, cause and effect, and evaluation*. (See Brewer, 1980; Faigley and Meyer, 1983; and Calfee and Curley, 1984.) But such categories are set up to account for expository prose. They do not represent all varieties possible in the written mode (telegram, memo, report, article, letter, note, etc.): i.e. Crystal and Davy's (1969:74) *modalities* within the written mode. Even less do they represent all modes of discourse within the spoken dimension.

Varieties possible in the spoken mode[4] include the distant correlatives of Crystal and Davy's modalities: *public lecture, political interview, political speech, radio phone-in, cassette letter, telephone recorded message, pedagogic interaction*, etc.

It is not clear at the present which parameters a taxonomy will have to take account of. The *spontaneous/non-spontaneous* distinction masks degrees of preparedness, from the impromptu, to the apparently unscripted but actually well-rehearsed. A second parameter, involving variation along the *public/ private dimension* is probably also relevant. So too is the relative *status and expertise of speaker* vis-à-vis audience.

A full and comprehensive taxonomy of discourse modes does not at this moment exist, and is certainly beyond the scope of this paper. However, the vagueness of many of the ad hoc terms used in work on discourse modes is a disadvantage. It is not even clear that we know what is meant by the term *conversation*. McGregor (1984) discusses the versatility of the term, and cites examples of *conversational exchange* in the literature:

> ... job interviews, telephone calls, jokes and story-telling episodes, teacher-pupil exchanges, and a range of recorded psychiatric, psychotherapeutic and psycho-logical investigative activities.
>
> McGregor (1984:73)

The absence of a fully worked-out, comprehensive taxonomy is not a reason for those with an interest in prosodic differentiation of modes to wait until such a taxonomy exists. On the contrary, it is a reason for prosodic studies of modes to be undertaken. The methodological principle needs to be established that prosodic studies of spoken discourse can provide at least one basis for organising a taxonomy of spoken texts, by relating discourse modes to each other along several prosodic dimensions at once, thus facilitating comparison of shared and non-shared features.

The prosodic features of spoken discourse which research can investigate include at least those enumerated by Crystal and Quirk (1964) or Crystal and Davy (1969): tone-unit (length, distribution, structure), tone choice, pitch range, prominence/ stress, loudness, rate, rhythmicality, pause, tension and paralinguistic/voice quality features.

3.0 Pitch[5] in Three Discourse Modes

Previous work on fundamental frequency in different types of text has focussed on the characteristics of texts conveying different emotions. Fonagy (1978) compares fundamental frequency (Fo) tendencies in 10 texts, exemplifying: 1) tenderness 2) anger 3) repressed anger 4) joy 5) fear 6) sadness 7) coquetry 8) disdain 9) longing 10) reproach, each text having been rendered by the same speaker. (For a full description of Fonagy's study, see Section 1.1.) In contrast, Graddol (this volume) examines Fo characteristics in two contrasting texts read aloud: a neutral technical prose text, and a dialogue. Graddol examines Fo trends in terms of mean, range, skew and kurtosis, and concludes that there are significant statistical differences between the two text types. (See Section 1.1 for additional comments on his study.)

The study reported here examined Fo in three discourse modes: **reading aloud, acting,** and **conversation**. The purpose of the three-way comparison was to analyse the Fo realisation of two dimensions in discourse mode differentiation: in **rehearsed** and **unrehearsed** material, and in material intended for **public multiple audience** (acting and reading aloud), as opposed to material intended for a **private, unique audience** (conversation).

3.1 Experimental Design

3.1.1 Material

The text **read aloud** was a short, self-contained prose narrative, and was adapted from a biographical account of childhood memories (see Appendix I). It was designed to last approximately 30 seconds in speaking time. The **acted** text was a constructed monologue (see Appendix II), which was designed to be interactive, but to have non-verbal input from the second party. This was to obviate the need for editing out everything other than the performance of the actor. Speakers were asked to act the text as if they were participating in a radio play. The **conversation** involved each speaker who produced the read aloud text and the acted text talking informally with the analyst in the recording setting. A certain amount of prompting by the analyst was necessary to get the conversation going, and after the first five minutes approximately, the talk alternated between *free exchange*[6] typical of symmetrical status participants (in which both parties feel relatively unconstrained about initiating a turn) and *constrained exchange* more typical of interview situations where one party feels relatively constrained about initiating a turn, by the status of the interviewer.

3.1.2 Speakers

Sixteen amateur actors, eight males and eight females, aged 24-49 provided the recordings. Each had taken part in at least five theatre productions, and several had experience of radio drama as well. They were asked to assist with a study of speaking styles by reading aloud the prepared narrative text in Appendix I; to act the memorised dramatic monologue in Appendix II, with no textual aid; and to talk informally with the analyst, as described above. A subset of the ten best speakers of the original 16 was selected, who represented the "best acting voices", in the view of a panel of three judges, all of whom were non-linguists with an interest in theatre.

3.1.3 Recording

The recordings were made in a very quiet sound-proofed (but not anechoic) room, with the microphone about 4 ins. (10cm) from the speaker's mouth. The tape recorder, a Dolby Super Seven Ferrograph (Half Track), was in an adjacent room on a direct connection lead, in order to eliminate recording hum as far as possible, and the recordings were made at 15 ins. (37.5cm)/ second.

3.1.4 Method of Analysis

The speech signal was fed through a 12 bit analogue to digital converter to a mini-computer installation[7] (Automation Alpha 2/40, produced by Cambridge Electronic Design). After low pass filtering (cut-off level at 4.5kHz), the signal was analysed at a sampling rate of 10KHz using an auto-correlation algorithm developed by Dubnowski, Schafer and Rabiner (1976). The algorithm includes a subroutine for correction of pitch doubling and pitch halving, which occurs when higher harmonics are dominant, and close to the frequency of the fundamental. While this subroutine is probably successful in smoothing out some false Fo readings, it is unlikely that all errors were eliminated.

Autocorrelation, like other short-term analysis Fo determination algorithms, provides a sequence of average estimates of Fo, but does so by measuring the similarity between two input functions: in this case the same signal correlated with itself, such that the lag forms the parameter of the autocorrelation function. The technique is based on finding the second peak of the autocorrelation function, the shift at which this peak occurs giving the pitch period. Autocorrelation algorithms have shortcomings which can be compensated for by pre-processing the signal, and in this case, centre clipping and infinite peak clipping was used. This process is claimed to be one of the most reliable (Hess, 1983:470).

3.1.5 Results

The software available for processing the results did not, unfortunately, include programs for calculating range, skew and kurtosis. Only mean and standard deviation values were derived.

The mean Fo value and standard deviation for each speaker, for each of the three discourse modes, is presented in Table 1.

		Time (Sec)	Mean Fo (Hz)	SD (Hz)
MALES				
READING	MG	33.2	96.5	26.3
ALOUD	DM	25.5	126.3	26.1
	IR	27.6	126.9	31.6
	TP	25.8	182.3	46.1
	AT	26.0	108.3	27.6
ACTING	MG	35.0	118.4	31.7
	DM	32.5	152.4	45.9
	IR	36.5	130.4	34.3
	TP	33.5	176.1	38.6
	AT	30.5	133.9	42.9
CONVERSATION	MG	30.0	100.8	29.7
	DM	30.0	116.9	21.2
	IR	30.0	98.9	14.4
	TP	30.0	100.8	21.1
	AT	30.0	86.3	11.6
FEMALES				
READING	JH	25.2	181.6	46.8
ALOUD	SB	26.8	192.5	46.2
	MD	29.8	256.6	73.3
	JT	25.8	209.0	55.0
	CC	31.8	226.2	49.2
ACTING	JH	27.0	204.4	49.7
	SB	27.0	218.5	69.9
	MD	28.4	288.5	94.9
	JT	27.5	248.9	87.3
	CC	36.2	239.0	55.4
CONVERSATION	JH	30.0	166.4	22.4
	SB	30.0	184.4	30.7
	MD	30.0	166.3	18.7
	JT	30.0	191.2	27.7
	CC	30.0	203.0	30.6

Table 1 Fo and SD (in Hz) for individual males and females in three discourse modes.

By averaging the mean Fo across all five male speakers, and across all five female speakers, for the three discourse modes, it is possible to see the relative Fo ranking of discourse modes.

	MALES		FEMALES	
	Mean Fo (Hz)	Mean SD (Hz)	Mean Fo (Hz)	Mean SD (Hz)
READING ALOUD	128.06	31.54	213.18	54.10
ACTING	142.24	38.68	239.86	71.44
CONVERSATION	100.74	19.60	182.26	28.02

Table 2   Mean Fo (in Hz) for grouped males and females in 3 discourse modes.

3.1.6 Discussion of Results

The Fo values for **males** are significantly higher for **acting**, than for **reading aloud**, and significantly higher for **reading aloud** than for **conversation**. ($p<.001$, with 2 df.) Exactly this ranking is reflected in the Fo values for **females**. Although the statistical analysis did not set out to analyse Fo *range* directly, the SD values give an indication of fluctuations around the mean[8]. It can be seen that the fluctuations around the mean are greatest for **acting**, as far as **males** are concerned, with the next highest in terms of range being **reading aloud**, and **conversation** involving the **smallest variation around the mean**: approximately half that of acting. For **females**, the mean SD for **acting** is highest, being approximately two and a half times the mean SD for **conversation**. Thus, we find independent evidence to substantiate Graddol's claim (this volume) that females make greater use of their pitch potential. His data showed that they make proportionately greater excursions from their pitch baseline than men do. We also find that the **ranking** of mean SD's for females is the same as the ranking of mean SD's for males: acting involves the greatest variation around the mean, then reading aloud, then conversation.

In other words, there is evidence that the Fo band occupied by the three discourse modes is **narrowest for conversation** and **widest for acting**, with reading aloud being intermediate between these two. There is also evidence that long term Fo tendencies tend to settle within a relatively **lower range of frequencies** for **conversation** than for **reading aloud**, which in turn occupies a relatively lower range of frequencies than acting.

The evidence from the study reported here, then, is that long-term pitch characteristics are significantly different in the three discourse modes selected: reading aloud, acting and conversation.

A more sophisticated statistical analysis of the pitch characteristics, such as is applied by Graddol (this volume) yielding measures of skew and kurtosis, might have facilitated the derivation of further information.

Six comments about the results are in order:-

1. The 'conversation' recorded fluctuated between 'free exchange/parity of initiation' and 'constrained exchange/non-parity of initiation' (i.e. between genuine conversation and interview-like exchanges). Auditory impression leads me to believe that relative pitch level drops, and relative variation around the mean **decreases** with **increase in intimacy/relaxation of tension**. However, since it is at least possible that there are different kinds of conversation, each with a characteristic pitch range, further contrastive work will be necessary to establish how far the result obtained is general for conversation.

2. It may be that the Fo values for reading aloud and acting are **closer** for this population than they would be for non-actors, simply because their skill at acting spills over into their reading aloud performance. Further work involving **non-actors** reading aloud and acting would be required to resolve this question.

3. It is not clear how far the artificiality of the recording session affected the results. It is conceivable that in a more 'natural' setting (e.g. a theatre or television studio) actors might feel more at liberty to use greater variation around their mean Fo value than was the case here. Comparison of acting voices in different settings would be necessary to resolve this issue, but uncontrolled recording conditions would undoubtedly raise problems for acoustic analysis.

4. The choice of approximately 30 seconds of each discourse mode for each speaker was more a matter of processing convenience than speaker "representativeness". There was no assumption that this speech span was adequate for an absolute measurement of the defining pitch character-istics of the selected discourse mode. A much longer speech span, perhaps twice or three times as long, might have been necessary for statistical certainty that the charactersitic measured was truly representative of the mode in question. Further research is needed to show what size of speech span is the minimum necessary in order for absolute measurement to be made of pitch tendencies in any selected discourse mode.

5. In order to identify a particular prosodic parameter (in this case, pitch) as signalling a particular social dimension, comparison between *acting* and *other* public modes (e.g. political speeches, sermons) would be required. In other words, before claims can be made that **high variation about a mean** is characteristic of **public address for a multiple audience**, and **small variation about a mean** is characteristic of **private communication for a unique, single audience**, measurement of Fo in several discourse modes involving public address for a multiple audience, and several discourse modes involving private communication for a unique audience, would be necessary.

213

6. Although statistically significant results were obtained for mean Fo level, and SD in Hertz values, the scale used -a linear one - may not be appropriate. In order to reflect pitch perception, the results would have had to be transposed to a log scale. Approximate musical interval equivalents of the SD's of Males and Females in the three discourse modes can be seen from Table 3.

Table 3 indicates that for Reading aloud, (Male SD 32Hz, Female SD 54Hz) the range in semi-tones is not significantly different for Males as opposed to Females. For Acting, (Male SD 38Hz, Female SD 72Hz) the range in semi-tones is not statistically different for Males as opposed to Females. And for Conversation, (Male SD 20Hz, Female SD 28Hz) again, the range for Females as opposed to Males is not significantly different. However, although one effect of the transformation is to reduce the degree of difference between Males and Females, the overall effect of pitch range difference in the three discourse modes is still preserved. Conversation still comes out with the narrowest pitch range, the SD corresponding to around 3 semi-tones.

Since so much depends on the scale selected, it is important that aims should be clear at the outset. The investigation reported here did not originally aim to represent the results in perceptual terms, but to make no reference to perception would be to ignore a very fundamental aspect of Fo. Clearly, the question of how analyses of Fo in extended discourse should be represented is open to debate. As Graddol points out in his paper (this volume), a linear scale may be more appropriate for perception of pitch values below 1kHz.

Further work is planned taking all these points into consideration.

MALES

SD (in Hz)		Hz	Range (in semi-tones)
READING ALOUD			
+32	160 Hz	161	4
		152	3
		143	2
		136	1
SD=32	Mean 128 Hz	128	
		120	1
		114	2
		107	3
		101	4
-32	96 Hz	95	5
ACTING			
+38	180 Hz	178	4
		168	3
		159	2
		150	1
SD=38	Mean 142 Hz	142	
		134	1
		127	2
		119	3
		112	4
-38	104 Hz	106	5
CONVERSATION			
+20		119	3
		112	2
		106	1
SD=20	Mean 100 Hz	100	
		94	1
		89	2
		84	3
-20		79	4

FEMALES

SD (in Hz)		Hz	Range (in semi-tones)
READING ALOUD			
+54	267 Hz	268	4
		253	3
		239	2
		226	1
SD=54	Mean 213 Hz	213	
		201	1
		190	2
		179	3
		169	4
-54	159 Hz	159	5
ACTING			
+72	312 Hz	320	5
		302	4
		285	3
		269	2
		254	1
SD=72	Mean 240 Hz	240	
		226	1
		214	2
		201	3
		190	4
		179	5
-72	168 Hz	169	6
CONVERSATION			
+28		216	3
		204	2
		193	1
SD=28	Mean 182 Hz	182	
		172	1
		162	2
-28		153	3

Table 3   Range converted from SD around Mean Hz value to semitones

215

4.0 Summary and Conclusion

This study examined pitch in three discourse modes (reading aloud, acting and conversation), performed by ten amateur actors.

From the mean standard deviation in Fo in the three discourse modes, it can be deduced that the largest fluctuations about the mean are to be found in acting, and the smallest in "intimate" conversation, with reading aloud intermediate between these. It can be said, then, that the sample of acting studied showed greater pitch variation than reading aloud or conversation, the standard deviation of pitch in acting being roughly twice that of conversation. In other words, there is evidence that conversation occupies a 'narrower pitch band' than the more public modes of acting and reading aloud.

In addition, it was found that the mean pitch value for conversation was significantly lower than reading aloud, and lower for reading aloud than acting. In other words, the samples of a simulated 'more public mode of address' studied are located at a higher average pitch level.

Females were found to exhibit larger fluctuation about the mean Fo value than males, and this was especially marked in acting. In other words, there is independent evidence of Graddol's finding (this volume) that females make greater use of their pitch range potential.

In conclusion, there are long-term pitch trends that do differentiate discourse modes, and there are sex-specific preferences in relation to the exploitation of pitch range.

Instrumental analysis of other socially well-definend groups, and other speech activities, is yet to be explored.

It may seem premature to speculate as to the reasons for the patterns identified. But on the other hand, description without explanation is an impoverished version of science.

Why is acting located at a higher average pitch level than conversation? Does heightened pitch act as a device for focusing attention? In dramatic performances, actors must 'drown out' competing stimuli and project the voice, in order to satisfy the minimum conditions of success. The size of the physical space which the voice must traverse, and the physical presence, between speaker and hearer, of stage props, proscenium and audience, mean that there are many competing stimuli that have to be overcome. The voice must be 'larger than life' in terms of its pitch and loudness characteristics. It is of interest that these two prosodic parameters, pitch and loudness, and also tempo, enter into child-addressed adult speech. Garnica reports that certain prosodic aspects of speech to 2-year-olds, 5-year-olds, and adults differ. She found more rising sentence-final pitch contours when addressing 2-year-olds (even on imperatives, which normally have falling contours); whispered **parts** of sentences to 2-year-olds, but not 5-year-olds; and addition of primary stresses resulting in **more than one** per sentence when addressing 2-year-olds (Garnica 1977: 80-81). Garnica[9] points out that these modifications function as 'attention getters'. They also function as an aid to utterance segmentation, since indication of the 'key words' in the utterance will serve to indicate which sub-units should be extracted first. Prosodic modification in speech to young children involves strategies for competing against the influx of multiple stimuli which the child is processing. Pitch heightening, and increased loudness can be shown to involve strategies that are effective in overcoming the two communication problems of 'scattered attention' and segmentation of utterances.

In acting, on the other hand, we find that *the whole discourse* is subject to pitch heightening, and very probably increase in loudness too (although the latter was not analysed in this study).

The reverse is true in conversation, where the relative average pitch level is lower, the significance of this being that a great deal of dyadic exchange is non- competitive. Conversation which becomes competitive exhibits pitch raising at turn competitive points (see French and Local, this volume).

Turning now to the question of the size of the fluctuations around the mean pitch value, here too, we find support for the theory that conversation is attempting a different task from acting. Acting must constantly fight against the mental fatigue of the hearers, who are required to do nothing other than listen silently (except at applause points). It must overcome the damping effect of non-participation by heightening the strength of the stimulus for the listener. Hence the much larger fluctuations around the pitch mean.

The significance of the difference between the sexes, as regards pitch range exploited, is discussed by Graddol (this volume) who suggests that powerful social conditioning forces constrain men to exploit a narrower pitch band than women do. Since men do not exploit their full pitch potential, which women do (or very nearly do), men cannot adopt this behaviour pattern without being perceived as taking over a female characteristic. The purpose of the pitch differentiation, then, is sex differentiation.

The speculative suggestion is, then, that heightening of pitch characteristics is attuned to attention-states in the hearer-organism, pitch heightening having the function of focusing and maintaining attention.

217

Footnotes:

1.   Beattie and Butterworth (1979) draw attention to the nature of Goldman-Eisler's (1968) corpus of spontaneous speech. Only "grammatically correct ... well constructed sentences ... logically consistent with the whole utterance were considered" (Goldman-Eisler, 1968: 36). It is not clear whether this selected corpus is unrepresentative of global trends, in terms of contrasts between speech styles.

2.   Barik's figures (81.6%) for the duration of speech as opposed to pause (18.4%), in the lecture mode, are very similar to the ratio of speaking (83%) to silence (17%) reported by Grosjean and Deschamps (1975) in French and English radio interviews.

3.   Percentage figure derived by the present writer from the raw data of Levin, Schaffer and Snow.

4.   I am indebted to the LAGB discussion of the relationship between speech and writing at the LAGB Spring meeting 1984 (Hull) and to Dick Hudson's summary of the discussion.

5.   In common with others writing on fundamental frequency extraction, I use the term **pitch** as a shorthand for Fo. Strictly speaking, pitch is a psychological phenomenon, for the identification of which hearers undoubtedly make use of linguistic information, such as word accent and rhythm.

6.   Levinson (1983: 284) defines conversation as "that familiar predominant kind of talk in which two or more participants freely alternate in speaking, which generally occurs outside specific institutional settings like religious services, law courts, classrooms and the like".

7.   I am extremely grateful to Dr F Nolan, Department of Linguistics, Cambridge University, for allowing the data to be run on his installation. Any errors arising from interpretation of the data are, of course, my own.

8.   See comments in Graddol, this volume on SD as an indicator of Fo range.

9.   Bard and Anderson (1983) obtained results in four experiments on perception of speech addressed to young children which are in direct opposition to Garnica's observations. They suggest that speech to young children is in fact more unintelligible than speech to adults. Their paper came to my notice too late for me to take full account of implications for the discussion of prosodic characteristics of speech.

Appendix I
Story to be read aloud

I remember one old boy - what was his name? - Battling Billy -shell shocked after the Boer War. He used to really get going if he had a drop too much. He'd dash out of his house in his red underwear, swearing like anything. He had a broom and a dustbin lid, and he'd charge at anybody watching him.

Well, the cops would come for him. What a pantomime. Always the same -Billy in the lockup till Maggie bailed him out.

Adapted from Kathleen Dayus: *Her People* (Virago Press)

Appendix II
Dialogue

Josie: Come on. We've gotta get going. Where's the gear?
           (Mart is silent)
           Listen, you're not chickening out, are you? If you
           think I'm in this on my own, you've got another think
           coming.
           (Mart turns his back)
           Oh, I get it. You're going into Holy Orders like your
           Mum always said you should.
           (Mart winces)
           Like hell you are. Come on. You need the money and so
           do I.
           (Mart looks at the floor)
           OK. I'll just give your old boss a ring.
           (Mart rises, furious and sullen, and fetches out a bag.)
           That's more like it.

DISCOURSE SPECIFIC PITCH BEHAVIOUR

David Graddol

1. Introduction

Most studies of voice pitch have been concerned with short term features of pitch movement within sentences, and their role in intonation and stress. Pitch of voice, however, is a paralinguistic as well as a prosodic phenomenon, and like other paralinguistic features of accent and voice quality, it simultaneously carries information of several different kinds. Abercrombie (1967) has referred to this information as *indexical,* distinguishing three principal categories:

a) those which indicate membership of a group
b) those which characterise the individual
c) those which reveal changing states of the speaker.

Characteristics of voice pitch which have as their domain stretches of talk longer than the sentence seem to belong more to the paralinguistic or indexical category than to the linguistic or prosodic category. Furthermore, long term features of pitch and voice quality are generally regarded as 'informative' rather than 'communicative' (Laver and Trudgill, 1979), since, insofar as they reflect anatomical contraints of a particular speaker's vocal apparatus, or a long term articulatory setting, they will not be available for conscious manipulation.

Several indexical aspects of pitch behaviour have attracted attention in the literature. A number of studies have shown that information contained in pitch contours is sufficient to allow listeners to identify individual voices from a fixed corpus (Atal, 1972; Abberton and Fourcin, 1978). In view of this fact, it is not surprising that long term pitch distributions have been used successfully for speaker recognition (Steffen-Batog et al, 1970). Measures of long term pitch distributions have also been suggested as a diagnostic tool in speech pathology (Fourcin and Abberton, 1976; Hirano, 1981). Interest in the third of Abercrombie's categories is reflected in studies by social psychologists in the perception of personality and emotional state. Pitch of voice is often one of the speech attributes taken into account in studies of task induced stress, (Hecker et al, 1968), displays of emotion (Fairbanks and Pronovost, 1939) and perception of personality types (Scherer, 1979).

Viewing long term pitch as primarily an individual and indexical character-istic may, however, be an oversimplification for several reasons. Firstly, pitch phenomena seem to display certain features at a discourse level which are similar to features of intonation at the sentence level. Paragraphing phen-omena (Lehiste, 1975, 1978 and 1979; Couper-Kuhlen, 1982) form one example. Other pitch related discourse features, such as turn taking (Cutler and Pearson this volume) and interruptions (French and Local this volume) are also tied to particular events and situations and cannot be regarded as indexical. Secondly, medium and long term pitch distributions must also reflect the structure of the short term temporal patterning, that is the phonetic shape of the intonational contours, which they comprise. If two discourses are differentiated by range of syntactic structures, sentence lengths, and sentence complexity, then this will be reflected in the intonation patterns observed, which in turn may be reflected in long term pitch distributions.

Any long term pitch distribution will, then, reflect at least three different sources of pitch variation:

1) It will reflect contraints imposed by the speaker's vocal anatomy.
2) It will reflect any habitual intonational patterning which is characteristic of an individual or group accent, or other distributional characteristics attributable to a particular articulatory setting.
3) It will reflect situational and discourse variables which are expressed in intonational structure and choice of pitch range.

This paper explores the extent to which the third source of pitch variation described above can be identified by the use of statistical techniques. Data will be reported from a pilot study which forms part of a longer investigation into paralinguistic features of long term pitch distribution.

1.1 Experimental Procedure

Fifteen men and fifteen women, all with university education, aged between 25 and 40 and working in academic or academic related grades at the Open University were selected for the study. All subjects spoke a variety of British English without strong regional affiliation. Each subject was recorded reading two passages, typed onto separate cards. The first passage consisted entirely of a single extended statement with several clauses taken from the introduction to the Illuminating Engineering Society's Code for Interior Lighting. The second passage was a constructed dialogue which required greater inflection and the use of question intonation. Subjects took a mean time of 14.3 seconds to read the first passage and 18.4 seconds to read the second. At the end of the recording session each subject was asked to phonate the vowel / ɑ:/ at as low a pitch as possible, being encouraged to work downwards until basal pitch was reached. After the recording session, subjects were weighed and measured for height at the University's medical room, in connection with another part of the experiment. Two male subjects who failed to report for measurement were subsequently dropped from the analysis, along with one male whose voice quality prevented reliable pitch measurement by the method adopted. The final sample thus consisted of 12 men and 15 women.

1.2 Analytical Technique

The pitch measurements for each subject were made on a micro-computer based installation which was designed and built for the purpose. The speech signal was first low pass filtered (250 Hz 24db/octave for men; 350 Hz 24db/octave for women). The time period between zero crossings in the filtered signal was measured by counting the number of pulses received from a crystal controlled clock (operating at 20 kHz for men, and 31.25 kHz for women) on an 8 bit counter. This arrangement created a low frequency cut off in measurement of 78 Hz for the men and 122 Hz for the women, except in the measurement of basal pitch where use of a different algorithm allowed the recovery of lower pitches. Resolution varied between 0.3 Hz at the lowest frequency to 3 Hz-4 Hz at the filter turnover frequency. The filter settings were chosen to ensure that the whole of a speaker's pitch range could be safely recorded without *ad hoc* alteration of the cut off frequency. This in turn meant that a number of second harmonic readings were inevitably included in the raw data. The raw data were checked for octave shifts resulting from second harmonic readings by software and reinterpreted where necessary. The data were then transferred to a mainframe computer for further statistical analysis.

2. Choice of Pitch Measures

2.1 General Considerations

The best method of characterising the complex pattern of pitch distribution which results from the analysis of any extended sample of speech will depend not only on the intrinsic properties of the time varying signal which the discontinuous pitch contour represents, but also on an understanding of what is salient to a hearer in extracting linguistic and social information. It is unfortunately the case that we know extremely little about either the phonetic characteristics of pitch contours, or about what acoustic cues are used by listeners (see Wells, this volume).

The lack of data about the phonetic level is partly due to a traditional emphasis by linguists on phonological aspects of intonation and a related distrust of instrumentation. This distrust is probably well founded in two respects. Acoustic analysis can all too easily focus attention too narrowly on one particular attribute of the speech soundwave, and obscure important interactions between features, such as the interaction between fundamental frequency, intensity and duration in intonation. This problem should be kept in mind when considering the data reported here which refer to patterns of variation in fundamental frequency only.

A second caveat concerns the accuracy of instrumental measurement. Voiced speech sounds are never strictly periodic, and their transient nature may give rise to a number of spurious effects in measurement, some of which, such as octave leaping when the second harmonic is tracked instead of the fundamental, are well known. What is less often realised is that pitch of voice

223

may at times be simply indeterminate (as may be the case in creaky voice) or may be ambiguous even when viewed by the most robust computational algorithms for pitch extraction (Noll, 1967). It is likely, furthermore, that instantaneous pitch is as indeterminate to the ear as to laboratory instruments. Since most of the experimental work on pitch perception which exists has not made use of naturally jittered speech, the response of the ear to such signals is incompletely understood. As insufficient information exists to allow salient parameters of long term pitch to be identified, it will be necessary to make use of standard distributional measures, although it is to be expected that some of these may ultimately prove to have little value in this application.

Pitch contours which graph fundamental frequency against time are the traditional method of displaying pitch of voice information. Such contour graphs, when related to segmental transcriptions of utterances, show much of the information on which pitch perception is based. Contour graphs are not suitable, however, for providing the summary statistics required in the study of long term pitch. A more useful method of summarising distributional data is provided by a histogram which shows how much time was spent at different pitches, or how many pitch periods of particular lengths were observed.

A single histogram can be used to characterise the pitch distribution in a sample of speech of any length and is thus a powerful summarising technique. The main information loss concerns the temporal organisation of individual pitch periods. Some of this temporal information (such as roughness in pitch, or speed of pitch movement) may be an important carrier of paralinguistic information. Although not used in this paper, some of this data can be recovered by the use of supplementary analyses.

2.2 Characterising the Histogram

Each histogram has a particular shape which can be characterised by standard descriptive statistics. Jassem (1971) suggests four main criteria which will be adopted here:

a) Measures of central tendency

The most widely used measure of central tendency is the arithmetic mean. Since period by period measurement of pitch may occasionally lead to a few spurious high frequency readings, to which a mean will be very sensitive, many studies have supplemented calculations of mean by median pitch measures. Mean pitch in this study was derived from the arithmetic mean of all measured periods. Median pitch was calculated as a time median -that is to say 50% of the time spent in voiced speech was occupied by periods above or below the median pitch. This leads to longer pitch periods being given more weighting than shorter periods, since a single period at 100 Hz occupies the same time interval as two periods at 200 Hz. Time normalisation was applied to all other measures where appropriate. Data reported here, although collected on a period by period basis, can thus be compared with data reported in other

224

studies where the more usual method of equal interval time-sampling has been employed. Since the mean and median pitch were found, as might be expected, to correlate well (p=.001) only the means will be reported in some analyses in order to simplify the presentation of data.

b) Measures of range

Some measure of the location and extent of the pitch range or compass of the voice is required. The simplest measure is to take the absolute highest and lowest pitches recorded, but this makes the measure very sensitive to single extreme readings and possible error data. Jassem (1971) suggested basing range measures on the Standard Deviation, taking 4 SDs to be the effective range. Other researchers have suggested taking the fifth percentile as the lower limit of the range, and the 95th percentile as the upper limit. The 90% measure is affected by the distribution of the data as well as the absolute range. A visual inspection of the histograms in this study showed that if odd extreme readings were ignored, then the absolute range used by an individual varied less than might appear from the speaker's 90% range measure. For this very reason the 90% measure was preferred by some early researchers (Lewis and Tiffin 1933) since it seemed a better estimate of a person's 'functional' range. The SD measure leads to a rather larger estimate of range, both in theory and practice, than the 90% measure. (Four times the standard deviation would include around 96% of the data in a normal distribution). In spite of the fact that distributions of long term pitch are commonly non-normal, the SD is useful in the calculation of parametric statistics which are regarded as sufficiently robust to use in this context. It proved useful, in this study, however, to distinguish between the upper and lower limits of range separately, and this was most easily done by using percentile information. Hence, both the SD and the 5th and 95th percentiles are reported.

c) The shape of the distribution: skew

Two other useful standard descriptive statistics are measures of skewness and kurtosis. A pitch distribution can be said to be positively skewed if it is assymetrical, containing more observations at lower than higher frequencies. Skew can be calculated in various ways, but perhaps the most widely used is Walker's coefficient of skew. A normal distribution has a coefficient of skew which is zero.

d) The shape of the distribution: kurtosis

Walker's coefficient of kurtosis measures a further possible deviation from a normal distribution, and represents the extent to which the distribution is more 'pointed' (leptokurtic) or 'flatter' (platykurtic) than normal. A normal distribution again has a coefficient of kurtosis which is zero. A positive coefficient implies that the distribution is more pointed than normal, and a negative coefficient implies a flatter than normal distribution. Kurtosis has been shown to be a useful measure in the identification of pathological voice quality (Fourcin and Abberton, 1976).

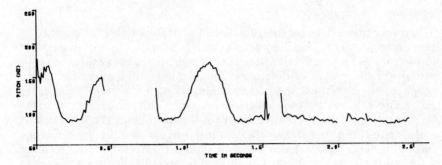

Figure 1a) Pitch contour.

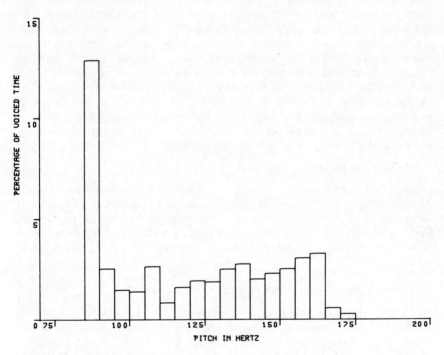

Figure 1b) Histogram.

Figure 1 Four ways of graphing pitch distribution

226

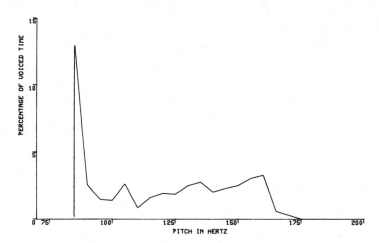

Figure 1C) Graph.

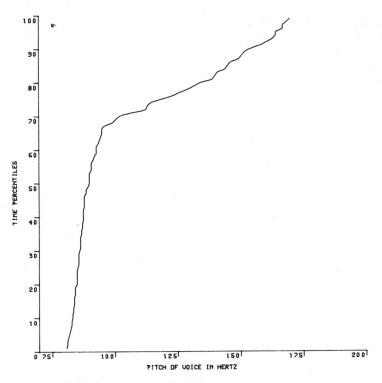

Figure 1d) Ogive or probability curve.

Figure 1 Four ways of graphing pitch distribution.

227

2.3 Choice of Scale

The characteristics just described can be regarded as properties of an individual histogram, that is, a particular graphical representation, and not of the raw data. Changing a scale or the class interval, for instance, alters the shape of the distribution. Measures of skew and kurtosis, in particular, will change if pitch is measured in terms of musical intervals. The musical scale is a logarithmic one and can be calibrated in octaves, semitones, or some smaller interval. The interval chosen here is the Cent (1 Cent = 1/100 semitone). Since the cent is an interval, and not an absolute measure, it can only be used by relating a given pitch to another fixed reference pitch. The reference pitch often used for this purpose is 16.35 Hz (four octaves below middle C) which is regarded as being at or below the threshold of pitch and hence a zero point on the scale. Figures 2a and 2b show the linear and log distributions respectively for one subject reading the 'lighting' passage. The abscissa of the log histogram is marked in Cents above 16.35 Hz. The class interval for the log scale is 50 cents (that is, each column is 1/4 tone wide) and for the linear scale 5 Hz.

Although the choice of scale is an important one, it is not clear whether a logarithmic or linear scale is more appropriate. The ear is known to perceive pitch in a roughly logarithmic fashion but many studies have shown that frequencies below about 1 kHz are perceived more linearly (Stevens and Volkmann, 1940). The ability to perceive slight differences in pitch also seems to alter as a function of frequency, the difference limen being more or less constant below around 2 kHz (Shower and Biddulph, 1931; Nordmark, 1968). These psychophysical findings might suggest that fundamental frequency in speech, which falls almost entirely in the linear region, should be graphed on a linear scale. The situation is made more complex, however, by the fact that a principal pitch detection mechanism in the ear relies more on the spacing of higher frequency harmonics than on the location of the fundamental component. Research into the perception of pure tones may not, therefore, be too relevant to this particular problem. A logarithmic scale not only changes the apparent distribution of pitch in a single sample, but makes a considerable difference to comparisons of range between men and women. When viewed in terms of musical intervals, the pitch range used by most women seems to be rather less than that used by most men. The opposite is true when these ranges are viewed in a linear scale. Whenever intervals in pitch must be compared at different frequencies, a log scale is to be preferred.

3. The Data

Table 2 gives the group means for the various measures proposed, the mean of the mean pitches, and the 5th and 95th percentiles are given in Hz. the SD is given in cents, to allow comparison between men and women, and the skew and kurtosis coefficients are taken from the logarithmic histograms of all speakers. Table 3 shows the data for each individual.

228

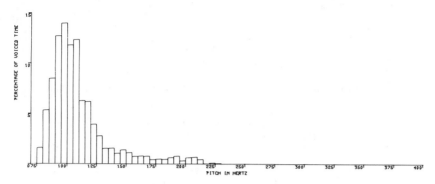

Figure 2a) Pitch distribution for male subject 2 reading the 'lighting' passage a) linear scale in Hz

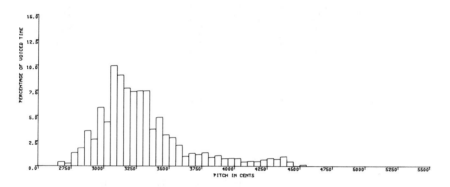

Figure 2b) Pitch distribution for male subject 2 reading the 'lighting' passage b) log scale in cents

	Linear	Log
Mean	114 Hz	3315 (Cents)
SD	26.7 Hz	344 (Cents)
Skew	1.82	1.26
Kurtosis	3.66	1.62
5th Percentile:	85 Hz	
95th Percentile:	173 Hz	

Table 1 Descriptive statistics for histograms 2a and 2b

229

Female Lighting Passage

Sub	5%	95%	Mean	Median	SD	Skew	Kurtosis	Basal
1	166	294	221	216	278	.0	.3	151
2	128	260	184	181	361	.17	-.21	135
3	154	216	181	178	177	.42	.96	146
4	134	244	181	174	285	.7	.86	163
5	123	315	218	214	392	-.25	-.2	126
6	160	269	210	209	252	0.0	-.09	137
7	182	276	227	228	247	-1.65	5.22	169
8	171	233	203	204	165	-.06	1.65	184
9	137	269	193	188	328	.19	-.25	166
10	140	306	212	209	390	.07	-.22	159
11	156	274	205	201	269	.46	.68	139
12	129	322	229	233	423	-.58	-.05	183
13	123	306	200	194	404	.34	-.46	141
14	176	303	233	231	286	-.66	2.85	177
15	155	303	208	199	330	.7	.44	133

Female Dialogue Passage

Sub	5%	95%	Mean	Median	SD	Skew	Kurtosis
1	135	343	233	228	385	-.05	.03
2	127	332	200	192	509	.35	-.83
3	155	240	193	188	244	.07	-.51
4	132	347	211	190	471	.47	-.66
5	123	343	221	208	492	-.09	-.93
6	167	303	217	211	338	.11	-.11
7	194	289	237	238	211	-.39	2.42
8	170	240	204	205	185	-.15	2.33
9	130	318	212	201	472	.11	-1.0
10	145	339	221	205	454	.26	-.87
11	153	343	227	209	418	.31	-.64
12	167	355	233	212	389	.51	-.23
13	134	339	211	197	484	.36	-.85
14	138	335	242	238	362	-.5	.75
15	151	355	229	206	476	.32	-1.06

Male Lighting Passage

Sub	5%	95%	Mean	Median	SD	Skew	Kurtosis	Basal
1	79	153	106	98	376	.92	.48	68
2	85	173	114	106	344	1.26	1.62	84
3	83	176	119	114	371	.85	.84	74
4	80	170	113	109	374	.75	.61	83
5	81	155	109	102	364	1.02	1.35	83
6	87	180	128	126	333	.18	.94	102
7	89	169	125	122	323	.3	.2	92
8	84	178	112	103	363	.99	.72	71
9	98	194	136	129	345	.47	.65	99
10	93	170	121	115	329	1.66	4.39	94
11	86	153	116	114	293	.27	.16	76
12	79	208	137	136	527	-.08	-1.01	111

Male Dialogue Passage

Sub	5%	95%	Mean	Median	SD	Skew	Kurtosis
1	80	172	114	111	404	.46	-.56
2	79	176	118	111	387	.83	.62
3	84	217	145	136	510	.08	-1.16
4	80	176	120	116	452	.40	-.51
5	84	243	137	120	567	.59	-.59
6	84	232	142	130	465	.40	-.17
7	85	232	135	123	478	.73	-.17
8	84	192	125	113	457	.44	-.93
9	85	238	147	131	500	.39	-.52
10	81	166	121	120	333	.16	.17
11	86	192	125	117	420	.52	-.60
12	78	232	143	136	517	.03	-.60

Table 3 Individual scores

	MALE		FEMALE			T-TEST	
	A	B	A	B		Male	Female
Mean	119	131	207	219		0.001	0.000
Mean	(3436	3602	4394	4492)	(Cents)		
4sd	1444	1828	1220	1568		0.000	0.000
Range	1222	1565	1092	1347		0.000	0.002
5% ile	85.3	82.0	148	147		0.08	0.70
95% ile	173	205	279	321		0.002	0.000
Skew	0.7	0.4	-0.0	0.1		0.07	0.30
Kurtosis	0.9	-0.4	0.7	-0.1		0.002	0.001

Table 2   Mean data for males and females in two reading passages A = 'lighting' passage; B = 'dialogue' passage

4. Discussion of Results

4.1 Discourse Variables

Table 2 shows that the two passages differ on several of the pitch measures. These differences can be summarised as follows.

1) The dialogue has a higher mean pitch and a more extensive pitch range in both men and women.
2) The upper range seems to be extended more than the lower range.
3) Distributions seem to be flatter in the dialogue passage.
4) There is a slight tendency for the men to show less positive skew in the dialogue passage compared to the lighting passage.

Whether or not these results are statistically significant will depend largely on whether the individuals follow a similar pattern to that of the overall means. The right hand column of Table 2 shows the results of related T-Tests. Only the differences in 5th percentile and differences in skew were not significant. The T-Tests show that, by and large, not only do all subjects modify their pitch behaviour when they read the second passage, but they do so in the same direction. This strongly suggests that the pitch distributions are reflecting some discourse specific features. These trends can be seen in Figure 3 which shows the probability curves for all subjects in both passages.

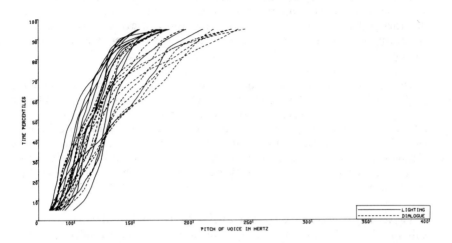

Figure 3a) Probability curves for males.

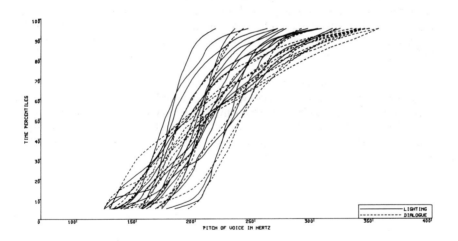

Figure 3b) Probability curves for females.

233

The implication of these results is that, given any pair of histograms, or any two sets of descriptive statistics, we will be able to identify which of the two reading passages they were derived from. The results do not imply that, given a randomised group of unpaired histograms, we will necessarily be able to sort them accurately into the two categories. This is because there may be sufficient variation between individuals to obscure the variation between reading passages.

This point was explored further by means of discriminant function analysis. This is a statistical technique which ascertains what variable, or combination of variables, best allows two or more groups of data to be differentiated. Use of discriminant analysis thus serves two purposes here. It will determine whether there are any intrinsic characteristics which distinguish the pitch distributions in the two passages, and it will give some idea as to which of the variables carry most of the discourse specific information.

The analysis was carried out in two ways. First, male and female data were submitted separately to the analysis. This was to provide for the possibility of sex differences in pitch behaviour. Second, male and female data were submitted to the analysis together. Since the large absolute differences in pitch between men and women would distort the results of this analysis, the mean, 5th percentile and 95th percentile were calculated in this analysis as the difference in cents from the overall mean pitch of the grouped data for each sex. The other variables made available to the discriminant program were range (5th percentile to 95th percentile), standard deviation, skew and kurtosis.

Two tables are provided for each analysis. The first gives the standardised discriminant function, which shows which variables were used in the function and how they were weighted. This function is then applied to each case in the data which is allocated to one of the two groups. The classification table shows how successful this application was, and how many cases in each group were misclassified.

Results for male subjects

Func 1

RANGE   0.72412
KURTOSIS -0.47278

Table 4 Standardised canonical discriminant function coefficients

Actual group	No. of cases	Predicted group membership 1	2
Group 1 MALE LIGHTING	12	11 91.7%	1 8.3%
Group 2 MALE DIALOGUE	12	2 16.7%	10 83.3%

Percent of "grouped" gases correctly classified: 87.50%

Table 5 Classification results for male subjects

Results for male subjects

Func 1

RANGE   8.52210
95th % -5.19299
5th %   4.30079
SD   -1.13665

Table 6 Standardised canonical discriminant function coefficients

235

Actual group	No. of cases	Predicted group membership 3	4
Group 3 FEMALE LIGHTING	15	12 80.0%	3 20.0%
Group 4 FEMALE DIALOGUE	15	3 20.0%	12 80.0%

Percent of "grouped" cases correctly classified: 80.00%

Table 7 Classification results for female subjects

Results for both sexes combined

Func 1

95th %	-1.31679
RANGE	0.80674
KURTOSIS	0.67957

Table 8 Standardised canonical discriminant function coefficients

Actual group	No. of cases	Predicted group membership 1	2
Group 1 LIGHTING PASSAGE	27	22 81.5%	5 18.5%
Group 2 DIALOGUE PASSAGE	27	6 22.2%	21 77.8%

Percent of "grouped" cases correctly classified: 79.63%

Table 9 Classification results for both sexes

236

The discriminant analysis shows that the two passages can be distinguished with surprising accuracy. It seems that less information is required to separate male readings than to separate female readings, but that a single discriminant function can be found which will work for both sexes. This function suggests that the measures which are most useful in this application are the upper limit of range, the range itself, and the degree of kurtosis. It is noteworthy that mean pitch did not appear in any of the functions, indicating that it has no particular discriminant value which is not included in other variables. Skew, also, seems to carry little discriminant information.

5. Conclusion

It has been shown that the statistical distribution of pitch in the reading aloud of short texts must be regarded as being, in part, a function of the textual material, and that this effect may be more pronounced than individual differences in pitch range and location. An explanation of the precise source of such differentiation must await a closer study of the distributional properties of intonational patterns.

THE ACQUISITION OF INTONATION BY INFANTS: PHYSIOLOGY AND NEURAL CONTROL

Philip Lieberman

1. Introduction

The study of linguistic behavior of human infants addresses one of the central questions of human biology and evolution - to what extent does human linguistic ability follow from innate, species-specific biological mechanisms. The research of the past thirty years has demonstrated that human speech is an integral part of human linguistic ability. The premise that I will develop in this paper is that many of the linguistically salient aspects of human speech begin to develop and can be seen in the vocal behavior of infants. These data indicate to me that the biological substrate of human speech involves an interplay between biological mechanisms that have other vegetative functions and neural and anatomical mechanisms that appear to have evolved primarily for their role in facilitating human vocal communication. These data thus refute Chomsky's (1980) claim that human linguistic ability follows from the presence of a unique, species-specific "language organ" that yields linguistic behavior disjoint from other aspects of human cognitive behavior or the social communications of other animals.

The "suprasegmental" aspects of human speech have not received much attention in recent studies of the development of human speech in relation to human language. The intonation, stress and general "melody" of speech constitute the suprasegmental component of speech. Although these aspects of speech are among the first that develop in human infants (Lewis, 1936), we still have much to learn concerning the biological bases, the development and the linguistic function of these aspects of human speech. The acoustic paramaters of the fundamental frequency of phonation, the amplitude of the speech signal and its timing all are relevant to the perception of the suprasegmental or "prosodic" features of human speech. Some of the linguistic functions of the prosodic features of human speech were explicitly noted since at least the 13th century. The instructions for the chanting of church music that can be found in old manuscripts, for example, recognize the "terminal" cues that segment the flow of speech into sentences and major syntactic units (Hadding-Koch, 1961). The role of intonation in segmenting the flow of speech into sentence-like units for syntactic analysis has been demonstrated in many independent linguistic, phonetic, acoustic and psycho-acoustic studies e.g., (Armstrong and Ward, 1926; Pike, 1945; Trager and Smith, 1951; Lieberman, 1967; Atkinson, 1973; Tseng, 1981). It is impossible to arrive at the meaning of a sentence unless you know what words go together. You again can test this hypothesis by simply taking a newspaper and moving the sentence beginning and ending punctuation over one word to the right. The result usually is incomprehensible since the "wrong" words have been grouped together. This segmenting function of intonation is its paramount *linguistic* function. Intonation can also transmit the attitude of the speaker with respect to the linguistic message that is transmitted by means of the words and rule-governed syntax of the language (Pike, 1945). However, this function is secondary to signalling the segments of speech to which we must apply the "rules" of our internal representation of our knowledge. In brief, without sentences, we cannot have human language.

2. The Breath-Group

The *breath-group* is the primary element that people use to segment the flow of speech into sentence-like units. The breath-group is organized about vegetative constraints of respiration and the physiology of the lungs and larynx. Its primary elements can be seen in the initial cries of the newborn infants and follow from the articulatory and respiratory maneuvers that are necessary to sustain life. Its full linguistic expression, however, involves behavioral patterns that are not present at birth, i.e., a complex pattern of articulatory control that involves reference to the probable length of a sentence **before** a sound is uttered, and linguistically motivated "over-rides" of the central and peripheral chemoreceptors that otherwise mediate respiration.

I shall start with a discussion of the acoustic parameters and articulatory and respiratory maneuvers that we can characterize as a breath-group.

In Figure 1, I have sketched a schematic diagram of the human respiratory system from the larynx down. This sketch does not seek to represent the actual anatomy of the human respiratory system; it is a functionally accurate model for the aspects of respiratory control that are germane to our enquiry. The model has only one lung, and the points that are relevant for one lung will be relevant for both lungs. Note the lung "balloon" in the model and the plungers that are attached to the side wall and bottom wall of the pleural chamber. The human respiratory system functions in an odd manner that reflects the fact that lungs evolved from the swim bladders of fish (Darwin, 1859; Negus, 1949). The swim bladders in fish are internal sacks into which a fish can pump air that has been filtered out of the water by the fish's gills. The swim bladders are elastic so that they can expand or contract to take up the volume of air that the fish needs to balance its weight against displaced water at a given depth. Air breathing animals retained the elastic sacks, which were connected to the outside atmosphere and filled by expanding the pleural space. Inspiration in human beings thus takes place when we expand the volume of the pleural space by moving the diaphragm downwards or the rib cage outwards. The plunger labelled *diaphragm* can exert force downwards to expand the pleural space. The plunger labelled *intercostals* can also move outwards to expand the

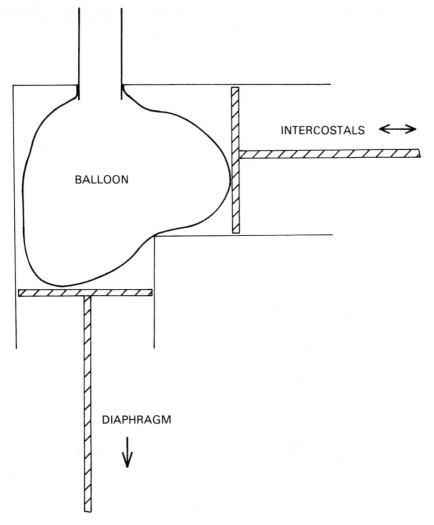

INTERCOSTALS ⟷

BALLOON

DIAPHRAGM

Figure 1 Schematic diagram of lower respiratory system

pleural volume. The pressure inside the sealed pleural space will fall as the volume increases because the product of the volume and pressure is equal to a constant. Since the inside of the lung balloon is open to the outside air, the lung balloon will expand as the pleural air pressure falls. The constant atmospheric air pressure will be manifested against the inside of the lung balloon as it stretches. As the lung balloon expands and stretches two things thus happen. Air flows into the lung, and energy is stored in the elastic walls of the lung balloon.

The lungs thus store energy that powers the *expiratory* phase of respiration during inspiration, as illustrated in Figure 2.

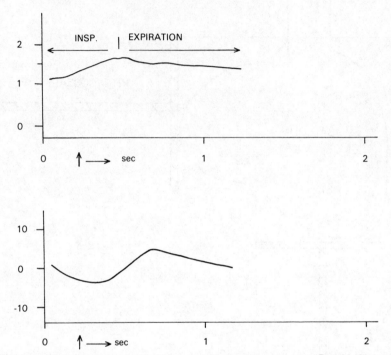

Figure   2 Lung volume in liters and air pressure in Cm H$_2$0 during quiet respiration

If you think of a rubber balloon it is clear that you store energy when you blow the balloon up. The energy that you store in the *elastic* balloon will force air out of the balloon when you release your hold on its open end. The intercostal and abdominal muscles can also squeeze inwards on the pleural space and contribute power for the expiration of air. The plungers that schematize these muscle groups in Figure 1, thus point inwards for the abdominals, and inwards and outwards for the intercostals. The intercostals in adult-like *Homo sapiens* can function both as inspiratory and expiratory muscles. The main force that powers the expiratory phase of respiration however is the *elastic recoil* force of the lungs, i.e., the elasticity of the lung "balloon". The difficulty that people have, for example, in breathing when they suffer from emphysema follows from the lungs losing their elasticity.

Figure 2 shows the lung volume functions and air pressure developed in the lungs that occurs during normal, quiet respiration in an adult human being (Lieberman, 1967). The inspiratory and expiratory phases of respiration have

242

almost the same duration. Inspiration is marked by air flowing into the lungs so the lung volume increases; expiration is manifested in the lung volume plot as a fall in the volume. Note that the alveolar air pressure, like the air pressure in the lungs, gradually falls during expiration. This follows from the gradual decrease in the elastic recoil force which is, of course, greater when the lungs are distended and which falls as the lung volume decreases. The rubber balloon analogy again is useful in thinking about this effect. If you blow up a balloon and release it, it will fly about quite fast at first when it is distended and the air pressure inside is highest. As the rubber balloon's volume decreases, the internal air pressure will fall and it will fly slower and slower.

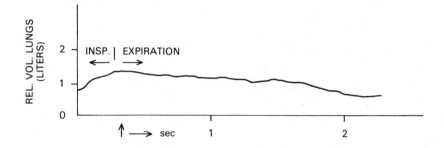

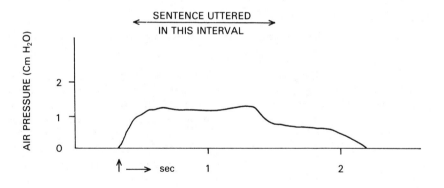

Figure 3 Lung volume and air pressure functions during speech over the span of a sentence

Figure 3 shows lung volume and air pressure functions for a speaker during the production of a sentence. Note the contrast with Figure 2. The duration of expiration is now long; it is keyed to the length of the sentence. The air pressure function moreover is relatively level throughout the expiration. Human speakers typically produce speech using a relatively steady alveolar air pressure that ranges from about 8 to 10 cm of H_2O. (Draper, Ladefoged and Whitteridge, 1960; Lieberman, 1967; Lieberman, 1968; Bouhuys, 1974). They moreover maintain this relatively steady air pressure function throughout the length of the expiration. The length of the expiration and the depth of the inspiration that precedes an expiration are moreover keyed to the length of the one sentence or sentence-like unit of speech that they are **going** to produce.

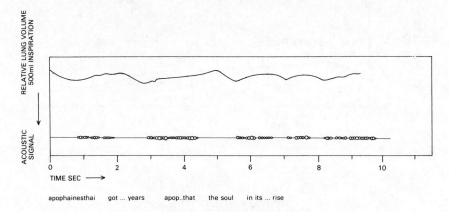

Figure 4   Lung volume functions for a speaker reciting several lines of a poem

Figure 4 shows lung volume functions for a speaker reciting a poem (Lieberman and Lieberman, 1973). Note that the length of the expiratory phase of respiration varies. It is determined by the line structure of the poem. Note too that a "deeper", i.e., a greater inspiration occurs when the speaker is going to produce a longer expiration. The speaker thus "programs" his respiratory activity in terms of the structure of the poem. He takes in more air before he starts on a long expiration. The speaker thus must have some knowledge of the duration of the utterance that he or she is going to produce. The psychological reality of the sentence thus is apparent at this level of observation.

The programing requirement is, however, more complex than simply taking more air into your lungs before a longer expiration.

244

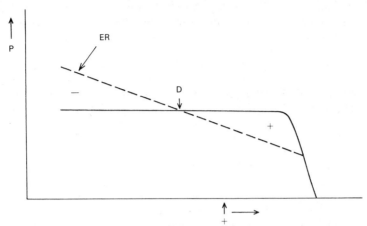

Figure 5 Diagram illustrated respiratory maneuvers that are necessary to produce a steady sublottal air pressure over the course of a long utterance

The sketch in Figure 5 is germane to a discussion of the maneuvers that people continually make when they talk, play wind instruments, or sing. The interrupted line represents the alveolar air pressure that would result if the elastic recoil function were the only force that the speaker brings into play. The solid line represents the steady alveolar air pressure that the speaker actually produces. The area to the left thus represents the "excess" pressure generated by the elastic lung recoil that the speaker must counter when she/he takes a large volume into her/his lungs at the start of a long expiration. "Excess" air pressure is countered by pulling outwards on the rib cage with the intercostal muscles. The intercostal "hold back" muscle function has to be adjusted to the initial depth of the inspiration and has to gradually decrease as the lung volume decreases. When the air pressure developed by the elastic recoil matches the "desired air pressure" at point "D", the speaker has to supplement the elastic recoil force with the "expiratory" component of the intercostals and the abdominal muscles. The programing is thus complex and must be keyed to the length of the sentence that the speaker intends to produce. At the end of the expiration the alveolar air pressure falls rapidly. This follows from the speaker's opening his larynx for inspiration and simultaneously starting to the transition to the negative air alveolar air pressure that is necessary for inspiration.

3. The Acquisition of Intonation by Infants

To briefly review the discussion, adult speakers typically lengthen the duration of the expiratory phase of expiration during speech. The length of an expiration is equal to the length of a sentence-like unit of speech. Adult speakers maintain a steady subglottal air pressure, during the non-terminal phase of the expiration. They effect this level air pressure by "holding back" on the elastic recoil force of the lungs with the intercostal muscles that can expand the rib-cage.

There is one crucial difference between the intonation signals that newborn infants produce and those typical of older human speakers. Newborn infants cannot regulate subglottal air pressure by a "hold back" intercostal muscle gesture. The hold back, i.e., inspiratory function of the intercostal muscles is a mechanical consequence of the fact that the ribs are angled downwards and outwards from the spine in human beings after the age of about three months. At birth, the ribs in newborn infants are almost perpendicular to the spine (Crelin, 1969). Newborn infants thus inherently cannot effect a steady subglottal air pressure by working against the air pressure generated by the elastic recoil of the lungs. The control of subglottal air pressure during long expirations requires a hold back function since the elastic recoil pressure at the start of the expiration will exceed the level of 8-10 cm H_2O that is normally used during speech. Newborn infants can generate the air pressure functions that occur in short breath-groups because the air pressure that results from the elastic recoil is quite low, in the order of 2 cm H_2O. Newborn infants can supplement this pressure with their abdominal muscles to generate the subglottal air pressures necessary for phonation. They cannot, however, regulate air pressure during long breath-groups because the increased lung volume generates a subglottal air pressure function that is initially too high. Although adult speakers tend to produce short breath-groups that again involve the simpler pressure regulation scheme of the newborn infant (Froscher, 1978), they can also produce very long breath-groups. Human infants begin to produce long episodes of phonation after their third month of life when their rib cage has restructured towards the adult configuration (Langlois et al, 1980).

The regulatory patterns that are involved in generating the air pressure functions typical of speech are quite complex even for the relatively "simple" situation that occurs when we produce short breath-groups and do not have to program an intercostal "hold back" function. The elastic recoil function still must be supplemented by the precisely coordinated activity of the "expiratory" intercostal and abdominal muscles. It is striking that newborn infants do as well as they do and it is reasonable to hypothesize an innately determined mechanism that has evolved to regulate subglottal air pressure during phonation. The presence of such an innate mechanism would not be surprising since the larynx clearly has evolved over a period of 300 million years to facilitate the production of sound at the expense of respiratory efficiency (Negus, 1949).

The data of Truby, Bosma and Lind (1965); Stark, Rose and McLagen (1975); and Langlois, Baken and Wilder (1980) all show a pattern of respiratory activity for newborn infants in which the expiratory phase is about five times longer than the inspiratory phase. Newborn infants appear to generate an initial positive alveolar air pressure by means of abdominal contraction about 100 msec before the onset of phonation. There also is an abrupt decrease in alveolar air pressure at the end of phonation as the infant goes into the inspiratory phase of respiration (Truby et al, 1965: 73).

Three aspects of the intonation patterns of normal human newborn cry are similar to the patterns that adult speakers usually use.

(1) The duration of the expiratory phase is usually longer than that of the inspiratory phase and can vary in duration. The cry patterns noted in Truby et al (1965) had expiratory phases whose durations varied over a two-to-one range.

(2) The alveolar air pressure function rapidly rises prior to the onset of phonation and then falls rapidly at the end of phonation as the infant enters the inspiratory phase of phonation. Phonation occurs until the end of expiration. The abrupt shift in the alveolar air pressure function at the end of phonation reflects a basic vegetative constraint since a negative air pressure is necessary for inspiration. The infant must maintain a positive air pressure during expiration so an abrupt transition must take place at the end of the expiratory cycle coincident with phonation. Numerous studies (Lieberman, 1967; Lieberman et al, 1969; Ohala, 1970; Atkinson, 1973; Shipp, Doherty and Morrissey, 1979) have found that the effect of changes in subglottal air pressure on the fundamental frequency of phonation is approximately 10 Hz/cm H_2O. Thus, all things being equal Fo will fall at the end of an expiration. If the larynx does not maintain its phonatory configuration until the end of phonation but instead begins to open towards its inspiratory position the terminal fall in Fo will be enhanced as the laryngeal muscles detension (Van den Berg, 1962; Atkinson, 1973).

Most traditional perceptually based phonetic theories e.g., (Armstrong and Ward, 1926; Pike, 1945; Trager and Smith, 1951) and many instrumental studies (Lieberman, 1967; Hadding-Koch, 1961; Vanderslice and Ladefoged, 1972; Atkinson, 1973; Tseng, 1981; Landahl, 1982) agree insofar as a falling of Fo and amplitude contour forms the *terminal* of a breath-group. The terminal intonation contour whose acoustic correlates are a falling Fo and amplitude thus is the cue that signals the end of a declarative sentence or phrase in most human languages (Lieberman, 1967). This signal follows from the vegetative constraints of respiration. It reflects the biological necessity of a transition in alveolar air pressure from the positive air pressure of expiration to the negative air pressure of inspiration.

(3) The third aspect wherein the newborn cry pattern's intonation is similar to the adult pattern, is that the Fo contour tends to be almost level in the

non-terminal portion of the breath-group. About 70 percent of the Fo contours noted in the spectrograms in Truby et al (1965) and the corpus that formed the data base sampled in Lieberman et al (1972) had a relatively steady non-terminal Fo contour. The other cry patterns involved either gross perturbations of the Fo pattern where the infant blew his/her vocal cords apart because of excessive subglottal air pressure relative to medial compression (Van den Berg, 1962) or exhibited other patterns of Fo variation. What was not noted was the steady "declination" that some recent studies claim in the "base form" for intonation (Maeda, 1976; Sorenson and Cooper, 1980; Pierrehumbert, 1979). The declination theory claims that a general fall in Fo throughout the breath-group characterizes the intonation contours of most languages. According to Pierrehumbert (1979) this hypothetical gradual fall in Fo follows from some as yet unknown, basic property of speech production that is manifested in the initial utterance of infants and children. The intonation pattern of newborn cry does not show a consistent Fo declination that fits any version of the declination theory. (Different versions of the declination theory characterize the hypothetical Fo fall in different ways.)

4. Overriding the Vegetative Regulatory System

There are a number of layered feedback mechanisms that monitor breathing in humans and other animals to ensure that the respiratory system meets the physiologic demands of both normal and strenuous activities. There are two "layers" of feedback control that make use of "chemoreceptors" that monitor the levels of dissolved CO_2 and oxygen, and the pH (the degree of acidity or alkalinity) of our blood and cerebrospinal fluid. These feedback mechanisms are basic in that they sustain the ventilatory conditions that are necessary to sustain life. They probably are "layered" to maintain redundancy in the life support system. However, we routinely override these regulatory systems when we talk, sing or play wind instruments.

The two layers of chemoreceptor actuated feedback are "central" and "peripheral" with respect to the brain. The central chemoreceptors are located near the ventrolateral surface of the medulla, or "spinal bulb" of the brain. The medulla is continuous with the spinal cord and is one of the "primitive" parts of the brain. The chemoreceptors are located in a part of the medulla that is relatively far from the traditional "respiratory centers" that regulate respiration. They monitor the CO_2 and pH of both the cerebrospinal fluid and the blood that perfuses the medulla. Peripheral chemoreceptors are located in two places, in the carotid bodies, near the bifurcation of the common carotid artery in the neck and in the aortic bodies, near the arch of the aorta. The aorta is the main artery that carries oxygenated blood from the heart. The peripheral chemoreceptors monitor pH and oxygen in the arterial blood (Bouhuys, 1974).

The central and peripheral chemoreceptor feedback system acts rapidly to make small changes in respiration. The central feedback system operates slowly but it can effect large changes in respiration. The chemoreceptors are quite sensitive. They, for example, initiate increased respiratory activity when you breathe in a closed room with a number of other people because the oxygen content of the "stale" room air is lower than it should be. The chemoreceptor feedback systems can operate rapidly; when you are breathing stale air a single breath of pure oxygen will lead to a temporary reduction of ventilation (Dejours, 1963).

Despite these redundant regulatory systems, adult human beings typically override the control pattern that prevails during quiet respiration when they talk. When you breathe room air and talk, ventilation per minute increases during speech. The ventilation rate can become quite high when you produce high flow sounds like [h] (Klatt et al, 1968). A significant decrease from normal blood CO_2 levels thus can occur during sustained speech during normal activity levels. In contrast, when it is necessary to transfer more air through the lungs to meet basic vegetative constraints, for example, during strenuous activities, speech production decreases the flow rate. Though speakers in some cases adapt patterns of respiration that maintain optimum air transfer with flow rates compatible with intelligible speech, they usually give priority to the flow rates that are necessary for speech production and override the regulatory mechanisms.

It again is unlikely that the ability to override these basic vegetative regulatory mechanisms is "learned" in the normal sense of that word. However, we do not know when infants begin to act in this mode or whether exposure to an environment in which they hear people talking is necessary to "trigger" genetically transmitted patterns of linguistic behavior. The generally poor quality of the intonation of deaf speakers (see Maassen this volume) suggests that some exposure to speech is necessary.

5. Early Imitation of Intonation

Traditional, perceptually based accounts of the acquisition of speech state that infants start to imitate the sounds that they hear towards 8 to 10 months (Lewis, 1936). Recent studies that make use of the techniques of instrumental analysis, however, show that the process of imitation can start much earlier. Acoustic analysis of a conversation between a Japanese-speaking mother and her six week old son, for example, shows the infant imitating the absolute Fo and shape of the mother's intonation (Rabson et al, 1982).

Figure 6 shows the mother's Fo contour for an utterance directed towards an adult (one of the members of the recording crew) immediately before she turned to talk to her infant son.

249

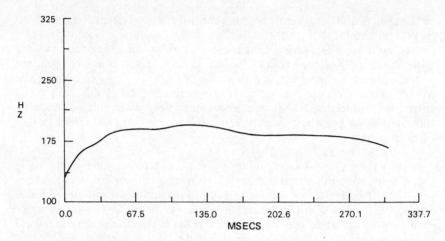

Figure 6 Utterance of mother addressing adult

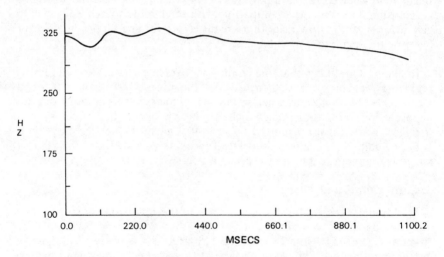

Figure 7 Contour of utterance [m] of as mother addresses infant

Figure 7 shows the Fo contour of the sustained m-like sounds that she directed towards her son. Note that the average Fo of the speech directed to the infant is over 300 Hz in contrast to the mother's average Fo of 200 Hz in her speech directed towards adults. The mother appears to be using a "motherese" register in which her average Fo is within the infant's Fo range (Keating and Buhr, 1978) facilitating imitation.

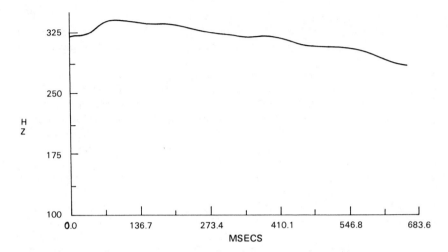

Figure 8 Contour of utterance of infant imitating mother

Figure 8 shows the Fo contour of the infant imitating the sound whose Fo is plotted in figure 7. The infant has matched both the absolute Fo and shape of the sound that his mother directed to him. Note, however, that the infant's imitation is only 680 msec long whereas the duration of the mother's utterance was 1100 msec. The infant at age six weeks lacks the rib cage anatomy that is neccessary to produce a long expiration at a controlled sub-glottal air pressure. He thus responds with a shorter intonation contour that however preserves the absolute Fo and shape of his mother's intonation contour. The infant's imitations of his mothers speech in this "conversation" involved three interchanges in which the infant's responses were limited to duration of approximately 700 msec. The mother appeared to initiate this conversation when she moved quite close to her son's face and he directed the first m-like sound, which his mother in turn imitated, followed by the infant imitating that sound, etc. Infants by these procedures may "learn" that it is appropriate to imitate speech sounds. There, of course, may be a genetically transmitted tendancy for children to imitate sounds and for mothers to acculurate their children to the imitation of speech. However, whether or not threr are any innate mechanisms that are specifically "designed" to facilitate the imitation of speech sounds, it is evident that the infants begin to imitate the intonation contours that occur in their native language at a very early age. These instrumental thjus are consistent with the traditional, oft repeated claim that children aquire the characteristic intonation patterns of their native language native language in the first year of life (Lewis, 1936).

By age three months infants can match the duration of their mother's intonation contours as well as the absolute Fo. The data of Sandner (1981) show a three-month old infant imitating the fundamental frequency contours

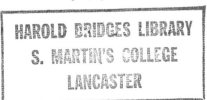
251

of his German-speaking mother during a five minute "conversation". The infant is imitating the detailed, non-terminal modulations of fundamental frequency that his mother produces. Sandner presents no physiologic data on the infant's subglottal air pressure; however, an adult human speaker would normally maintain an even subglottal air pressure and imitate the details of the non-terminal fundamental frequency contour by adjustments of the laryngeal muscles (Ohala, 1970; Atkinson, 1973). It otherwise would be extremely difficult, if not impossible, to imitate a long, detailed fundamental frequency contour. The speaker would have to compensate for the constantly changing subglottal air pressure that would be generated by the decreasing elastic recoil function. As we have noted, phonation during newborn cry, where subglottal air pressure is not regulated tends to be interrupted with intervals of aspiration when the vocal cords are blown apart by an excessively high subglottal air pressure. The infant in Sandner's study thus in all likelihood was regulating subglottal air pressure using his intercostal muscles. It is difficult to see how a three-month old infant could have "learned" to regulate his subglottal air pressure since the developement of his rib cage would not have allowed him to use his intercostal muscles to regulate air pressure **until** the third month of life (Langlois et al, 1980). In other words, the infant in Sandner's study appears to regulate subglottal air pressure and imitates intonation contours as **soon** as his anatomy develops to the point where he can regulate subglottal air pressure. The pattern of anatomy and muscular control suddenly appears. It thus is quite likely that the neural muscular control pattern for the regulation of subglottal air pressure is innately determined.

The control of subglottal air pressure and laryngeal muscle control in children who have been deaf from birth is usually extremely poor. Whether this means that an innate propensity for control exists, that must be exercised within a "critical period" is unclear.

6. Linguistic "Base-Forms"

The study of the acquisition of intonation by infants can yield some insight into the nature of the "base form" of intonation. It is obvious that children learn to speak without any formal instruction. We do not have to resolve the issue of whether language acquisition in children rests on a language-specific neural ability or not, to make use of the fact that children **do** somehow manage to extract the linguistically salient aspects of speech from the "noise" that they encounter in life. Jakobson (1940) thus proposed that the sequence in which children acquired the distinctive speech contrasts of their first language yields an insight into the linguistic hierarchy of the speech code. A long-term study at Brown University has followed the development of speech in normal infants from birth to ages that range from three to four years (Lieberman, 1980). One aspect of this study involves the acoustic and linguistic analysis of the intonation contours that children use in their initial one-word utterances. Landahl (1982) in these studies, shows that the Fo contours of these one-word utterances are quite similar to the contours that adult speakers of American English usually use to segment speech into meaningful sentences.

Acoustic analyses of the intonation of declarative sentences of American English show that the linguistically salient acoustic cue that usually delimits the scope of a sentence is a breath-group *terminal* abrupt fall in Fo accompanied by a concomitant fall in the amplitude of the speech signal (Lieberman, 1967; Vanderslice and Ladefoged, 1972; Atkinson, 1973). In Figures 9, 10 and 11 Fo contours of some of the first one-word utterances of a 70 week-old girl are presented (Landahl, 1982).

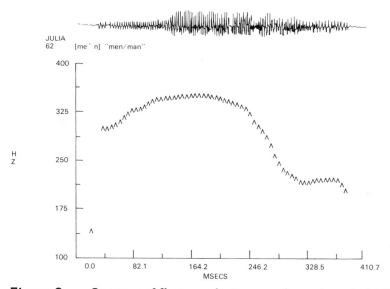

Figure 9 **Contour of first word utterance 'men/man' of 70 week old girl (Landahl, 1980)**

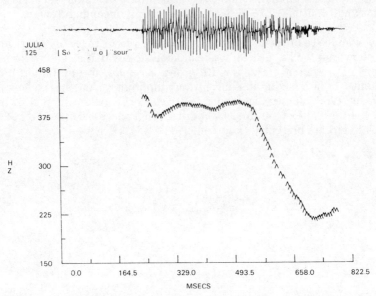

Figure 10 First word utterance 'sour' of 70 week old girl (Landahl, 1980)

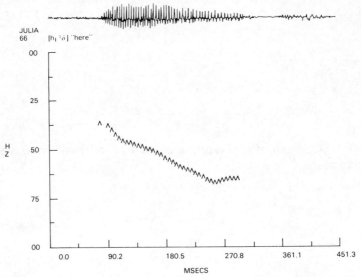

Figure 11   First word utterance 'here' of 70 week old girl (Landahl, 1980)

254

Note that the Fo contour in Figure 10 which corresponds to the word *sour* initially is level and then falls. In Figure 9 the Fo that occurred for the one-word "sentence" *man* is presented. Note that there again is a terminal Fo fall; the non-terminal Fo contour is again relatively flat after an initial rise. In Figure 11 the Fo contour for the utterance *here* shows a gradual fall throughout the breath-group. Figure 11 shows a "declination" or fall throughout the breath-group, the other two samples do not. The one-word utterances analyzed in Landahl (1982) which are derived from the spontaneous speech of three children show that declination does not typically characterize these utterances. The most general acoustic cue is a terminal fall in Fo. Thus, if the general claim of Jakobson (1940) is correct, and children acquire the "base form" for the intonation of American English, these data show that it does not consist of a "declination", contrary to the claims of Pierrehumbert (1979) who asserts that declination is a linguistic "universal" that can be seen in the initial utterances of children.

According to proponents of the declination theory of intonation, speakers consistently segment the phrases of a sentence into syntactic units by "programming" a declination, i.e., a gradual fall in Fo. Since local perturbations in Fo can occur as the consequence of the speaker's stressing words, the claim of the declination theory is that there will be either a gradual fall in the "valleys" of the Fo contour across a sentence (Maeda, 1976) or in the peaks of the Fo contour (Pierrehumbert, 1979; Sorenson and Cooper, 1980). The non-terminal portion of the breath-group does sometimes gradually fall for most speakers and may consistently fall for some speakers, but the effect is not general (Lieberman and Tseng, 1980; Lieberman et al, 1982; Tseng, 1981).

Figure 12 for example, shows the Fo contour that was derived for an adult male speaker of American English when he produced the sentence, *Good, which one?* in normal discourse (Lieberman and Tseng, 1980). Note that the peaks in Fo at $T = 50$ and 260 msec have the same absolute value, contrary to the claims of declination theorists. The terminal fall at 640 msec ends at a lower value than the initial Fo "valley" at 120 msec as the declination theory of Maeda (1976) claims, but this relation also would hold for breath-group theories, since the terminal fall is, by definition supposed to have a lower value than non-terminal Fo's.

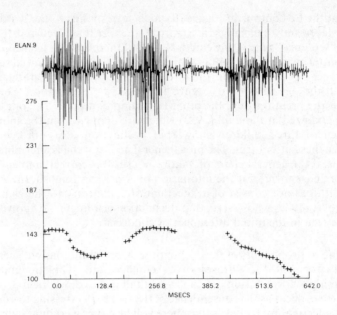

Figure 12 Utterance contour of sentence Good, which one?' said by American male

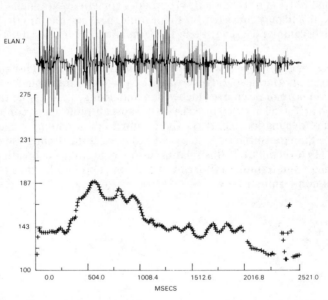

Figure 13 Same male uttering 'Remember, we talked about the alternative solution'

Figure 13 shows the Fo contour that this same speaker produced when he uttered the sentence, *Remember, we talked about the alternative solution.* There is an Fo prominence on the word *remember* which yields the percept of *stress* or *prominence* on this word (Fry, 1958; Lieberman, 1960). Neither the Fo "peaks" or "valleys" however, show a general "declination" if we discount this initial peak.

The communicative function of level versus falling non-terminal Fo contours is not clear. Pike (1945), in his comprehensive phonetic study of the intonation of American English, attempted to show that different intonation contours conveyed particular attitudes of the speaker. Pike, however, concluded that the attitudinal value of the intonation contour was not independent of the lexical content of the words of a sentence. Umeda (personal communication), who has studied a large corpus of Fo contours of sentences uttered in the course of sustained discourse, suggests that Fo "declination" may be a discourse effect that serves to introduce a "new" topic in a conversation. Umeda's data show that an initial Fo peak, like that in Figure 13, serves as an acoustic "paragraph" marker in discourse. Umeda also notes that some speakers continually make use of this acoustic clue in virtually all of their sentences. The declination theory makes too strong a claim about the form of the non-terminal Fo contour of the breath-group. Some of the data cited in support of the declination theory are misleading; if Fo contours that are essentially level are averaged with ones that do fall, the average is bound to be a contour that will fall. The claim of the declination theory that all Fo contours must fall is clearly wrong.

7. Concluding Comments

The acoustic and linguistic analysis of cry and speech production in infants and young children demonstrates that human linguistic behavior is structured by physiologic mechanisms. Some of these mechanisms appear to be primarily adapted for vegetative, non-linguistic functions. In this sense human linguistic ability follows from our general, biological endowment. Other aspects of speech production which are manifested quite early in an infant's life appear to involve physiologic mechanisms that are adapted for communication. The biological bases of human linguistic ability thus involve a mosaic that, like other aspects of human behavior, reflects the course of hominid evolution in that it involves mechanisms that occur in other animals and certain specializations that characterize hominids.

257

THE ROLE OF TEMPORAL STRUCTURE AND INTONATION IN DEAF SPEECH

Ben Maassen

1. Introduction

In general, the speech of deaf people is difficult to understand for naive listeners. Prelingually deaf children especially must overcome great difficulties in acquiring skills for verbal communication. Deafness is a hearing handicap that is so severe that understanding spoken language mainly by hearing will never be possible (usually this is assumed to be the case at a hearing loss of 90 dB ISO or more). The prefix 'prelingual' means that the hearing loss is congenital or acquired so early in life, that no substantial speech- or language-development had taken place; that is before the age of 2 years 6 months (Uden, 1968). Without special education deaf children remain deaf-mute. For a better understanding of the characteristics of deaf-speech, the special way in which these children acquire spoken language must be considered.

During the process of speech-acquisition a hearing child tries to match its own acoustic products with an external norm that is auditorily defined, i.e. the acoustic products of other people. In this learning process attention is directed to the intended acoustic results: speech sounds. The child thereby gradually acquires the articulatory processes by which these products are achieved, including the corresponding tactile and kinesthetic feedback-patterns. These processes themselves, however, remain in the background. Articulation proceeds automatically, reaching consciousness only under exceptional circumstances (e.g. when the speaker stumbles).

For a prelingually deaf child the situation is completely reversed. Lacking most of the *product information*, it has to rely almost entirely on *process information* (Povel, 1974a, 1974b). Not only its own articulations are defined as movements of the articulatory organs, but also the norms the child is trying to imitate must be explicitly described in terms of production. The only support comes from tactile and kinesthetic feedback, possibly supplemented with visual feedback when a mirror is used. As we will see, this shift in modality from the auditory to the tactile, kinesthetic and visual senses is partly reflected in the typical errors deaf speakers produce: they are inclined to confuse those sounds or err in those speech-characteristics that are hardest to discriminate on the basis of the feedback available to them. Information on their own intonation patterns and those of others thereby appears to be particularly difficult to transmit.

Apart from the question of the type of deviations deaf speakers produce as compared to hearing speakers, one might ask: to what extent do these errors affect intelligibility? It is not at all necessarily the case that the most frequent error is also the most detrimental to intelligibility. The experimental literature on speech perception has shown that acoustic distortions, produced by the experimenter, can easily be overcome by the listener, if only the distortions are introduced more or less systematically. For instance, lengthening every phoneme by a factor of two or making the Fo-contour monotonous (both manipulations get near typical deaf-errors) hardly affect intelligibility. Therefore, from these studies one can conclude that a mere inventory of errors, although perhaps a prerequisite for further research, does not answer the question why deaf speakers are difficult to understand. As a consequence, an inventory of errors does not answer the practical question as to which deviations teachers of the deaf should spend most energy on if they want to improve the intelligibility of their pupils.

Two methods for assessing the (relative) importance of different error types will be described: the 'correlational method' and the 'speech transformation method'. Most research on deaf speech in the literature has followed the *correlational method*. According to this method, errors in deaf speech are divided into distinct, articulatorily and auditorily relevant dimensions, like errors in consonants, vowels and suprasegmental attributes. The significance of the different dimensions is assessed by calculating multiple correlations with intelligibility-scores. Those error types are considered most damaging, which best predict unintelligibility.

The second way to tackle this question is by using the *speech transformation method*. According to this method, deviations in deaf speech are artificially corrected with the help of computer programs, after which the improvement in intelligibility is measured in perception experiments. This method has become available as a result of recent developments in digital speech technology. Techniques for manipulating speech signals in the temporal domain and for changing Fo-contours are now relatively easy to apply. The speech transformation method derives part of its attractiveness from the fact that it directly simulates speech training, without bothering pupils and teachers with a restricted, experimentally controlled training programme.

In what follows, research in the literature, performed according to the correlational method, will first be presented. After a brief overview of the segmental deviations in deaf speech, special emphasis is put on temporal structure and intonation. These latter aspects have been the main subject-matter of the speech transformation method, which will be described next. This method has been applied by the author together with Dr. Povel on a speech sample of deaf Dutch children. The important role of suprasegmental aspects as determinants of intelligibility according to the correlation studies could not be corroborated. Possible explanations for this discrepancy will be discussed.

2. Correlational Studies

The first extensive investigation, in which an attempt was made to explain the low intelligibility of deaf speech in terms of acoustic and articulatory deviations, stressed the importance of suprasegmental errors (Hudgins and Numbers, 1942). In this study 192 deaf and hearing impaired children participated and a total number of 1900 sentences was analysed. The authors divided the factors upon which intelligibility depends into two main classes. The first class, *specific factors*, consisted of 7 categories of consonant errors and 5 categories of vowel errors. These were not defined according to standard phonetic features (like voicing, place and manner of articulation) but were rather a summary inventory of actually occurring errors. For instance, frequent deviations were: consonant omissions, errors in abutting or adjacent consonants, splitting up a diphthong into two separate vowels, or dropping one component so that it became a monophthong. These factors are now better known as segmental aspects.

The second class of errors distinguished by Hudgins and Numbers, consisted of *general factors* (or suprasegmental aspects). These appeared much harder to analyse. While errors in accentuation, grouping and phrasing were lumped together into one category labelled 'speech rhythm', the authors noted that "Other defects such as defective voice quality, false intonation and monotonous speech, while present could not be systematically analysed into quantitative terms and are not included in the study" (Hudgins and Numbers, 1942; 307). Nevertheless, a significant correlation between correct rhythm and intelligibility was reported (r=0.73) which was even slightly higher than the absolute correlation between consonant errors and intelligibility (r=0.70).

This extensive investigation of Hudgins and Numbers was followed by many others. The most important methodological variations between studies relate to type of speaker (ranging from 'hard-of-hearing' (hearing loss 30 dB) to 'deaf' (hearing loss of at least 90 dB), procedure of eliciting the speech samples (picture naming or picture description, read out sentences), type of listener for determining intelligibility (educators and teachers of the deaf, phoneticians, naive listeners) and error categories. All studies agree, however, in dividing errors into segmental and suprasegmental categories. We will first give a brief survey of the first error type - results are fairly consistent on this point - before discussing suprasegmentals more thoroughly. For the sake of clarity, methodological details will only be mentioned when they are directly relevant for interpreting results. The major part of the investigated speech-material consists of sentences read by children between 8 and 14 years of age with a hearing loss of at least 60 dB.

2.1. Segmental errors

2.1.1. Consonant errors

A general finding is that consonant errors are more harmful to intelligibility than vowel errors.

The most frequent consonant errors noted in deaf speech are consonant omissions (McGarr and Osberger, 1978). Hudgins and Numbers (1942) found a very high negative correlation (r=−0.56) between omission of releasing consonant and intelligibility (Hudgins and Numbers, 1942). Consonants with their place of articulation in the centre or back of the mouth were more frequently omitted than labial, dental or alveolar consonants (Levitt and Smith, 1972; Smith, 1975; Levitt, Smith and Stromberg, 1976).

The second important category consists of consonant-substitutions. Especially voiced plosives (/b/, /d/, /g/) and fricatives (/ ð /, /v/, /z/) are often replaced by their voiceless cognate (/p/, /t/, /k/ and / θ /, /f/, /s/ respectively) (Hudgins and Numbers, 1942; Markides, 1970; Nober, 1967; McGarr and Osberger, 1978). Calvert (1961) and Monsen (1976, 1978) found that these confusions were mainly due to temporal distortions. Normally, a voiceless sound is produced with **longer** duration than its voiceless cognate, while the preceding vowel is **shorter**; deaf speakers in general do not make this distinction. The remaining consonant substitutions relate mostly to **manner** of articulation (/m/ → /p/, /b/; /s/ → /st/); place-errors are far less frequent (Levitt and Smith, 1972).

The third most important consonant-error category of the investigation by Hudgins and Numbers (1942) consisted of errors in compound consonants. The correlation with intelligibility was r=−0.44. Since errors in this category consisted either of dropping one of the components (e.g. /str-/ of 'street' becomes /st-/ or in a failure to fuse the members (so that /str-/ becomes /s t r-/), in later studies these errors are treated as consonant omissions or suprasegmental errors respectively. Remaining consonant errors, like the very frequent nasalisations, affect intelligibility to a lesser extent.

2.1.2 Vowel Errors

Deaf speakers often neutralise vowels; almost all studies report this phenomenon. According to Handzel (1956) and Monsen and Shaughnessy (1978) this is mainly due to insufficient variation in the second formant. More significant for intelligibility are substitutions by a different, often unrelated vowel (Hudgins and Numbers, 1942; Markides, 1970). Levitt and Smith (1972) found to be particularly frequent confusions on the dimension tense-lax (/e/ vs. /ɛ/, /o/ vs. /ɔ/, /a/ vs. /ɑ/). Most authors reported a tendency to monophthongise diphthongs by dropping one of the components; alternatively, like compound consonants, diphthongs are often articulated too slowly, resulting in two separately spoken vowels and thereby in the addition of an extra syllable.

2.2. Suprasegmental errors

Whereas results on segmental errors are quite uniform, the literature diverges widely with respect to prosodic or suprasegmental features of deaf speech. This is mainly due to the fact that no reliable phonetic transcription system exists for suprasegmental aspects. It requires a well-developed analytic ability on the part of the listener to perceive, for instance, pitch-movements independently from accents. Attempts to elaborate a transcription system for one of the suprasegmental aspects of which the acoustic correlates are still largely unknown, i.e. voice quality (Laver and Hanson ,1981), are only of recent date and not yet generally introduced into the field. As a consequence, investigators of the deaf have been forced to apply error-categories based on subjective impressions.

2.2.1 Judgements on rhythm and intonation

Despite the fact that transcription methods had not been standardised, correlational studies have recognised the significance of prosodic deviations in deaf speech. Hudgins and Numbers (1942) divided the sentences into three rhythm-categories: normal rhythm, abnormal rhythm and non-rhythmic. As was noted above, in spite of this crude division a very high correlation was found with intelligibility ($r=-0.73$). Moreover, high negative correlations (around $r=-0.50$) were found with consonant and vowel errors.

Smith (1975) asked three speech-pathologists to rate sentences spoken by deaf speakers on 19 binary categories pertaining to suprasegmental aspects: three categories for voice-quality, two for voice-pitch, two for phonatory control, two for intonation, two for stress, four for fluency and four for rate of speech. A factor-analysis on this material revealed two fairly significant factors. One related to poor phonatory control, which included intermittent phonation and inappropriate variations of pitch and loudness; the other factor related to rate of speech production. Together these two factors accounted for 50% of the variance. Phonatory control showed a partial correlation (i.e. after elimination of segmental effects) with intelligibility of $r=-0.39$. These results were corroborated by Levitt, Smith and Stromberg (1976) on the same corpus of sentences to which they added speech samples of 30 deaf and hearing children: phonatory control and rate of speech production again appeared the most important factors. Moreover, these authors brought the subjective ratings into relation with acoustic measurements. Judgements on pitch level, insufficient or excessive variability of intonation, rate of production and intermittent and spasmodic phonation not only showed the highest consistency between raters, but also correlated significantly with Fo and temporal measurements. No such acoustic correlates could be found for errors of voice quality and inappropriate stress.

263

There are two other studies in which temporal phenomena and pitch-movements stand out as important determinants of speech quality. McGarr and Osberger (1978) correlated ratings of speech-pathologists on phonation and prosody with judgements on intelligibility. Phonation errors and errors in absolute pitch-level showed only a moderate correlation (r=−0.36). Pause insertion, incorrect stress location and inappropriate sentence intonation - together labelled prosodic errors - appeared far more important (r=−0.64). In the second study, Parkhurst and Levitt (1978) asked a trained speech-pathologist to rate incorrect pitch-movements and temporal distortions. The latter category included inappropriate lengthening and pause insertions. In a multiple linear regression analysis, both appeared good predictors of intelligibility.

Instead of relying on subjective ratings, an alternative way of studying suprasegmentals of speech starts from measurement of the most relevant acoustic parameters. In the above discussion we saw that the acoustic correlates of accentuation, phonation and sentence intonation are mainly temporal structure and Fo-contour. By shifting from ratings to measurements, one loses out on perceptual relevance of the variables under study, but gains in accuracy and reliability of measurement.

2.2.2 Temporal structure

In general deaf people speak much more slowly than hearing speakers (Hudgins, 1934; Voelker, 1935); lengthening by a factor 1.5 to 2 is not uncommon (Nickerson et al in Gold, 1980). More important than mere speech rate for intelligibility, however, are the **relative** deviations in the temporal domain. Deaf speakers produce a lot of them. It was noted that they do not systematically produce voiceless plosives and fricatives with longer durations (and shorter preceding vowels) than their voiced cognates, as hearing speakers do. Monsen (1974) found that in deaf speech the shortest /i/ was longer than the longest /I/; hearing speakers showed more variability in vowel duration depending on context: only within the same context an /i/ is somewhat (40 msec.) longer than an /I/.

While there is some dispute about whether this kind of temporal phenomenon belong to the segmental or to the suprasegmental domain, a clearly prosodic phenomenon is the finding of Nickerson e.a. (in Gold, 1980) that deaf children fail to produce a difference between the durations of stressed and unstressed syllables. Through this lack of differentiation, the verb "sub**ject**" spoken by a deaf speaker is indiscriminable from the noun "**sub**ject" (Ando and Canter, 1969). The resulting 'staccato' speech is frequently reported (Angelocci, 1962; Boothroyd, Nickerson and Stevens (in Gold 1980)). Moreover, deaf speakers insert pauses in inappropriate places, not only between words but even within words. As a consequence, the grouping of syllables is incorrect (Hudgins, 1934; Nickerson et al (in Gold, 1980)), and they are often spoken separately (Stark and Levitt, 1974). This 'syllabic speech' strongly affects intelligibility (Levitt, Smith and Stromberg, 1976).

2.2.3 Intonation

Incorrect location of word and sentence accent is not only caused by temporal distortions, but to an even larger extent by incorrect pitch-movements. According to Sussman and Hernandez (1979) pitch control in the deaf speaker is inadequate for marking stress. Deaf speech is characterised by a monotonic pitch contour (Hudgins and Numbers, 1942; Levitt, Smith and Stromberg, 1976). Owing to insufficient control of the vocal cords, Fo variations are often restricted to those variations that - by physiological properties of the speech organs -directly result from changes in duration and intensity. This monotony gives the speech an unnatural quality. In addition, deaf speaker's pitch is often too high (Angelocci, Kopp and Holbrook, 1964; Calvert, 1961; Smith, 1975), this being mainly caused by an increased subglottal pressure and tension of the vocal cords. Willemain and Lee (1971) hypothesised that the reason for the high pitch is that the deaf speaker uses extra vocal effort to give him an awareness of the onset and progress of voicing. Finally, some investigators (Martony, 1968; Smith, 1975; Parkhurst and Levitt, 1978) reported that some deaf speakers produce excessive pitch-changes, which can give rise to inappropriate accentuations.

3. Speech Transformation Method

A very serious handicap of the correlational method is caused by the fact that, in natural speech, acoustic dimensions do not vary independently. An example is the relation between duration and spectrum of a vowel: vowels that are reduced in duration are also neutralised (Koopmans-van Beinum, 1981). The reason why such interrelations between acoustic parameters cause a problem for the correlational method is the following. Suppose two deaf speech errors, A and B, show a strong interrelationship. Suppose further that only error A is detrimental to intelligibility. Since it is the case that error B shows a tendency to occur together with error A, also B will be negatively correlated with intelligibility. Despite this negative correlation, however, correction of error B will have little or no effect on improving intelligibility (Gold, 1980). Thus a high negative correlation between an error and intelligibility does not guarantee that correction of this error will be effective.

This drawback is avoided by the speech transformation method. Instead of calculating the correlation between an error and intelligibility, the impact of the error is assessed directly by correcting it artificially and measuring the subsequent improvement in intelligibility. The diagram shown in Figure 1 illustrates the procedure. Deaf speech is fed into the computer and digitalised. Specialised programs carry out transformations that apply to the temporal structure, intonation or sound spectrums in the different dimensions of speech. After each manipulation the sentences are converted back to an analogue signal and recorded on tape. The effect is evaluated by performing an intelligibility test: the sentences are presented to naive listeners who write down what they can understand.

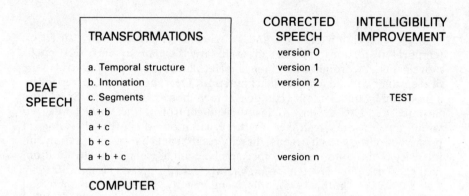

Figure 1   Schematic drawing of the speech transformed method

By executing two or more transformations on the same speech signal combined corrections can also be produced and interactions evaluated.

The method simulates experimentation with speech-training programmes. It thereby bypasses not only the practical and ethical problems that adhere to teaching and education experiments, but also the recurrent difficulty of correlated acoustic variables. How can a speech therapist be certain that only the intended aspects improve? John and Howarth (1965) gave deaf children a short training in temporal aspects; there was a high (relative) increase in intelligibility. Boothroyd, Nickerson and Stevens (in Gold, 1980) showed that after a training programme of 450(!) hours with visual feedback on duration of stressed and unstressed syllables, only the actually trained sentences improved; there was hardly any transfer to other sentences. In neither of these studies was it possible to exclude the possibility that other than temporal aspects had changed.

An added advantage of the speech transformation method is that there are no natural limits on what can be manipulated. It is not necessary to wait for a specific phenomenon under study to show up in the speech sample, because infrequent characteristics can be produced artificially. If the investigator does not restrict himself to correction of only actually occurring errors, require-ments of representativeness of the collected speech sample are not as severe as they are in the correlational method. The latter method demands a large speech sample, in which also infrequent characteristics and interactions are represented. The speech transformation method is limited only by technical considerations. So far, it has been applied mainly to temporal structure and intonation.

266

3.1 Speech synthesis

Huggins (1978) used the M.I.T. speech synthesizer developed by Klatt in 1972. In order to calculate segment durations and intonation contours this program requires for each syllable a stress specification (0 = no stress; 1 = primary stress; 2 = secondary stress). Spectral properties of speech sounds remain unaffected by this part of the program. Huggins synthesized sentences with an intelligibility score of 86%, when all parameters were specified optimally. By interchanging 0's and 1's of the stress specificiations the same sentences were generated with a deviant temporal structure, a deviant intonational pattern and a combination of both. Sentences that were only temporally distorted reached an intelligiblity score of 52%, and only intonationally distorted sentences a score of 67%. When both transformations were applied simultaneously, intelligibility dropped to 48%. Huggins concluded that suprasegmental aspects play an important role in the speech-perception process. His subjects reported that temporal and intonational deviations were misleading, since they put the listener on the wrong track.

With the same computer program, Bernstein (1977) synthesised 9 sentences in which, as well as temporal errors, segmental errors were also introduced that were derived from a sample of 24 words and 12 sentences spoken by a deaf child. He thus simulated deaf speech. As expected, intelligibility decreased when more consonant errors were introduced. Temporal deviations, however, only had an effect in sentences that already contained many consonant errors; temporal distortions alone did not impair intelligibility.

3.2 Temporal corrections of deaf speech

In a pilot experiment Maassen and Povel (1977) and Maassen (1978) corrected temporal deviations of five sentences spoken by three deaf children. Each phoneme of the deaf utterances was made equal in duration to the corresponding phoneme of a norm utterance: the same sentence spoken by a hearing child. The improvement in intelligibility for four of the five sentences was slight and significant for only one sentence. Quality judgements of all four sentences significantly favoured the corrected versions. The fifth sentence significantly deteriorated in intelligiblity as well as in quality.

In a more extensive investigation Osberger and Levitt (1979) gradually reduced temporal differences between deaf and hearing utterances. The original corpus of 36 deaf utterances received a mean intelligibility score of 36%. After elimination of pauses -step one - intelligibility dropped to 20%. In step two, a relative correction, the ratio of stressed to unstressed syllables in the deaf utterances was made equal to the corresponding ratio's in a norm utterance, by changing (mostly shortening) the durations of unstressed vowels. The norm utterances were obtained by having the same sentences also spoken by a hearing child. Now intelligibility rose to 34%. The third step was an absolute correction: duration of each phoneme was made equal to that of the corresponding phoneme in the norm utterance. (An exception was made for fricatives, affricates and plosives; these remained unchanged since they were already shorter in the deaf utterance.) Intelligibility dropped again to 24%. Also combinations of pause elimination (step one) and corrections of phoneme durations (steps two and three) had a negative effect on intelligibility (<20%). Like Bernstein, Osberger and Levitt found an interaction with segmental errors. However, this interaction went in the opposite direction: temporal corrections (step two) only improved intelligibility of sentences containing **few** segmental errors (less than 30%).

3.3 Temporal and Intonation Correction

In the study to be discussed now the effects of both temporal structure and intonation were evaluated. In this investigation, which will be fully reported in Maassen and Povel (in preparation) 30 Dutch sentences spoken by ten deaf children[1] were manipulated. Corrections in the temporal domain formed a replication and an extension of the set produced by Osberger and Levitt (1979). Each sentence was transformed into six different versions. In the first, the *syllabic relative* version, duration ratios between stressed and unstressed syllables were made equal to those of a norm utterance; the norm sentences were spoken by a hearing child of the same age and sex. The second version was a *phonemic relative* version. Here every phoneme of the deaf utterance got the same relative duration as the corresponding phoneme of the norm. (Only burst periods of plosives remained unaffected.) In the third, *phonemic absolute* version, phoneme durations of the deaf utterances were made equal to those of the norms. Versions four, five and six were respectively one, two and three plus pause elimination.

Together with the original utterances, these temporal corrections resulted in seven versions per sentence. These were presented to different groups of naive listeners (between-subject design), who wrote down what they understood. Intelligibility scores were calculated and expressed as percentages of words correctly understood. For three sentences the manipulations caused a dramatic fall in intelligibility; the transformations obviously had failed, which is ascribed to some unknown technical complication. Of the remaining 27 sentences, version 0 (the original) received a mean score of 18% (see Table 1).

0	1	2	3	4	5	6
18%	17%	21%	17%	16%	19%	14%

Table 1   Mean intelligibility scores expressed in percentage of words correctly understood, of the original sentence (version 0) and the six temporal corrections (version 1 to 6).

268

The best version was the phonemic relative one (version 2); also for the version with pause elimination, this correction (version 5) received the highest score. Elimination of pauses itself decreased intelligibility.

These are not firm conclusions, however. Although an analysis of variance showed a significant overall-effect for correction ($p < 0.05$), none of the versions stood out significantly better than the original utterance. This was caused by the fact that the best correction was not the same for all sentences. For 14 sentences, version 2 stood out as the most intelligible; intelligibility increased significantly from 25% to 30% ($p < 0.02$). For the remaining sentences, either the syllabic relative or the phonemic absolute correction brought about a comparable increase in intelligibility, which was significant only for the first group. It may be concluded that correction of only the temporal structure yields a small improvement in intelligibility.

On the other hand, quality judgements clearly favoured the temporally corrected versions. The phonemic relative correction (version 2) was preferred to the original utterance (version 0) by 75% of the subjects; this result is highly significant ($p < 0.01$). Preference rates of the phonemic absolute (56%) and the syllabic relative versions (49%) approached chance level. As with intelligibility scores, elimination of pauses had a negative effect.

In a first attempt to correct intonation, entire Fo contours of the norm utterances were transposed onto the deaf utterances. This method appeared to be unsuccessful. Since the Fo contour of the norm had to be synchronised with the receiving deaf utterance, such that syllables were matched and voicing of phonemes was kept intact, Fo movements were stretched or compressed in time. This gave a very unnatural result.

For this reason we decided to make use of the intonation grammar of Hart and Cohen (1973) and Hart and Collier (1975). This rule system, when used as a generative grammar, needs as input a sentence plus a specification of the syllables that should be stressed. The system delivers as output a stylised Fo contour, a pattern of Fo movements, which forms an acoustic realisation of the accent structure.

Three alternative contours were generated for each sentence, referred to below as Variants 1 to 3. The first two started from a 'neutral' stress specification assigned by a panel of three judges using the Sentence Accent Assignment Rule of Gussenhoven (1983). This we will call the linguistic accent structure (LAS). In Variant 1, the LAS was realised with the most probable Fo stylisation given by the grammar. Variant 2 was produced by using the simplest option of the grammar, which consists in a rise-fall pattern on each stressed syllable, a contour of peaks. The rationale behind this procedure was that this variant is probably the easiest to learn for a deaf speaker. The third variant was also a contour of peaks, but now the rise-fall patterns were placed on the syllables that were realised as accented by the deaf speakers themselves, yielding the deaf accent structure (DAS).

These three variants applied to the original utterance yielded intonation-versions 1, 2 and 3. In order to investigate a possible interaction with temporal manipulations, the same contours were also implemented on the best temporal version of each sentence. These were intonation corrections 4, 5 and 6.

Intelligibility was measured in the same way as in the earlier experiment. LAS corrections, whether realised as the most probable contour or as simple peaks (i.e. versions 1 and 2) caused an increase in intelligibility from 18% to 25%. Version 3, DAS realised as peaks, received a score of 23%. Although the mean increase in intelligibility caused by temporal corrections was from 18% to 24%, temporal corrections did not affect intelligibility when they were combined with intonation corrections: versions 4, 5 and 6 were not better understood than 1, 2 and 3.

Quality judgements did show an additive effect for temporal and intonation corrections. Whereas the LAS-version with the realistic contour (version 1) was preferred to the original by 72% of the subjects, the addition of temporal corrections raised this score to 84%. For the contours of peaks (versions 2 and 5) preferences were less extreme (62% and 70% respectively). The conclusion must be that, like temporal correction, correction of intonation improves the quality of the sentences, but has only a small effect on intelligibility.

4. Summary and Conclusion

The question of the role of suprasegmental aspects in deaf speech was approached from two different angles, from the production side and from the perception side. From the point of view of production, the question is one that asks: what are the typical prosodic characteristics of deaf speech? From the point of view of perception the question is: what is the (relative) contribution of these errors to the low intelligibility of deaf speech?

In the literature the characteristics of deaf speech fall into two categories: segmental and suprasegmental. The most frequent consonant errors, which belonged to the first category, had to do with consonant clusters, voicing of plosives and fricatives, manner of articulation rather than place and consonant omissions. Vowel errors, also classified as segmental errors, were mainly neutralisation, tense-lax confusions and errors in diphthongs. Suprasegmental errors were judged by raters as errors in rhythm, accentuation, sentence intonation, voice quality, rate of speech production and phonatory control. As far as could be determined, the most important acoustic correlates of these auditive impressions appeared to be temporal structure and Fo contour.

These converging data in the literature correspond to observations on our own speech material. In a preliminary investigation, an inventory of errors was made with strikingly similar results (Maassen, 1983). There it is argued that the most difficult problem for deaf speakers is not what articulatory movements must be performed - i.e. which muscles must be contracted - but that the main problem resides in the force and duration of the muscle tensions and their mutual temporal alignment. Many of the most frequent segmental and suprasegmental errors can be interpreted in this way. Suprasegmental errors relate directly to force and timing: rate of speech production, including speed of articulatory transitions, is mainly a matter of timing; pitch, pitch movements and intensity are related to tension in the vocal cords and subglottal pressure.

Both suprasegmental deviations and a major proportion of the segmental deviations can be viewed as force and timing errors. Errors in the voicing of plosives and fricatives are mainly due to incorrect duration; consonant omissions can be ascribed to articulatory laxness (Hudgins and Numbers, 1942; Levitt, Smith and Stromberg, 1976); also manner of articulation has to do with force, and splitting up consonant clusters is a matter of timing. Furthermore, the vowel errors termed neutralisation and tense-lax confusions are tension errors, while splitting up a diphthong pertains to timing.

These results suggest that deaf speakers experience problems especially with those segmental and suprasegmental characteristics that for a correct realisation mainly depend on force of articulation, duration and temporal alignment.

In order to ascertain the perceptual relevance of the errors, two methods were described, the correlational method and the speech transformation method. Results obtained with these methods showed only partial agreement. Whereas correlational studies attached an important role to suprasegmental errors as determinants of intelligibility, speech transformation studies do not entirely corroborate these results: correction of suprasegmental errors yielded only a small improvement in intelligibility. An explanation for this discrepancy can be found in the main limitation of the correlational method, which is caused by the fact that acoustic parameters are not independent. In most studies, high correlations were found between segmental and suprasegmental error categories. Although partial correlation techniques are especially designed to handle this problem, these techniques are inherently unsatisfactory for resolving the problem. A serious and quite obvious restriction lies in the fact that only those variables that form part of the inventory can be taken account of in the investigative design. This means that an exhaustive inventory of errors is required. Moreover, the relevant parameters must be divided into the right categories, because only categories that are included in the inventory as **independent** can be taken account of. Thus, both overlaps and hiatuses confound the results.

An example of this phenomenon is given by the preliminary correlational study mentioned earlier (Maassen, 1983). A deviating result was the low (negative) correlation between suprasegmental errors and intelligibility and, quite unexpectedly, a **positive** correlation between accentuation errors and intelligibility. The following explanation was proposed. Accentuation errors showed a significant **negative** correlation with consonant omissions, the most harmful consonant error; sentences with many accentuation errors thus contained few consonant omissions. Retrospectively, this was not surprising. Accent errors involve mainly too much accentuation, hardly ever too little accentuation. Apparently, accented syllables are pronounced more carefully, contain fewer consonant omissions and are therefore more intelligible.

We may conclude from this overview, that no dramatic improvement in intelligibility must be expected when speech pathologists succeed in teaching their pupils to have better control over their speech production where suprasegmental aspects are concerned. This is not to say that the wholistic, synthetic speech-training method should be abandoned; many of the more serious errors in deaf speech have to do with timing, force and integration of articulatory movements. Correction of prosodic features may actually improve the quality of deaf speech and lead to a considerable increase in the acceptability of their everyday communication.

Footnotes:

1. *The children were pupils of the Institute for the Deaf in St. Michielsgestel, The Netherlands. They were all prelingually deaf and were educated according to the 'oral reflective method' (Uden, 1968, 1974). At the time of study these children were 12 to 14 years old.*

2. *The research presented in this chapter has been supported by a grant from the Netherlands Organization for the Advancement of Pure Research (ZWO).*

I wish to thank Dirk Povel, Carlos Gussenhoven and Paul Eling for reviewing an earlier draft of this chapter.

REFERENCES

Abberton E & Fourcin A J (1978) 'Intonation and speaker identification.' *Language & Speech* 21, 305-318.

Abercrombie D (1967) *Elements of General Phonetics*. Edinburgh: Edinburgh University Press.

Abercrombie D (1974) 'Syllable quantity and enclitics in English.' In Abercrombie D, Fry D B, Macarthy P A D, Scott N S & Trim J L M (eds) *In Honour of Daniel Jones*. London: Longman, 216-222.

Allerton D J & Cruttenden A (1974) 'English sentence adverbials: their syntax and their intonation in British English.' *Lingua* 34, 1-29.

Anderson S R (1978) 'Tone features.' In Fromkin (ed) *Tone: a Linguistic Survey*. London, New York: Academic Press, 133-175.

Ando K & Canter J (1969) 'A study of syllabic stress in some English words as produced by deaf and normally hearing speakers.' *Language & Speech* 12, 247-255.

Angelocci A (1962) 'Some observations on the speech of the deaf.' *Volta Review* 643, 403-405.

Angelocci A, Kopp G & Holbrook A (1964) 'The vowel formants of deaf and normal hearing eleven to fourteen-year-old boys.' *Journal of Speech and Hearing Disorders* 29, 156-170.

Armstrong L E & Ward I C (1926) *Handbook of English Intonation*. Leipzig and Berlin: B G Teubner.

Ashby M G (1978) 'A study of two English nuclear tones.' *Language & Speech* 21, 32-6.

Atal B S (1972) 'Automatic speaker recognition based on pitch contours.' *Journal of the Acoustical Society of America* 52, 1687-1697.

Atkinson J R (1973) 'Aspects of intonation in speech: implications from an experimental study of fundamental frequency.' PhD dissertation, University of Connecticut, Storrs.

Atkinson J & Drew P (1979) *Order in Court*. London: MacMillan.

Bailey C (1979) 'Phrasierung und Intonation im Englischen.' *Working Papers in Linguistics No. 5*. Technische Universität Berlin.

Bald W D (1980) 'English tag questions and intonation.' *Anglistentag 1979* Berlin: TUB-Dokumentation, Kongresse und Tagungen, Heft 7, 263-89.

Ballmer T & Brennenstuhl W (1981) *Speech Act Classification*. Berlin, Heidelberg, New York, Tokyo: Springer Verlag.

Bard E G & Anderson A H (1983) 'The unintelligibility of speech to children.' *Journal of Child Language* 10, 265-292.

Barik H C (1979) 'Cross-linguistic study of temporal characteristics of different types of speech materials.' *Language & Speech* 20, 116-126.

Bauer L, Dienhart J M, Hartvigson H H & Kvistgaard Jakobsen L (1980) *American English Pronunciation*. Copenhagen: Glyndendal.

Beattie G W (1979) 'Contextual constraints on the floor-apportionment function of speaker gaze in dyadic conversation.' *British Journal of Social and Clinical Psychology* 18, 391-392.

Beattie G W (1981) 'The regulation of speaker turns in face-to-face conversation: some implications for conversation in sound-only channels.' *Semiotica* 34, 55-70.

Beattie G W (1982) 'Turn-taking and interruption in political interviews: Margaret Thatcher and Jim Callaghan compared and contrasted.' *Semiotica* 39, 93]4.

Beattie G W & Butterworth B (1979) 'Contextual probability and word frequency as determinants of pauses and errors in spontaneous speech.' *Language & Speech* 22, 201-211.

Beattie G W, Cutler A & Pearson M (1982) 'Why is Mrs Thatcher interrupted so often?' *Nature* 300, 744-747.

Bell A (1977) 'Accent placement and perception of prominence in rhythmic structures.' In Hyman L M (ed) *Studies in Stress and Accent: Southern California Occasional Papers in Linguistics*, 4 (Department of Linguistics, University of Southern California: Los Angeles, California).

Bennett A (1980) 'Interruptions and the interpretation of conversation.' Tucson: University of Arizona. Mimeo.

van den Berg J W (1962) 'Modern research in experimental phoniatrics.' *Folia Phoniatrica* 14, 18-149.

Bernstein J (1977) 'Intelligibility and simulated deaf-like segmental and timing errors.' *IEEE International Conference on Acoustics, Speech and Signal Processing* 244-247.

Bing J M (1979) *Aspects of English Prosody*. Indiana University Linguistics Club, Bloomington, Indiana.

Bird S (1966) 'Determination in Bambara.' *Journal of West African Linguistics* 3, 5-11.

Boe L-J & Rakotofiringa H (1975) 'A statistical analysis of laryngeal frequency: its relationship to intensity level and duration.' *Language & Speech* 18, 1-13.

Bolinger D (1958) 'A theory of pitch accent in English.' *Word* 14, 109-149.

Boomer D S & Dittman A T (1962) 'Hesitation pauses and juncture pauses in speech.' *Language & Speech* 5, 215-220.

Boomer D S & Laver J D M (1968) 'Slips of the tongue.' *British Journal of Disorders of Communication* 3, 1-12.

Bouhuys A (1974) *Breathing*. New York: Grune and Stratton.

Brazil D (1975) *Discourse Intonation 2*. English Language Research Monographs, Birmingham: University of Birmingham.

Brazil D, Coulthard M & Johns C (1980) *Discourse Intonation and Language Teaching*. London: Longman.

Brewer W F (1980) 'Literary theory, rhetoric and stylistics.' In Spiro R J, Bruce B C & Brewer W F (eds) *Theoretical issues in Reading Comprehension*. Hillsdale, New Jersey: Lawrence Erlbaum Associates, 211-239.

Bristow G (1980) 'Speech training with colour graphics.' PhD dissertation, Cambridge University.

Brown G (1977) *Listening to Spoken English*. London: Longman.

Brown G (1982) 'Intonation, the categories given/new and other sorts of knowledge.' University of Edinburgh Linguistics Department, mimeographed.

Brown G (1983) 'Prosodic structure and the given/new distinction.' In Cutler A & Ladd D R *Prosody: Models and Methods* Berlin, Heidelberg, New York, Tokyo: Springer Verlag, 67-77.

Brown G, Currie K L & Kenworthy J (1980) *Questions of Intonation*. London: Croom Helm.

Buhr R D (1980) 'The emergence of vowels in an infant.' *Journal of Speech and Hearing Research* 23, 75-94.

Butterworth B (1980a) 'Evidence from pauses.' In Butterworth B (ed) *Language Production Vol. 1: Speech and Talk*. London, New York: Academic Press, 155-176.

Butterworth B (1980b) 'Some constraints on models of language production.' In Butterworth B (ed) *Language Production Vol. 1: Speech and Talk*. London, New York: Academic Press, 423-459.

Button G (1977) 'Remarks on conversational analysis.' *Analytic Sociology* 1, 2: D09 - S01.

Calfee R C & Curley R (1984) 'Structure of prose in the content areas.' In Flood J (ed) *Understanding Reading Comprehension* Barksdale, Newark: International Reading Association, 161-180.

Calvert D R (1961) 'Some acoustic characteristics of the speech of the profoundly deaf.' PhD dissertation, Stanford University.

Carnochan J (1960) 'Vowel harmony in Igbo.' *African Language Studies* I, 155-163.

Chafe W L (1970) *Meaning and the Structure of Language*. Chicago: Chicago University Press.

Cheshire J (1982) *Variation in an English Dialect*. Cambridge: Cambridge University Press.

Chomsky N (1980) In Piattelli-Palmarini M (ed) *Language and Learning: the Debate between Jean Piaget and Noam Chomsky*. London: Routledge & Kegan Paul, 35-82, 107-130, 310-324.

Chomsky N (1981) *Lectures on Government and Binding*. Dordrecht: Foris Publications.

Chomsky N (1982) *Some Concepts and Consequences of the Theory of Government and Binding*. Cambridge Massachusetts, London: MIT Press.

Clemmer E J, O'Connell D C & Loui W (1979) 'Rhetorical pauses in oral reading.' *Language & Speech* 22, 397-405.

Cole P & Morgan J L (eds) (1975) *Syntax and Semantics Vol. 3: Speech Acts*. London, New York: Academic Press.

Collier R (1975) 'Perceptual and linguistic tolerance in intonation.' *International Review of Applied Linguistics* 13: 293-308.

Corsaro W (1977) 'The clarification request as a feature of adult interactive styles with young children.' *Language in Society* 6, 183-207.

Coulthard M & Brazil D (1981) 'The place of intonation in the description of interaction.' In Tannen D (ed) *Analyzing Discourse: Text and Talk*. Washington: Georgetown University Round Table on Language and Linguistics, 94-112.

Coulthard M & Montgomery M (eds) (1981) *Studies in Discourse Analysis*. London: Routledge & Kegan Paul.

Couper-Kuhlen E (1982) 'Intonational macrostructures: aspects of prosodic cohesion.' Paper given at 1982 BAAL Seminar on *Intonation and Discourse*, Aston University, Birmingham.

Coustenoble H N & Armstrong I E (1934) *Studies in French Intonation*. Cambridge: Heffer.

Crystal D (1969) *Prosodic Systems and Intonation in English*. Cambridge: Cambridge University Press.

Crystal D (1975) *The English Tone of Voice*. London: Arnold.

Crystal D & Davy D (1969) *Investigating English Style*. London: Longman.

Crystal D & Davy D (1975) *Advanced Conversational English*. London: Longman.

Crystal D & Quirk R (1964) *Systems of Prosodic and Paralinguistic Features in English*. The Hague: Mouton.

Currie K L (1978) 'Recent investigations in intonation.' *Work In Progress*, 11. Department of Linguistics, University of Edinburgh.

Cutler A (1977) 'The context-dependence of "intonational meanings".' *Chicago Linguistic Society* 13: 104-115.

Cutler A (1982) *Slips of the Tongue and Language Production*. Berlin: Mouton (Linguistics, Special Issue 19-7/8).

Cutler A (1983) 'Speakers' conceptions of the function of prosody.' In Cutler A & Ladd D R (eds) *Prosody: Models and Measurements*. Berlin, Heidelberg, New York, Tokyo: Springer Verlag, 79-91.

Cutler A & Ladd D R (eds) (1983) *Prosody: Models and Measurements*. Berlin, Heidelberg, New York, Tokyo: Springer Verlag.

Cutler A & Pearson M (1985) 'On the analysis of turn-taking cues.' (Paper in this Volume.)

Darwin C (1859) *On the Origin of Species*. Facsimile reprint of first edition. London: J Murray.

Davy D (1968) 'A study of intonation and analogous features as exponents of stylistic variation, with special reference to a comparison of conversation with written English read aloud.' MA thesis, University of London.

Dayus K (1981) *Her People*. London: Virago Press.

Deakin G (1981) 'Overlap and gradient relationships in English intonation.' *Melbourne Working Papers in Linguistics* 7, 39-77.

Dejours P (1963) 'Control of respiration by arterial chemoreceptors.' In *Regulation of Respiration, Annals of the New York Academy of Sciences* 109, 682-695.

Dell F, Hirst D J & Vergnaud J-R (eds) (1983) *La Forme Sonore du Langage*. Paris: Hermann.

Draper M H, Ladefoged P & Whitteridge D (1960) 'Expiratory pressures and air flow during speech.' *British Medical Journal* 1, 1837-1843.

Dubnowski J J, Schafer R W & Rabiner L R (1976) 'Real-time digital hardware pitch detector.' *IEEE Transactions, ASSP* 24, 2-8.

Duez D (1982) 'Silent and non-silent pauses in three speech styles.' *Language & Speech* 25, 1, 11-28.

Duncan S (1972) 'Some signals and rules for taking speaking turns in conversations.' *Journal of Personality and Social Psychology* 23, 283-292.

Duncan S (1973) 'Toward a grammar for dyadic conversation.' *Semiotica* 9, 29-47.

Duncan S (1974) 'On the structure of speaker-auditor interaction during speaking turns.' *Language in Society* 2, 161-180.

Duncan S (1975) 'Interaction units during speaking turns in dyadic face-to-face conversation.' In Kendon A, Harris R M & Key M R (eds) *The Organization of Behavior in Face-to-Face Interaction*. The Hague: Mouton.

Edelsky C (1981) 'Who's got the floor?' Mimeo. Tempe: Arizona State University.

Faigley L & Meyer P (1983) 'Rhetorical theory and readers' classifications of text types.' *Text* 3, 4, 305-325.

Fairbanks G M & Pronovost W (1939) 'An experimental study of the pitch characteristics of the voice during the expression of emotion.' *Speech Monographs* 6, 87-104.

Faure G (1948) *Manuel Pratique d'Anglais Parlé*. Paris: Hachette.

Firbas J (1980) 'Post-intonation-centre prosodic shade in the modern English clause.' In Greenbaum S, Leech G & Svartvik J (eds) *Studies in English Linguistics for Randolph Quirk*. London: Longman, 125-33.

Firth J R (1935) 'The techniques of semantics.' In *Papers in Linguistics 1934-51*. London: Oxford University Press (1957 reprint), 7-33.

Firth J R (1948) 'Sounds and prosodies.' *Transactions of the Philological Society* 1948.

Firth J R (1957) 'A synopsis of linguistic theory 1930-1955.' In *Studies in Linguistic Analysis*. Oxford: Basil Blackwell.

Fonagy I (1978) 'A new method of investigating the perception of prosodic features.' *Language & Speech* 21, 34-49.

Foster S (1981) 'Interpreting child discourse.' In French P & MacLure M (eds) *Adult-Child Conversation*. London: Croom Helm, 268-286.

Fourcin A J & Abberton E (1976) 'The laryngograph and the voiscope in speech therapy.' In Loebel E (ed) *Proceedings of the XVIth International Congress on Logopedics and Phoniatrics Interlaken, 1974*, 116-122. S Karger AG: Basel.

French P (1983) 'Problem statements and directives: some aspects of control sequences in infant classroom interaction.' In Shwarze C & von Stechow A (eds) *Ergebnisse und Methoden in Moderner Sprachwissenschaft* Vol 12. Köln: Narr.

French P & Local J (1982) 'Turn-competitive incomings.' Paper given at 1982 BAAL Seminar on *Intonation and Discourse*, Aston University, Birmingham; and (1985) 'Prosodic features and the management of interruptions.' (Paper in this volume.)

Fries C C (1964) 'On the intonation in "yes-no" questions in English.' In Abercrombie D, Fry D B, MacCarthy P A D, Scott N S & Trim J L M (eds) *In Honour of Daniel Jones*. London: Longman, 245-54.

Fromkin V A (ed) (1973) *Speech Errors as Linguistic Evidence*. The Hague: Mouton.

Fromkin V A (ed) (1978) *Tone: A Linguistic Survey*. London, New York: Academic Press.

Fromkin V A (ed) (1980) *Errors in Linguistic Performance*. London, New York: Academic Press.

Froscher M M (1978) 'The effects on respiratory function of sense-group duration.' PhD dissertation, Columbia University.

Fry D B (1958) 'Experiments in the perception of stress.' *Language & Speech* 1, 125-152. Reprinted in Fry D B (ed) (1976) *Acoustic Phonetics*. Cambridge: Cambridge University Press, 401-424.

Fujisaki H & Sudo H (1979) 'A model of the synthesis of pitch contours of connected speech.' *Annual Report of the Engineering Research Institute of Tokyo* 28, 53-60.

Garnica O K (1977) 'Some prosodic and paralinguistic features of speech to young children.' In Snow C E and Ferguson C A (eds) *Talking to Children: Language Input and Acquisition*. Cambridge: Cambridge University Press, 63-88.

Garvey C (1977) 'The contingent query: a dependent act in conversation.' In Lewis M M and Rosenblum L A (eds) *Interaction, Conversation and the Development of Language*. New York, London: Wiley, 63-93.

Gibbon D (1976) 'Perspectives on Intonation Analysis.' *Forum Linguisticum* 9, Bern: Lang.

Gimson A C (1980) *An Introduction to the Pronunciation of English*. (3rd Edition) London: Arnold.

Gold T (1980) 'Speech production in hearing-impaired children.' *Journal of Communication Disorders* 13, 397-418.

Goldberg J A (1979) 'Amplitude shift: a mechanism for the affiliation of utterances in conversational interaction.' In Schenkein J (ed) *Studies in the Organization of Conversational Interaction*. London, New York: Academic Press.

Goldman-Eisler F (1968) *Psycholinguistics: Experiments in Spontaneous Speech*. London, New York: Academic Press.

Goldsmith J (1974) 'English as a tone language.' Ms. MIT.

Gosling J (1981) 'Kinesics in Discourse.' In Coulthard M & Montgomery M (eds) *Studies in Discourse Analysis*. London: Routledge and Kegan Paul, 158-183.

Graddol D (1985) 'Discourse specific pitch behaviour.' (Paper in this volume.)

Graddol D & Swann J (1983) 'Speaking fundamental frequency: some physical and social correlates.' *Language & Speech* 26, 351-366.

Grosjean F & Deschamps A (1973) 'Analyse des variables temporelles du français spontané, II. Comparaison du français oral dans la description avec l'anglais (description) et avec le français (interview radiophonique).' *Phonetica* 28, 191-226.

Grosjean F & Deschamps A (1975) 'Analyse contrastive des variables temporelles de l'anglais et du français: vitesse de parole et variables composantes, phénomènes d'hesitation.' *Phonetica* 31, 144-184.

Grutzmacher M & Lottermose W (1937) 'Über ein Verfahrern zur tragheitsfreien Aufzeichung von Melodiekurven.' *Akustische Zeitschrift* 2, 242-248.

Gussenhoven C (1983) 'Van fokus naar zinsaksent: een regel voor de plaats van het zinsaksent in het Nederlands.' *GLOT*, 6. Reproduced (English translation) in Gussenhoven C (1984) *On the Grammar and Semantics of Sentence Accents*. Dordrecht: Foris Publications, 63-91.

Gussenhoven C (1983) 'Focus, mode and the nucleus.' *Journal of Linguistics*. 19, 377-417.

Gussenhoven C (1984) 'Stress shift and the nucleus.' In Gussenhoven C *On the Grammar and Semantics of Sentence Accents*. Dordrecht: Foris Publications, 291-313.

Gussenhoven C (1985) 'The intonation of "George and Mildred": post-nuclear generalisations.' (Paper in this volume.)

Hadding-Koch K (1961) *Acoustic-Phonetic Studies in the Intonation of Southern Swedish. Traveaux de l'institut de phonétique de Lund No 3*. Lund: CWK Gleerup.

Hadding-Koch K, Studdert-Kennedy M (1964) 'An experimental study of some intonation contours.' *Phonetica*, 11, 175-185. Reprinted in Fry D B (ed) *Acoustic Phonetics*. Cambridge: Cambridge University Press, 431-441.

Halliday M A K (1967a) *Intonation and Grammar in British English*. The Hague: Mouton.

Halliday M A K (1967b) 'Notes on transitivity and theme in English, Part 2.' *Journal of Linguistics* 3, 177-244.

Halliday M A K (1970) *A Course in Spoken English: Intonation*. London: Oxford University Press.

Handzel L (1956) 'Acoustic analysis of vowels in deaf children, by means of the "visible speech" apparatus.' *Folia Phoniatrica* 8, 237-246.

Hart J't & Cohen A (1973) 'Intonation by rule: a perceptual quest.' *Journal of Phonetics* 1, 309-327.

Hart J't & Collier R (1975) 'Integrating different levels of intonation analysis.' *Journal of Phonetics* 3, 235-255.

Haycraft J & Creed T (1973) *Choosing your English*. BBC English by Radio and TV. Birmingham: Camelot Press Ltd.

Hecker M H L, Stevens K N, Von Bismark G & Williams C E (1968) 'Manifestations of task induced stress in the acoustic speech signal.' *Journal of the Acoustical Society of America* 44, 993-1001.

Helfrich H (1979) 'Age markers in speech.' In Scherer K R & Giles H (eds) *Social Markers in Speech*. Cambridge: Cambridge University Press, 63-107.

Heritage J (1978) 'Aspects of the flexibilities of natural language use.' *Sociology* 12, 1, 79-103.

Hess W (1983) *Pitch Determination of Speech Signals*. Berlin, Heidelberg, New York, Tokyo: Springer Verlag.

Hill L A (1975) *Stress and Intonation Step by Step*. London: London University Press.

Hirano M (1981) *Clinical Examination of Voice*. Berlin, Heidelberg, New York, Tokyo: Springer Verlag.

Hirst D J (1977) *Intonative Features: A Syntactic Approach to English Intonation*. (Janua Linguarum Series Minor No 139.) The Hague: Mouton.

Hirst D J (1980) 'Pitch features for tone and intonation.' *Travaux de l'Institut de Phonétique d'Aix en Provence* 6, 177-191.

Hirst D J (1981a) 'Un modèle de production de l'intonation.' *Travaux de l'Institut de Phonétique d'aix en Provence* 7, 297-311; shortened version in Rossi et al, 1981, *L'Intonation: de l'Acoustique à la Sémantique*. Paris: Klincksieck.

Hirst D J (1981b) 'Phonological implications of a production model of intonation.' In Dressler W, Pfeiffer D & Rennison J (eds) *Phonologica 1980. Proceedings of the Fourth International Phonology Meeting*. Vienna: Institut für Sprachwissenschaft der Universität Wien.

Hirst D J (1983a) 'Prosodie et structures de données en phonologie.' In Dell, Hirst & Vergnaud (eds) *La Forme Sonore du Langage*. Paris: Hermann.

Hirst D J (1983b) 'Structures and categories in prosodic representations.' In Cutler & Ladd (eds) *Prosody: Models and Measurements*. Berlin, Heidelberg, New York, Tokyo: Springer Verlag, 93-109.

Hirst D J (1983c) 'Interpreting intonation: a modular approach.' *Journal of Semantics* (in preparation).

Hirst D J (1985) 'Phonological and acoustic parameters of English intonation.' (Paper in this volume.)

Höfer I, Wallbott H, Scherer K R (in preparation) 'Messung Multimodaler Stressindikatoren in Belastungssituationen: Person-und Situationsfaktoren.' To appear in Krohne H W (ed) Angstbewältigung in Leistungssituationen. Weinheim: Edition Psychologie, forthcoming.

Hollien H & Majewski W (1977) 'Speaker identification by long-term spectra under normal and distorted speech conditions.' *Journal of Acoustical Society of America* 62, 975-980.

Horii Y (1975) 'Some statistical characteristics of voice fundamental frequency.' *Journal of Speech and Hearing Research* 18, 192-201.

Horii Y (1979) 'Fundamental frequency perturbation observed in sustained phonation.' *Journal of Speech and Hearing Research* 22, 5-19.

Householder F (1957) 'Accent, juncture, intonation and my Grandfather's reader.' *Word* 13, 234-245.

Huckin T N (1977) *An Integrated Theory of English Intonation*. Ann Arbor: University Microfilms Xerox.

Hudgins C V (1934) 'A comparative study of the speech co-ordination of deaf and normal subjects.' *Journal of Genetic Psychology* 44, 1-48.

Hudgins C V & Numbers F C (1942) 'An investigation of the intelligibility of the speech of the deaf.' *Genetic Psychology Monographs* 25, 289-392.

Hudson R A (1984) 'The higher level differences between speech and writing.' BAAL/LAGB CLIE Working Paper No. 3.

Huggins A W F (1978) 'Speech timing and intelligibility.' In Requin J (ed) *Attention and Performance VII*. Hillsdale, New Jersey: Lawrence Erlbaum Associates, 279-297.

van der Hulst H & Smith N (1982) *The Structure of Phonological Representations*. Dordrecht: Foris.

Hymes D (1972) 'Models of the interaction of social life.' In Gumperz J J & Hymes D (eds) *Directions in the Ethnomethodology of Communication*. New York, London: Holt, Rinehart, Winston, 35-71.

Jackson K H (1953) *Language and History in Early Britain*. Edinburgh: Edinburgh University Press.

Jakobson R (1941) 'Kindersprache, Aphasie und Allgemeine Lautgesetze.' Uppsala: Almqvist. Translation 1968 *Child Language Aphasia and Phonological Universals*. The Hague: Mouton.

Jarman E & Cruttenden A (1976) 'Belfast intonation and the myth of the fall.' *Journal of the International Phonetic Association* 6, 4-12.

Jassem W (1952) 'Intonation of conversational English (educated Southern British).' *Travaux de la Societé des Sciences et des Lettres de Wroclaw*, Ser A, No 45.

Jassem W (1962) 'Akcent jezyka Polskiego.' (Accent in Polish.) Prace Jezykoznawcze, Komisja Jezykoznawstwa PAN, No 31, Wroclaw.

Jassem W (1971) 'On the pitch and compass of the speaking voice.' *Journal of the International Phonetic Association*, 1, 59-68.

Jassem W (1983) *The Phonology of Modern English*. Warszawa: Panstwowe Wydawnictwo Naukowe.

Jassem W & Demenko G (1981) 'Normalization and mathematical description of linguistically relevant pitch curves.' *Proceedings of the Fourth FASE Symposium on Acoustics and Speech*. Venice, 145-148.

Jassem W & Demenko G (1985) 'On extracting linguistic information from Fo traces.' (Paper in this volume.)

Jassem W & Kudela-Dobrogowska K (1980) 'Speaker-independent intonation curves.' In Waugh L R & van Schooneveld C H (eds) *The Melody of Language*. Baltimore: University Park Press, 135-148.

Jefferson G (1972) 'Side sequences.' In Sudnow D (ed) *Studies in Social Interaction*. New York: Free Press, 294-338.

281

Jefferson G (1973) 'A case of precision timing in ordinary conversation.' *Semiotica* 9, 47-96.

Jefferson G (1981) 'The abominable "ne?": a working paper exploring the phenomenon of post response pursuit of response.' Occasional Paper No. 6, Department of Sociology, University of Manchester.

Jefferson G & Schegloff A (1975) 'Sketch: some orderly aspects of overlap in natural conversation.' Paper delivered at December 1975 meeting of the American Anthropological Association. Mimeo. Department of Sociology, University of California, Los Angeles.

John J E & Howarth J N (1965) 'The effect of time distortions on the intelligibility of deaf children's speech.' *Language & Speech* 8, 127-134.

Johns-Lewis C M (1985) 'Prosodic differentiation of discourse modes.' (Paper in this volume.)

Johns-Lewis C M (forthcoming) 'The role of prosody in the perception of discourse modes.' In Coulthard M (ed) *Talking About Text*. Birmingham: English Language Research, University of Birmingham.

Jones D (1909) *Intonation Curves*. Leipzig: G B Teubner.

Jones D (1940) *Phonetic Readings in English*. (26th Edition) Heidelberg: C Winters Universitätsbuchandlung.

Jones D (1975) *An Outline of English Phonetics*. (9th Edition) Cambridge: Cambridge University Press.

Jones D M (1949) 'The accent in modern Welsh.' *Bulletin of the Board of Celtic Studies* XIII, 63-64.

Jones R O (1967) 'A structural phonological analysis and comparison of three Welsh dialects.' MA dissertation. University College of North Wales, Bangor.

Keating P & Buhr R D (1978) 'Fundamental frequency in the speech of infants and children.' *Journal of the Acoustical Society of America* 63, 567-571.

Kelly J (1974) 'Phonology and African Linguistics.' *African Language Studies* XV, 97-109.

Kendon A (1967) 'Some functions of gaze direction in social interaction.' *Acta Psychologica* 26, 22-63.

Kingdon R (1958) *The Groundwork of English Intonation*. London: Longman.

Kirk R E (1968) *Experimental Design: Procedures for the Behavioural Sciences*. Belmont, California: Brooks/Cole.

Klatt D H, Stephens K N & Mead J (1968) 'Studies of articulatory activity and airflow during speech.' *Annals of the New York Academy of Sciences* 155, 42-54.

Klinghardt H & de Fourmestraux M (1911) *Französische Intonationsübungen*. Göthen: Schultze.

Klinghardt H & Klemm G (1920) *Übungen zum Englischen Tonfall*. Göthen: Schultze.

Knowles G (1974) 'Scouse: the urban dialect of Liverpool.' PhD dissertation, University of Leeds.

Knowles G (1978) 'The nature of phonological variables in Scouse.' In Trudgill (ed) *Sociolinguistic Patterns in British English*. London: Edward Arnold, 80-90.

Koopmans - van Beinum F J (1980) 'Vowel contrast reduction. An acoustic and perceptual study of Dutch vowels in various speech conditions.' Dissertatie Universiteit van Amsterdam.

Kreckel M (1981) *Communicative Acts and Shared Knowledge in Natural Discourse*. London, New York: Academic Press.

Kubzdela H (1976) 'An analogue fundamental frequency extractor.' *Speech Analysis and Synthesis* Vol 3, PWN, Warsaw, 269-279.

Labov W (1972) *Sociolinguistic Patterns*. Oxford: Basil Blackwell.

Labov W & Fanshel D (1977) *Therapeutic Discourse: Psychotherapy as Conversation*. London, New York: Academic .

Kubzdela H (1976) 'An analogue fundamental frequency extractor.' *Speech Analysis and Synthesis* Vol 3, PWN, Warsaw, 269-279.

Labov W (1972) *Sociolinguistic Patterns*. Oxford: Basil Blackwell Press.

Ladd D R (1978) 'Stylized intonation.' *Language* 54, 517-40.

Ladd D R (1980) *The Structure of Intonational Meaning: Evidence from English*. Bloomington: Indiana University Press.

Ladd D R (1981) 'A first look at the semantics and pragmatics of negative questions and tag questions.' *Papers from the Seventeenth Regional Meeting of the Chicago Linguistics Society* 164-71.

Ladd D R (1983) 'Phonological features of intonational peaks.' *Language* 59, 721-759.

Ladd D R, Scherer K R & Silverman K (1985) 'An integrated approach to studying intonation and attitude.' (Paper in this volume.)

Landahl K (1982) 'The onset of structured discourse: a developmental study of the acquisition of language.' PhD dissertation, Brown University.

Langlois A, Baken R J & Wilder D N (1980) 'Pre-speech respiratory behaviour during the first year of life.' In Murray T & Murray J (eds) *Infant Communication: Cry and Early Speech*. Houston, Texas: College Hill Press.

Lariviere C (1975) 'Contributions of fundamental frequency and formant frequencies to speaker identification.' *Phonetica* 31, 185-197.

Lass N J, Kelley D T, Cunningham C M & Sheridan K J (1980) 'A comparative study of speaker height and weight identification from voiced and whispered speech.' *Journal of Phonetics* 8, 195-204.

Lass R (1976) *English Phonology and Phonological Theory*. Cambridge: Cambridge University Press.

Laver J D M (1980) *The Phonetic Description of Voice Quality*. Cambridge: Cambridge University Press.

Laver J D M & Hanson R (1981) 'Describing the normal voice.' In Darby J K (ed) *Evaluation of Speech in Psychiatry*. New York: Grune and Stratton, 51-78.

Laver J D M & Trudgill P (1979) 'Phonetic and linguistic markers in speech.' In Scherer K R & Giles H (eds) *Social Markers in Speech*. Cambridge: Cambridge University Press, 1-32.

Leben W (1976) 'The tone in English intonation.' *Linguistic Analysis* 2 (1), 69-108.

Lee W R (1960) *An English Intonational Reader*. London: Macmillan.

Lee W R (1980) 'A point about the rise-endings and fall-endings of yes-no questions.' In Waugh L R & van Schooneveld C H (eds) *The Melody of Language*. Baltimore: University Park Press, 165-8.

Lehiste I (1975) 'The phonetic structure of paragraphs.' In Cohen A & Nooteboom S G (eds) *Structure and Process in Speech Perception*. Berlin, Heidelberg, New York, Tokyo: Springer Verlag, 195-203.

Lehiste I (1978) 'Experimental studies in the phonology of discourse.' In Eadie W (ed) *Directions in Communication*. Proceedings of the Ohio Conference on Communication, Ohio University, Athens, 17-44.

Lehiste I (1979) 'Perception of sentence and paragraph boundaries.' In Lindblöm B & Öhman S (eds) *Frontiers of Speech Communication Research*. London, New York: Academic Press, 191-202.

Lehiste I (1980) 'Phonetic characteristics of discourse.' *Transactions of the Committee on Speech, Acoustical Society of Japan* 4, 26-38.

Leiter K (1980) *A Primer on Ethnomethodology*. London: Oxford University Press.

Leon P R (1972) 'Ou sont les études de l'intonation?' *Proceedings of the 7th International Congress of Phonetic Sciences*. The Hague: Mouton, 113-150.

Leon P R & Martin P (1969) *Prolégomènes à l'étude des structures intonatives*. Montreal: Didier.

Levin H, Schaffer C A & Snow C (1982) 'The prosodic and paralinguistic features of reading and telling stories.' *Language & Speech* 25, 43-54.

Levinson S (1980) 'Speech Act Theory: the state of the art.' *Language and Linguistics Teaching: Abstracts* 13.1, 5-24.

Levinson S (1983) *Pragmatics*. Cambridge: Cambridge University Press.

Levitt H & Smith C R (1972) 'Errors of articulation in the speech of profoundly hearing-impaired children.' *Journal of the Acoustical Society of America* 51, 102(A).

Levitt H, Smith C R & Stromberg H (1976) 'Acoustical, articulatory and perceptual characteristics of the speech of deaf children.' In Fant G (ed) *Proceedings of the Speech Communication Seminar 1976*. New York, London: Wiley, 129-139.

Lewis D & Tiffin J (1933) 'A psychophysical analysis of individual differences in speech.' *Archives of Speech* 1, 43-60.

Lewis M M (1969) *Infant Speech, a Study of the Beginnings of Language*. New York: Harcourt Brace.

Liberman A M, Harris K S, Hoffman H S, Griffith B C (1957) 'The discrimination of speech sounds within and across phoneme boundaries.' *Journal of Experimental Psychology* 54, 358-368.

Liberman M Y (1975) 'The intonational system of English.' MIT dissertation. Reproduced by Indiana University Linguistics Club, 1978, Bloomington, Indiana.

Liberman M Y & Prince A (1977) 'On stress and linguistic rhythm.' *Linguistic Inquiry* 8, 249-336.

Liberman M & Sag I (1974) 'Prosodic form and discourse function.' *Chicago Linguistic Society* 10: 416-427.

Lieberman M R & Lieberman P (1973) 'Olson's "Projective Verse" and the use of breath control as a structural element.' *Language and Style* 5, 287-298.

Lieberman P (1960) 'Some acoustic correlates of word stress in American-English.' *Journal of the Acoustical Society of America* 33, 451-454.

Lieberman P (1965) 'On the acoustic basis of the perception of intonation by linguists.' *Word* 21, 40-54.

Lieberman P (1967) *Intonation, Perception and Language.* Cambridge MA: MIT Press.

Lieberman P (1978) 'Direct comparison of subglottal and esophageal pressure during speech.' *Journal of the Acoustical Society of America* 43, 1157-1164.

Lieberman P (1980) 'On the development of vowel production in young children.' In Yeni-Komshian G H, Kavanagh J F & Ferguson C A (eds) *Child Phonology, Volume I: Production.* London, New York: Academic Press, 113-142.

Lieberman P (1985) 'The acquisition of intonation by infants: physiology and neural control.' (Paper in this volume.)

Lieberman P, Harris K S, Wolff P & Russell L H (1972) 'Newborn infant cry and nonhuman primate vocalizations.' *Journal of Speech and Hearing Research* 14, 718-727.

Lieberman P, Knudsen R & Mead J (1969) 'Determination of the rate of change of fundamental frequency with respect to subglottal air pressure during sustained phonation.' *Journal of the Acoustical Society of America* 45, 1537-1543.

Lieberman P & Tseng C Y (1980) 'On the fall of the declination theory: breath-group versus "declination" as the base form for intonation.' *Journal of the Acoustical Society of America* Supplement 1.

Lindström O (1976) *Aspects of English Intonation.* Göteborg: Acta Universitatis Gotheburgensis.

Local J K (1975) 'The role of non-segmental features in the sex-identification of Tyneside children.' Paper read to Graduate Linguistic Seminar, Newcastle, University School of English.

Local J K (1978) 'Studies towards a description of the development and functioning of children's awareness of linguistic variability.' PhD dissertation, University of Newcastle-upon-Tyne.

Local J K (1982) 'Modelling intonational variability in children's speech.' In Romaine S (ed) *Sociolinguistic Variation in Speech Communities.* London: Edward Arnold.

Local J K (1985) 'Patterns and problems in a study of Tyneside intonation.' (Paper in this volume.)

Local J K and Pearson M (1980) 'Some physical properties of three English tones.' *York Papers in Linguistics* 8, 207-218.

Local J K, Wells W H G & Sebba M, in preparation.

Loveday L (1981) 'Pitch, politeness and sexual role: an exploratory investigation into pitch correlates of English and Japanese politeness formulae.' *Language & Speech* 24, 71-88.

Maassen B A M (1978) 'Verstaanbaarheid van Spraak van Doven.' Doctoraalscriptie Katholike Universiteit Nijmegen.

Maassen B (1983) 'Fouten in dovenspraak en hun relatie met verstaanbaarheid.' *Tijdschrift voor Logopedie en Audiologie.*

Maassen B (1985) 'The role of temporal structure and intonation.' (Paper in this volume.)

Maassen B & Povel D J (1977) 'De temporele struktuur als heid van Spraak van Doven.' Doctoraalscriptie ,Katholike Universiteit Nijmegen.

Maassen B (1983) 'Fouten in dovenspraak en hun relatie met verstaanbaarheid.' *Tijdschrift voor Logopedie en Audiologie.*

Maassen B & Povel D (in preparation) 'The effect of improving temporal structure on the intelligibility of deaf speech.'

Maassen B & Povel D (in preparation) 'The effect of improving intonation on the intelligibility of deaf speech.'

MacGarr N S & Osberger M J (1978) 'Pitch deviancy and intelligibility of deaf speakers.' *Journal of Communication Disorders* 11, 237-247.

McGregor G (1982) 'Intonation and meaning in conversation.' *Language and Communication* 2, 123-131.

McGregor G (1984) 'Conversation and communication.' *Language and Communication* 4, 71-83.

Maclay H & Osgood C E (1959) 'Hesitation phenomena in spontaneous English speech.' *Word* 15, 19-44.

Maeda S (1976) 'A characterization of American English intonation.' PhD dissertation, MIT.

Markel J D & Gray A H (1976) *Linear Prediction of Speech.* Berlin, Heidelberg, New York, Tokyo: Springer Verlag.

Markides A (1970) 'The speech of deaf and partially-hearing children with special reference to factors affecting intelligibility.' *British Journal of Disorders of Communication* 5, 126-140.

Martony J (1968) 'On the correction of the voice pitch level for severely hard-of-hearing subjects.' *American Annals of the Deaf* 113, 195-202.

Meltzer L, Morris W N & Hayes D P (1971) 'Interruption outcomes and vocal amplitude: explorations in social psychophysics.' *Journal of Personality and Social Psychology* 18, 392-402.

Menn L & Boyce S (1982) 'Fundamental frequency and discourse structure.' *Language & Speech* 25, 341-383.

Millar J B & Wagner M (1983) 'The automatic analysis of acoustic variance and speech.' *Language & Speech* 26, 145-158.

286

Milroy L (1980) *Language and Social Networks*. Oxford: Basil Blackwell.

Monsen R B (1974) 'Durational aspects of vowel production in the speech of deaf children.' *Journal of Speech and Hearing Research*, 17, 386-398.

Monsen R B (1976) 'The production of English stop consonants in the speech of deaf children.' *Journal of Phonetics* 4, 29-41.

Monsen R B (1978) 'Toward measuring how well hearing-impaired children speak.' *Journal of Speech and Hearing Research* 21, 198-219.

Monsen R B & Shaughnessy D (1978) 'Improvement of vowel articulation of deaf children.' *Journal of Communication Disorders* 11, 417-424.

Negus V E (1949) *The Comparative Anatomy and Physiology of the Larynx*. New York: Hafner.

Nober E H (1967) 'Articulation of the deaf.' *Exceptional Child 33, 611-621.*

Nolan F (1983) The Phonetic Bases of Speaker Recognition. Cambridge: Cambridge University Press.

Noll A M (1967) 'Cepstrum pitch determination.' *Journal of the Acoustical Society of America* 41, 293-309.

Nordmark J O (1968) 'Mechanisms of frequency discrimination.' *Journal of the Acoustical Society of America* 44, 1533-1540.

O'Connor J D & Arnold G F (1961) *Intonation of Colloquial English*. London: Longman (2nd Edition 1973).

Ohala J (1970) 'Aspects of the control and production of speech.' *UCLA Working Papers in Phonetics* No. 15.

Ohala J & Ewen W (1973) 'Speed of pitch change.' *Journal of the Acoustical Society of America* 53, 345.

Öhman S (1967) 'Word and sentence intonation: a quantitive model.' Speech Transmission Laboratory (Stockholm), *Quarterly Progress and Status Report* 1967(2), 20-54.

Oller D K (1973) 'The effect of position in utterance on speech segment duration in English.' *Journal of the Acoustical Society of America* 54, 1235-1247.

Osberger M J & Levitt H (1979) 'The effect of time errors on the intelligibility of deaf children's speech.' *Journal of the Acoustical Society of America* 66, 1316-1324.

Palmer H E (1922) *English Intonation with Systematic Exercises*. Cambridge: Heffer.

Parkhurst B G & Levitt H (1978) 'The effect of selected prosodic errors on the intelligibility of deaf speech.' *Journal of Communication Disorders 11, 249-256.*

Pellowe J (1970) 'Establishing some prosodic criteria for a classification of speech varieties.' Newcastle: University of Newcastle, School of English. Mimeo.

Pellowe J (1980) 'Establishing variant intonation systems.' York Papers in Linguistics 8, 97-144.

Pellowe J & Jones V (1978) 'On intonational variability in Tyneside speech.' In Trudgill P (ed) *Sociolinguistic Patterns in British English*. London: Edward Arnold, 101-121.

Pellowe J & Jones V (1979) 'Establishing intonationally variable systems in a multidimensional linguistic space.' *Language & Speech* 22, 97-116.

Pellowe J, Nixon G, Strang B & McNeany V (1972) 'A dynamic modelling of linguistic variation: the Urban (Tyneside) Linguistic Survey.' *Lingua* 30, 1-30.

Peters A M (1983) *The Units of Language Acquisition*. Cambridge: Cambridge University Press.

Pierrehumbert H J (1979) 'The perception of fundamental frequency declination.' *The Journal of the Acoustical Society of America* 66, 363-369.

Pierrehumbert J B (1980) 'The phonology and phonetics of English intonation.' PhD dissertation, MIT.

Pike K L (1945) *The Intonation of American-English*. University of Michigan: Ann Arbor.

Platt J (1977) 'The sub-varieties of Singapore English.' In Crewe W (ed) *The English Language in Singapore*. Singapore, Kuala Lumpur, Hong Kong: Eastern Universities Press, 83-95.

Postal P M (1971) *Cross-over Phenomena*. New York: Holt, Rinehart & Winston.

Povel D J (1974a) 'Evaluation of the vowel corrector as speech training device for the deaf.' *Psychological Research* 37, 71-80.

Povel D J (1974b) 'Articulation correction of the deaf by means of visually displayed acoustic information.' Doctoral Dissertation, University of Nijmegen.

Psathas G (ed) (1979) *Everyday Language: Studies in Ethnomethodology*. New York: Irvington.

Quirk R, Greenbaum S, Leech G & Svartvik J *A Grammar of Contemporary English*. London: Longman.

Quirk R, Svartvik J, Duckworth A P, Rusiecki J P L & Colin A J T (1964) 'Studies in the correspondence of prosodic to grammatical features in English.' In *Proceedings of the IXth Congress of Lingustics* (Boston 1962). The Hague: Mouton, 679-91. Reprinted in Quirk R (1968) *Essays in English Language: Medieval and Modern*. London: Longman, 120-35.

Rabson S, Lieberman P & Ryalls J (1982) 'Imitation of intonation by Japanese speaking infants.' *Journal of the Acoustical Society of America* Supplement 1.

Ragsdale J D & Silvia C F (1982) 'Distribution of kinesic hesitation phenomena in spontaneous speech.' *Language & Speech* 25, 185-190.

Rando E (1980) 'Intonation in Discourse'. In Waugh L R & van Schooneveld C H *The Melody of Language*. Baltimore: University Park Press, 243-77.

Rossi M, di Cristo A, Hirst D J, Martin P & Nishinuma Y (1981) *L'Intonation: de l'Acoustique à la Sémantique*. Paris: Klincksieck.

Rutter D R, Stephenson G M, Ayling K & White P A (1978) 'The timing of looks in dyadic conversation.' *British Journal of Social and Clinical Psychology* 17, 17-21.

Sacks H, Schegloff E & Jefferson G (1974) 'A simplest systematics for the organisation of turn-taking for conversation.' *Language* 50, 696-735.

Sandner G W (1981) 'Communication with a three-month old baby.' *Proceedings of the Thirteenth Annual Child Language Research Forum*. Stanford University.

Schegloff E A (1973) 'Recycled turn beginnings.' Paper delivered to Summer Linguistics Institute, L.S.A. Michigan.

Schenkein J (ed) (1978) *Studies in the Organisation of Conversational Interaction*. London, New York: Academic Press.

Scherer K R (1971) 'Randomised splicing: a note on a simple technique for masking speech content.' *Journal of Experimental Research in Personality* 5: 155-159.

Scherer K R (1979a) 'Nonlinguistic vocal indicators of emotion and psychopathology.' In Izard C E (ed) *Emotions in Personality and Psychopathology*. New York: Plenum Press.

Scherer K R (1979b) 'Personality markers in speech.' In Scherer K R & Giles H (eds) *Social Markers in Speech*. Cambridge: Cambridge University Press, 147-209.

Scherer K R (1981) 'Speech and emotional states.' In Darby J (ed) *The Evaluation of Speech in Psychiatry and Medicine*. New York: Grune & Stratton, 189-220.

Scherer K R (1982) 'Methods of research on vocal communication: paradigms and parameters.' In Scherer K R & Ekman P (eds) *Handbook of Methods in Non-verbal Behaviour Research*. Cambridge: Cambridge University Press, 136-198.

Scherer K R & Giles H (eds) (1979) *Social Markers in Speech*. Cambridge: Cambridge University Press.

Scherer U & Scherer K R (1979) 'Psychological factors in bureaucratic encounters: determinants and effects of interactions between officials and clients.' In Singleton W T, Surgeon P, & Stammers R B (eds) *The Analysis of Social Skill*. (NATO Conference Series, Series III (Human Factors) Volume II). New York, London: Plenum Press, 315-328.

Schmerling S F (1976) *Aspects of English Sentence Stress*. Austin: University of Texas Press.

Schroder M C (1976) 'Implementation of pitch detection extraction techniques with regard to their usefulness in linguistic research.' Institut für Phonetik der Universität zu Köln, Bericht No. 5, Köln.

Schubiger M (1958) *English Intonation: Its Form and Function*. Tübingen: Max Niemeyer.

Schubiger M (1961) 'Review of Kingdon (1958).' *English Studies*. 42, 51-5.

Schubiger M (1965) 'English intonation and German modal particles: a comparative study.' *Phonetica* 12, 65-84. Reprinted in Bolinger D (ed) (1972) *Intonation: Selected Readings*. Harmondsworth: Penguin Books, 175-93.

Schubiger M (1980) 'English intonation and German modal particles II: a comparative study.' In Waugh L R & van Schooneveld C H (eds) *The Melody of Language*. Baltimore: University Park Press, 279-98.

Searle J (1969) *Speech Acts*. Cambridge: Cambridge University Press.

Searle J (1975) 'Indirect speech acts.' In Cole P & Morgan J L (eds) *Syntax and Semantics Vol 3: Speech Acts*. London, New York: Academic Press, 59-82.

Selkirk E O (1978) 'On prosodic structure and its relation to syntactic structure.' *Proceedings of the Conference on Mental Representation of Phonology*. Distributed by Indiana University Linguistics Club, 1980.

289

Shipp T, Doherty E T & Morrissey (1979) 'Predicting vocal frequency from selected physiologic measures.' *Journal of the Acoustical Society of America* 66, 678-684.

Shower E G & Biddulph R (1931) 'Differential pitch sensitivity of the ear.' *Journal of the Acoustical Society of America* 3, 275.

Siertsema B (1980) 'Sidelights on tag questions.' In Waugh L R & van Schooneveld C H (eds) *The Melody of Language*. Baltimore: University Park Press, 299-314.

Silverman K E A, Ladd D R & Scherer K R In press. 'Intonation and attitude: empirical tests of theoretical assumptions.' To appear in Lüer G (ed) *Bericht über den 33 Kongress der Deutschen Gesellschaft für Psychologie in Mainz 1982.* Göttingen.

Silverman D, Scherer K R & Ladd D R (1982)*Can Suprasegmental Congruence Cues be Detected in Short Dialogues?* Internal Report, Department of Psychology, University of Giessen, West Germany. (Mimeo.)

Smith C R (1975) 'Residual hearing and speech production in deaf children.' *Journal of Speech and Hearing Research* 18, 795-811.

Sorensen J M & Cooper W E (1980) 'Syntactic coding of fundamental frequency in speech production.' In Cole R A (ed) *Perception and Production of Fluent Speech*. Hillsdale, New Jersey: Lawrence Erlbaum Associates, 399-440.

Stark R & Levitt H (1974) 'Prosodic feature reception and production in deaf children.' *Journal of the Acoustical Society of America* 55, S63(A).

Stark R E, Rose S N & McLagen M (1975) 'Features of infant sounds: the first eight weeks of life.' *Journal of Child Language* 2, 202-221.

Steffen-Batog M (1966) 'Versuch einer strukturellen Analyse der polnischen Aussagemelodie.' *Zeitschrift für Phonetik* 19, 397-440.

Steffen-Batog M, Jassem W & Gruszka-Koscielak H (1970) 'Statistical distribution of short term Fo values as a personal voice characteristic.' In Jassem W (ed) *Speech Analysis and Synthesis* 11, 195-206.

Stevens S S & Volkmann J (1940) 'The relation of pitch to frequency: a revised scale.' *The American Journal of Psychology* 53, 329-353.

Stewart J M (1971) 'Niger-Congo, Kwa.' *Current Trends in Linguistics* 7, 179-212.

Strang B (1968) 'The Tyneside Linguistic Survey.' Paper read to International Congress of Dialectologists, 1965, Marburg. *Zeitschrift für Mundartforschung* NF4, 787-794.

Stubbs M (1983) *Discourse Analysis*. Oxford: Basil Blackwell.

Sundberg J (1979) 'Maximum speech of pitch change in singers and untrained subjects.' *Journal of Phonetics* 7(2), 71-79.

Sussman H & Hernandez M (1979) 'A spectographic analysis of the suprasegmental aspects of the speech of hearing-impaired adolescents.' *Audiology and Hearing Education* 5, 12-16.

Svartvik J & Quirk R (1980) *A Corpus of English Conversation*. Lund: Gleerup.

Thomas A (1979) 'A lowering rule for vowels and its ramifications in a dialect of North Welsh.' *Occasional Papers in Linguistics and Language Learning No. 6: Papers in Celtic Phonology.* (The New University of Ulster.)

Thomas C H (1967) 'Welsh intonation - a preliminary study.' *Studia Celtica* 2, 8-28.

Thudicum G (1926) *Manual Pratique de Diction Française à l'Usage des Étrangers* (5me édition). Genève: Libraire Kundig.

Trager G L & Smith H L (1951) *Outline of English Structure.* Washington: American Council of Learned Societies (revised edition, 1957). Norman, Oklahoma: Battenburg Press.

Truby H M, Bosma J F & Lind J (1965) *Newborn Infant Cry.* Upsala: Almquist and Wiksell.

Trudgill P (1974) *The Social Differentiation of English in Norwich.* Cambridge: Cambridge University Press.

Trudgill P (ed) (1978) *Sociolinguistic Patterns in British English.* London: Edward Arnold.

Tseng C Y (1981) 'An acoustic phonetic study on tones in Mandarin Chinese.' PhD dissertation, Brown University.

van Uden A M J (1968) 'A world of language for deaf children.' The Institute for the Deaf, Saint Michielsgestel. Mimeo.

van Uden A M J (1974) 'Dove Kinderen leren spreken.' Doctoral Dissertation, University of Nijmegen.

Uldall E (1964) 'Dimensions of meaning in intonation.' In Abercrombie D et al (eds) *In Honour of Daniel Jones.* London: Longman, pp 271-279. Reprinted in Bolinger D (1972) *Intonation.* Harmondsworth: Penguin, 250-259.

Vanderslice R & Ladefoged P (1972) 'Binary suprasegmental features and transformational word-accentuation rules.' *Language* 48, 4, 819-838.

Voelker C H (1935) 'A preliminary strobophotoscopic study of the speech of the deaf.' *American Annals of the Deaf* 80, 243-259.

Wang W S-Y (1967) 'Phonological features of tone.' *International Journal of American Linguistics* 33, 93-105.

Watkins T A (1953) 'The accent in Cwm Tawe Welsh.' *Zeitschrift für Celtischer Philologie* XXIV, 6-9.

Waugh L R & van Schooneveld C H (eds) (1980) *The Melody of Language.* Baltimore: University Park Press.

Wells W H G (1980) 'Information Focus.' Unpublished mimeo. Department of Language, University of York.

Wells W H G (1985) 'An experimental approach to the interpretation of focus in spoken English.' (Paper in this volume.)

Willemain T & Lee F (1971) 'Tactile pitch feedback for deaf speakers.' *Volta Review* 73, 541-553.

Williams B (1985) 'An acoustic study of some features of Welsh prosody.' (Paper in this volume.)

Williams C E, Stevens K N (1972) 'Emotion and speech: some acoustical correlates.' *Journal of the Acoustical Society of America* 52: 1238-1250.

Woo N (1969) *Prosody and Phonology*. PhD dissertation, MIT. Reproduced by Indiana University Linguistics Club, Bloomington, Indiana.

Wootton T (1981a) 'Conversation Analysis.' In French P & MacLure M (eds) *Adult-Child Conversation*. London: Croom Helm, 99-110.

Wootton T (1981b) 'Two request forms for four-year-olds.' *Journal of Pragmatics* V, 511-523.

Wulf W A, Shaw M, Hilfinger P N & Flon L (1981) *Fundamental Structures of Computer Science*. Reading Massachusetts, London: Addison-Wesley.

Yngve V (1970) 'On getting a word in edgewise.' *Papers from the Sixth Regional Meeting, Chicago Linguistic Society* 567-578.

Zimmerman D & West C (1975) 'Sex roles, interruptions and silences in conversation.' In Thorne B & Henley N (eds) *Language and Sex: Difference and Dominance*. Massachusetts: Newbury House.

SUBJECT INDEX

AUTHOR INDEX